Developing International Strategies

Rudolf Grünig • Dirk Morschett

Developing International Strategies

Going and Being International for Medium-sized Companies

 Springer

Prof. Dr. Rudolf Grünig
Chair of Management
University of Fribourg
Fribourg
Switzerland

Prof. Dr. Dirk Morschett
Chair for International Management
University of Fribourg
Fribourg
Switzerland

ISBN 978-3-642-24724-8   e-ISBN 978-3-642-24725-5
DOI 10.1007/978-3-642-24725-5
Springer Heidelberg Dordrecht London New York

Library of Congress Control Number: 2011941382

Printed on acid-free paper

Springer is part of Springer Science+Business Media (www.springer.com)

Preface

The strategies for going and being international form the focus of this book. It begins with an introduction to internationalization and to strategic planning. This is followed by the presentation of the strategy development processes for going international for new markets and for going international for production and sourcing. The book ends with recommendations for the strategic planning in international companies.

Many of the concepts, approaches and ideas presented in this book come from the academic teachers of the authors. The authors would like to express their gratitude to Richard Kühn, University of Berne, and Joachim Zentes, Saarland University, for their positive influence and long lasting support. Other ideas come from practice. We are therefore indebted to the many managers who have allowed us to share their strategic work.

In addition, we would like to address our special thanks to two persons. This book could not have been produced without the considerable talents of Anthony Clark who translated large sections of the book and improved the language of the other parts. Thekla Schulthess merits special thanks for her excellent work in typing the text, designing the figures and further editorial work.

August 2011
Rudolf Grünig, Dirk Morschett

Brief Contents

Contents

List of figures

List of insets

0 Introduction

0.1 Internationalization of society and economy

Internationalization or globalization touches every aspect of human society, extending well beyond economic relationships to areas such as social structures, work and leisure patterns, the spread of knowledge, concerns about the natural environment, and the causes and resolutions of armed conflicts. In response to these and many other areas in which the world has grown together in complex ways, we now routinely speak of the Global Village.

Though the world economy represents only one aspect of internationalization, it stands out as being of particular importance. When globalization is mentioned, most people in the world think first of its economic impact. Although it would be a gross oversimplification to see economic relations as the sole cause of internationalization within a complex set of various and interdependent elements, the economy undoubtedly has a great influence and is thus to a considerable extent responsible for the phenomenon.

Yet even if we focus only on economic globalization, the phenomenon remains extremely complex. There is no theory available which is adequate to account fully for these changes and which would allow a reliable prediction of future developments. And, considering how complex the phenomenon is, there is very unlikely to be an adequate theory in the near future.

0.2 Aims of the book and its target audience

Although we may be unable to fully explain it and to make future predictions, internationalization will certainly continue. And it will represent a great challenge to most large and medium-sized companies. This is where our book makes its contribution, putting forward concrete suggestions for action so that companies can thrive in their increasingly internationalized environment.

Most large companies have already gone international, accumulating sales in many different markets and making use of an international network in order to source and produce as favourably as possible. But this is not so true of medium-sized companies. Many medium-sized firms experience internationalization only as an attack on their home market. New competitors introduce products which are cheaper, and not always of lower quality, and these impact negatively on the turnover and margins of existing companies. To help solve this problem, our book adopts the perspective of such middle-sized companies and shows ways in which they might profit from globalization rather than merely suffering from it.

The book is aimed above all at company executives. It is intended to serve as a support for the development of strategies for going and staying international. It is also suitable as learning material for university or other Higher Education students, especially those following a master's level course or EMBA program.

0.3   Framework for going and being international

This book is based on a framework for going and being international, which is displayed in **Figure 0.1**. The different elements in the framework will now be briefly introduced.

Internationalization begins with analysis of the home market. If external analysis reveals that the home market is growing or has stabilized at a high level, and that competitive intensity is below average, then a company may decide not to enter new country markets. In this situation, the company is not obliged to take such risks because there are enough opportunities in the home market. And if internal analysis shows that the company can source and produce competitively in the homeland, then internationalization is not a requirement for the company to perform well on the production side.

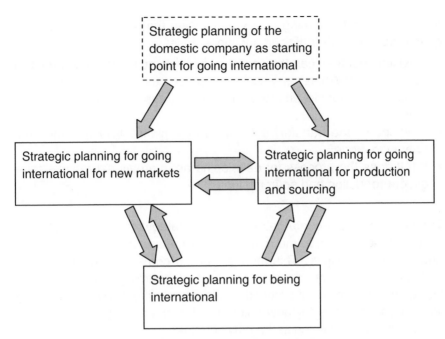

Figure 0.1: Framework for going and being international

But often both external and internal analysis gives a different result. In the home market the company is faced with an erosion of its sales and pressure on prices, and this trend seems likely to continue. Furthermore, internal analysis may also show increasing competitive weaknesses in the company's sourcing and production in its homeland. As well as high costs, the company may increasingly encounter difficulties in access to important resources, such as qualified personnel.

The erosion of sales and margins means that the company needs to enter new geographical markets in order to compensate for the fall in contribution margins at home. This immediately raises a number of difficult questions:

- Based on the competitive situation, which country markets offer the best opportunities? What products and services could be successfully marketed in these countries?
- What is the best mode to open up the target markets in order to achieve success?
- How is the internationalization strategy for new markets developed?

If production and sourcing problems indicate that the company should go international, other difficult questions arise:

- In which countries can the company build up sustainable competitive advantages? Where is access to resources easier or cheaper? Which value-adding activities should be transferred to other countries?
- How should the transfer of activities take place? Which is the best operation mode?
- What does the process for developing an internationalization strategy for production and sourcing look like?

The newly developed internationalization strategy for new markets may indicate that success in the markets is only possible if products can be offered more cheaply. This means that the company must be on the look-out for ways of reducing the cost of sourcing and production. However, the transfer of production and sourcing to new countries may lead to opportunities for new sales. Customer contacts can be developed and sales achieved in the new countries.

Once the first steps have been taken in new countries, whether motivated by the need for increased sales or by improvements on the production side, sooner or later the coordination and optimization of the whole system will become an important issue. Usually the most effective way to do this is by developing a corporate strategy, a number of business strategies and a number of functional strategies, which together take full account of the company's international activities. Questions which will need to be addressed include:

- To what extent should the activities in the various countries and in the different product groups be integrated and managed centrally? To what extent is local autonomy an important factor to guarantee the responsiveness required to serve local customers successfully?
- What is the strategic structure of the internationalized company? What are its strategic businesses?
- What will be the target turnover and market share for each product group in each country market? What are the objectives for the operation units? How will the investment budget be allocated?
- Can products or services be standardized?
- How is the value creation process built up? What is produced and what is sourced and where? Which international operation modes

should be adopted? Which exceptions should be allowed, and on what grounds?

- How can we structure the planning process?

The corporate strategy and the business strategies of an international company can themselves provide the motivation for the development of new strategies for going international. If it becomes clear that future success once again requires increased sales and/or better production and sourcing conditions then the internationalization process must continue. But a more positive view is also possible: the international company's corporate strategy or business strategies can reveal new opportunities which require the development of new strategies for going international.

0.4   Overview of the book

As can be seen from **Figure 0.2,** there are five parts to this book. The structure of the book follows the framework for going and being international explained in Section 0.3.

Part I introduces internationalization. Chapter 1 provides a selection of facts and figures and Chapter 2 goes on to consider the drivers and conditions which might lead a company to extend its activities geographically. As the focus of this book is on recommendations for action rather than description and explanation, these chapters do not attempt a comprehensive account of the complexities of economic globalization, but merely offer an overview.

Part II is an introduction to strategic analysis and planning, both in general and in the context of going and being international. Chapter 3 explains the concept of strategic planning with an emphasis on the purpose of strategy planning. Chapter 4 outlines the reasons for going international and chapter 5 presents the documents and processes of strategic planning in the international context.

Introduction

Part I
Internationalization
Facts and drivers

Part II
Strategic planning in general and in the international context
Documents and processes of strategic planning in general and in the international context. Strategic planning leading to internationalization.

Part III
Strategies for going international for new markets
Strategic issues and planning process for going international for new markets.

Part IV
Strategies for going international for production and sourcing
Strategic issues and planning process for going international for production and sourcing.

Part V
Strategies for being international
Strategic issues and planning process for an international company.

Closing remarks

Figure 0.2: Structure of the book

Part III looks at strategies for going international for new markets. First Chapter 6 shows how potential markets can be analysed and assessed. Next Chapter 7 presents possible entry modes, together with their advantages and disadvantages. Finally Chapter 8 sets out a process for determining an internationalization strategy for new markets.

Part IV looks at going international for production and sourcing. It is structured in the same way as Part III. Chapter 9 first considers the question of evaluating new production and sourcing locations. Chapter 10 confronts the choice of foreign operation mode, and then Chapter 11 recommends a process for developing an internationalization strategy for production and sourcing.

Part V explains strategic planning once activities have been internationalized. First Chapter 12 looks at the level of integration and responsiveness. In Chapter 13, the definition of strategic businesses in international companies is discussed. Then Chapter 14 considers the issue of defining strategic objectives. The next chapter looks at how market offers may be adapted to different country markets. Chapter 16 deals with determining the international value creation process and discusses the operation mode of an international company and its businesses. Finally Chapter 17 shows how to run the strategy planning process in an international company.

Chapter 18 offers concluding remarks.

0.5   Note to readers

Developing strategies for going and being international represents a problem of great complexity. As Section 0.3 shows, there are many relevant perspectives which need to be included in the analysis and planning. If the book is to be of genuine assistance to strategy development practice, it must not attempt to disguise this real complexity with unhelpful simplifications.

Despite this, the authors have tried to present these complex themes in as straightforward and reader-friendly a fashion as possible:

- On the whole the text has short sentences which should be easy to understand. We prefer to be clear, even if we need to repeat ourselves sometimes, rather than to attempt elegant prose.
- Each part is introduced by a short text explaining the content and, where necessary, the reasons for the structure. This should enable the reader to skip topics which deal with familiar matters or which are not a current point of interest and to concentrate on the parts and chapters which seem most important in the light of existing knowledge and needs.
- Whenever possible, basic ideas are presented in visual form.
- Within the text, numerous insets present practical examples which show the relevance and application of the recommended methods. This should make the ideas in the book easier to put into practice.
- An index is provided to enable rapid access to topics of special interest.

Despite the complexity of the subject, we very much hope that the book remains understandable and helpful. And in particular, we hope that this text will prove useful in practice.

Part I

Internationalization

Part I introduces the phenomenon of internationalization. There are two chapters.

Chapter 1 offers facts and figures on internationalization.

- Section 1.1 presents and interprets selected data from the KOF Index of Globalization. This index, created by the Swiss Federal Institute of Technology in Zurich, takes a very wide view of internationalization, including both social and political dimensions alongside economic trends. As a result, the KOF Index provides an excellent introduction to the phenomenon.
- In accordance with the aims of this book, Section 1.2 narrows the focus to economic globalization and provides an overview of trade and Foreign Direct Investments (FDI) based on an interpretation of data from the World Bank. In addition, two insets look specifically at the textile and garment industry of Vietnam and at the Swiss watch industry. These two very different cases offer contrasting examples of strongly internationalized industries.

Chapter 1 thus provides emphatic evidence for the rapid progress of globalization and especially for the internationalization of the world economy.

Chapter 2 goes on to examine the causes of the phenomenon. There are four sections:

- Section 2.1 sets out a framework for the internationalization of a company. The framework distinguishes three elements: drivers, external conditions and explanatory models. The following three sections of the chapter look at each of these factors in turn.
- Section 2.2 examines the drivers. Strategic management literature identifies six factors which can drive the internationalization of a company. In two insets it is shown how combinations of these drivers led to internationalization in two specific cases.
- Section 2.3 considers the external conditions, which is the second element in the framework for internationalization. An inset presents

the World Trade Organization (WTO), which has contributed significantly to economic globalization by promoting the removal of customs and other trade barriers. A second inset shows how more favourable conditions can lead to the expansion of international trade.

- Finally Section 2.4 presents what the authors consider to be the most powerful explanatory models for internationalization. The first of these is the theory of cost advantages. An inset presents a comparison of cost positions in different countries for certain products. A second explanation of the internationalization of companies is provided by the law of the experience curve.

1   Facts and figures about internationalization

1.1   Internationalization in general

The KOF Index of Globalization offers a helpful and longsighted view of internationalization. Produced by the Swiss Federal Institute of Technology in Zurich, it looks at the phenomenon in very broad terms taking into account economic, social and political internationalization. The index published in 2010 covers the period from 1970-2007. For this reason, the facts and numbers which follow do not take account of the financial and economic crisis of 2008-2009. However, this is anything but a disadvantage, since strategic management publications, like the strategies themselves, need to be oriented towards longer term trends and not the vagaries of the marketplace (KOF, 2010a, p. 1).

The KOF Index is based on 24 variables. Beyond the overall Index of Globalization there are three sub-indices (Dreher, 2006, pp. 1091 ff.; KOF, 2010b).

- The sub-index for **Economic Globalization** includes first of all figures for specific economic movements like trade and FDI. In addition, restrictions like tariffs and non-tariff barriers are included.
- The **Social Globalization** of a country is measured by personal contact, information flow and cultural proximity. Personal contact includes measures such as foreign population as a percentage of total population and telephone traffic with other countries. Information flow includes data on internet use and the availability of television sets. This is because these media cross borders and play a central role in spreading information and ideas internationally. Cultural proximity measures the internationalization of consumption by including, among other things, data on the numbers of McDonald's restaurants and IKEA stores.
- The sub-index for **Political Globalization** uses variables such as the number of foreign embassies and membership of international organizations.

The variables used to compute the index and the three sub-indices all yield a number for each country ranging from 1 (lowest) to 100 (highest). The variables and the sub-indices are all weighted, using principal component analysis (Dreher, 2006, pp. 1091 ff.; KOF, 2010b).

Figure 1.1 gives figures for the Index of Globalization from 1970 through 2007 for the world, for Switzerland, and for Vietnam. Switzerland and Vietnam have been chosen as two countries which differ both from the world average and from each other:

- For the world as a whole, the graph shows a trend in which scores are continually rising. Over the 37 years represented in the graph the index climbed from 35 to 57, representing an increase of more than 60%. After the fall of the Berlin Wall in 1989 scores rose particularly strongly. However, social internationalization has stagnated since 2001. The KOF figures thus clearly suggest a gap between the economic and political integration of the world's countries on the one hand and social integration on the other. One manifestation of this gap might be the regular popular protests seen at G8 summit meetings.

- In 1970 Switzerland was at a much higher level of internationalization than the world as a whole. This is true both for the overall index and for all three sub-indices. Up to the year 2000 the overall internationalization index and the two sub-indices for Economic Globalization and Social Globalization continued to climb, moving above 90. For the overall index the rise from 1970 - 2000 equates to more than 55%. The Political Globalization sub-index was already at 97 in 1993. Since 2000, scores have fallen off slightly, though they remain extremely high. This slight fall should not be taken to indicate that Switzerland's internationalization has decreased.   As explained above, for each variable per country and year the highest value is transformed into the index value 100 and the lowest value into the index value 1. The scores in between are calculated in a linear way. This means that the fall in the index value for Switzerland may be attributable to a fall in its relative score, compared with other countries.

- Until 1975, the end of the war, Vietnam had a very low index value of 24. And in the period to 1995 the index value did not climb very far; Vietnam's internationalization at that time was based almost entirely on political moves. But since 1995 internationalization in Vietnam has been in full swing, building above all on improved social integration. The sub-index for social internationalization rose from 14 in 1995 to 31 in 2007, an increase of over 120%.

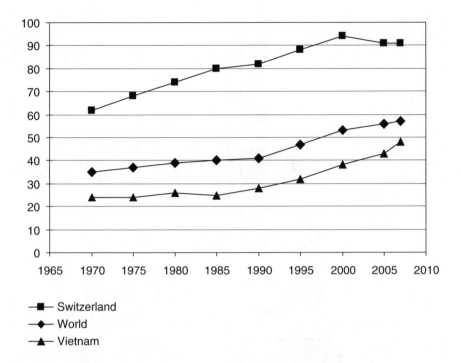

Figure 1.1: KOF Index of Globalization 1970 to 2007 for the world, for Switzerland and for Vietnam (data from KOF, 2010c; KOF, 2010d)

Internationalization has progressed to a very different extent in the various countries. **Figure 1.2** gives the indices for eight countries for the year 2007:

- Switzerland, Germany and Poland are strongly internationalized. In these three countries social and political internationalization have progressed even further than economic international links, which are also strong.
- Thailand and China can be found in the upper mid range of countries. The degree of economic globalization corresponds to the country's overall Globalization Index. The lower level of social internationalization is balanced by strong political internationalization. Vietnam is in the lower mid range. The relatively high degree of economic internationalization is offset by low social internationalization.
- Bangladesh and Burundi are examples of nations with low levels of internationalization. The low globalization index is the result of low

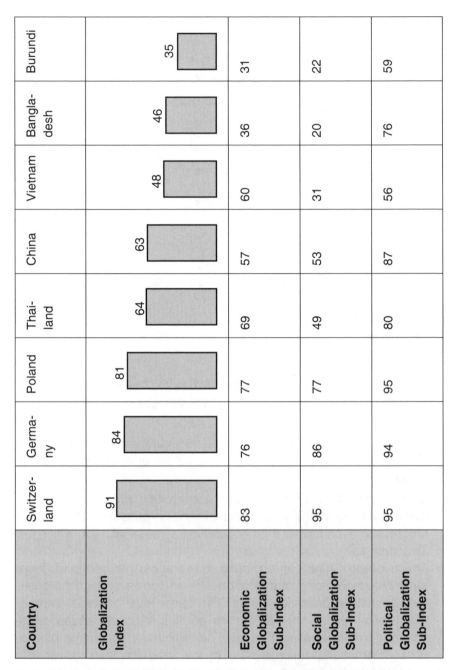

Country	Switzer-land	Germa-ny	Poland	Thai-land	China	Vietnam	Bangla-desh	Burundi
Globalization Index	91	84	81	64	63	48	46	35
Economic Globalization Sub-Index	83	76	77	69	57	60	36	31
Social Globalization Sub-Index	95	86	77	49	53	31	20	22
Political Globalization Sub-Index	95	94	95	80	87	56	76	59

Figure 1.2: KOF Globalization Indices 2007 for selected countries
(data from KOF, 2010e)

economic and social globalization. This is compensated for by a high degree of political integration in the international community.

In summary, the long-term indices indicate a very remarkable increase in the globalization of our world since 1990. However, the indices for 2007 reveal vast differences between individual countries, both for the overall index and for the different sub-indices.

It is economic internationalization which is of particular relevance to the aims of this book and so Section 1.2 will now look more specifically at this.

1.2   Internationalization of the economy

Four key indicators provide evidence of the tendency for the economies of different countries to become increasingly enmeshed:

- The first two are exports and imports of goods and services. "Exports of goods and services represent the value of all goods and other market services provided to the rest of the world. They include the value of merchandise, freight, insurance, transport, travel, royalties, license fees and other services. ... They exclude compensation of employees and investment income" (World Bank, 2010). In the same way "imports" embraces all goods and market services provided by the rest of the world. We can only identify an increase in globalization when exports and imports grow faster than the Gross Domestic Product (GDP). For this reason these two scores are expressed as percentages of GDP.
- The other two indicators derive from the Foreign Direct Investments (FDI), and are "net [outflows] or inflows of investment to acquire a lasting interest in or management control over an enterprise operating in an economy other than that of the investor. It is the sum of equity capital, reinvested earnings, other long-term capital and short term capital, as shown in the balance of payments" (World Bank, 2010). Enmeshment occurs as firms in the country under consideration invest in other countries. But economies also become enmeshed when the investment takes place in the reverse direction. This means that both outflows and inflows are relevant. To show the

trend to internationalization, annual outflows are expressed as percentages of GDP.

- Trade and FDI are to be seen as complementary approaches (Graham 1997, pp. 29 ff.): FDI creates cross-border trade. Production facilities based outside the home country will often rely on components imported from the home country. And the products produced outside the home country will be marketed in various countries, typically also being exported back to the home market. In many cases it is the FDI which creates the possibility of opening up new markets. This is particularly so if the products produced outside the home country are significantly cheaper than those produced at home.

Figure 1.3 shows changes in exports, imports, FDI outflows and FDI inflows expressed as percentages of GDP for the years 1988 to 2007. The table gives figures for the world as a whole, for Switzerland, and for Vietnam. The data can be interpreted as follows:

- Exports worldwide climbed from 18% in 1988 to 29% in 2007. This corresponds to an increase of over 60% in the period of twenty years. In the same period GDP went up by more than 80%. What this means is that in these twenty years exports almost tripled. If we look at the world as a whole, the volumes of imports and of exports are logically equal. For this reason there is no figure here for imports. Until 1996, Foreign Direct Investments represented just 1% of GDP. But after this the figure begins to rise. In 2007 as much as 5% of the world's GDP was being invested outside the home country. But here we cannot observe the same steadily increasing trend as we found for exports. FDI figures are influenced by the downturns and upturns of the economic situation.
- If we now look at the figures for Switzerland, in 1988 exports were already 36% of GDP, twice the figure for the world as a whole. By 2007 exports had grown to 56% of GDP. But Switzerland does not only have high exports. As a country with limited natural resources, its imports are also very high. Imports rose from 34% of GDP in 1988 to 47% in 2007. However, over the twenty years Switzerland's overall trade surplus has grown. The FDI figures are also impressive. Outflows grew from 4% of GDP in 1988 to 13% in 2007. And while Swiss companies have been making significant investments in other countries, Switzerland itself has also been an attractive target for foreign investors. Foreign investment into Switzerland also in-

creased in the period under consideration and since 1997 has re-
mained well above the world average.

- The figures for Vietnam are significantly different from those for
Switzerland, showing a trade deficit. But what stands out most is the
scale of the increases over the period under consideration. Exports
as a percentage of GDP have risen by more than 1800% and imports by over 500%. If we add the fact that GDP itself has risen by
more than 6 times in this period, we can see that exports of products
and services from Vietnam have risen by a factor of more than 100
in the last twenty years! Vietnam has not made significant investments in other countries, but Vietnam has become an important re-
cipient of FDI. These investments have greatly contributed to the
country's export growth. As **Inset 2.1** will show, many of the exports
originate from production facilities set up by foreign companies.

Figure 1.4 shows the international economic integration of six specific
countries for the year 2007. The countries divide clearly into three
pairs. Switzerland and Germany are economically successful countries
with strong international connections. Their economic success is based
not only on a trade surplus, but is also rooted in FDI outflows. Because
of their economic success, the countries are themselves attractive targets for foreign investors. Next, Thailand and Vietnam are strongly
integrated with other countries through imports and exports of goods
and services. While Vietnam still has a trade deficit, Thailand has a
positive trade balance. FDI inflows will lead to further increases in exports and in the medium term both these countries will become economically stronger, with Vietnam transitioning to a trade surplus in the
medium term. Finally, Bangladesh and Burundi are much less enmeshed. Imports and exports are both much lower. Unlike in Vietnam,
here the trade deficits are not combined with FDI inflows. These countries currently lack the foreign investments which would be needed to
boost their exports.

Up to now we have looked at economic internationalization at the mac-
ro-economic level. But for strategic planning industry perspectives are
also important. **Inset 1.1** and **Inset 1.2** describe internationalization in
two different industries in different countries. These are the textile and
garment industry in Vietnam and the watch industry in Switzerland.

World: Exports in % of GDP

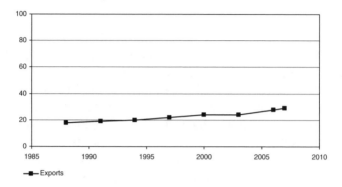

Switzerland: Exports and imports in % of GDP

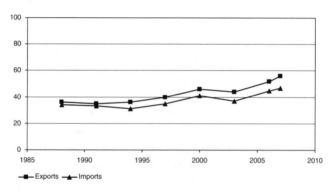

Vietnam: Exports and Imports in % of GDP

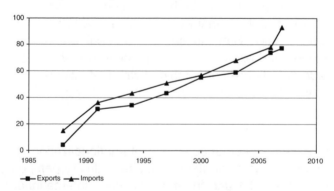

Figure 1.3: Economic internationalization 1988 to 2007 for the world, Switzerland and Vietnam (data from World Bank, 2010)

World: FDI outflow in % of GDP

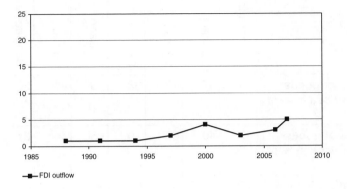

Switzerland: FDI outflow and inflow in % of GDP

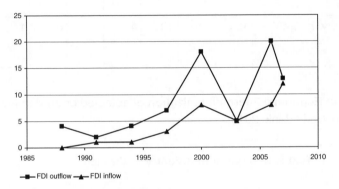

Vietnam: FDI outflow and inflow in % of GDP

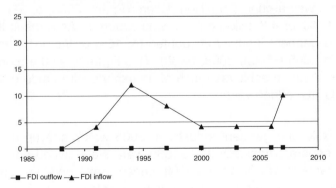

Figure 1.3: Economic internationalization 1988 to 2007 for the world, Switzerland and Vietnam (continued)

Country	Switzerland	Germany	Vietnam	China	Thailand	Poland	Bangladesh	Burundi*
Exports of goods and services in % of GDP	56	47	77	38	73	41	20	11
Imports of goods and services in % of GDP	47	40	93	30	65	44	27	47
FDI outflow in % of GDP	13	5	0	0	1	1	0	0
FDI inflow in % of GDP	12	2	10	4	5	6	1	0

* Data for 2006

Figure 1.4: Economic internationalization of selected countries for 2007
(data from World Bank, 2010)

⌐ Inset 1.1: Textile and garment industry in Vietnam

In 2005 the domestic product of the textile and garment industry in Vietnam was around 5.5 billion dollars (Pham, 2008, p. 37). Of this some 90%, or 4.8 billion dollars, was exported. As a result the textile and garment industry accounted for 15% of Vietnam's total exports in 2005 (Pham, 2008, p. 37). This figure is all the more striking, as Vietnam achieves much of its exports with crude oil, where there is little added value.

The textile and garment industry in 2005 was made up of around 2,800 separate firms. Of these, 560 were state-owned enterprises, 1,280 were privately owned Vietnamese firms, and the remaining 960 were FDI enterprises. The industry employs more than 2.1 million people, or just under 5% of all workers (Pham, 2008, pp. 35 ff.).

The FDI enterprises are mostly owned by Asian companies. Almost 95% of the capital invested has come from East and Southeast Asia. But the industry's exports go predominantly to the US and Canada (56%) and to Europe (15%) (Pham, 2008, pp. 35 ff.).

Of these exports, it can be assumed that a large proportion originates from FDI enterprises. These companies were established in order to gain access to qualified workers with moderate wages. Investors from countries like Taiwan, South Korea and Japan enjoy immediate cost advantages when they can produce in Vietnam, rather than in the home country. In 2005, hourly wages in the textile and clothing industry were USD 8 for Taiwan and USD 7 for South Korea. In Japan the figure was USD 28. Compare these figures with the average for Vietnam, less than USD 0.5 (Dicken, 2009, p. 257). The transfer of production to Vietnam has not changed the customer relationships. Companies continue to supply their traditional markets in the US and Europe from their production facilities in Vietnam.

FDI enterprises have not only created jobs in Vietnam, but have also developed competences in design, production and sales. As a result, in the medium term it can be expected that the performance of other firms, the state-owned enterprises and privately owned Vietnamese companies, to improve as well. This will in turn increase exports from these companies too.

Inset 1.2: Watch industry of Switzerland

The Swiss watch industry is largely concentrated in the region known as the Jura and along the southern foot of the Jura mountains. In a few hundred square miles there is an industry cluster (Porter, 1990, pp. 179 ff.) which enjoys a dominant position in the worldwide market's upper price segment and luxury segment. The upper price segment comprises products priced at CHF 500 to CHF 2,000 ex works. The luxury segment has watches with an ex works price of more than CHF 3,000 (Federation of the Swiss Watch Industry, 2010a). Retail prices are about three times as much as the ex works price.

The Swiss watch industry is very strongly geared towards exports. More than 90% of the watches are exported. In addition, foreign tourists account for a large proportion of those watches which are sold in Switzerland. **Figure 1.5** shows watch exports for 1970-2007:

- Up to the early 1970s, the Swiss watch industry was active in all price segments. The watches all had mechanical movements.
- The invention of the electronic watch brought dramatic changes. The number of watches produced each year in Switzerland fell from 60 million in 1973 to only 15 million in 1983. Foreign made quartz watches forced the cheaper mechanical watches from Switzerland out of the market. As a result of the disappearance of these cheaper watches, the average price for a mechanical watch rose from CHF 39 in 1973 to CHF 164 in 1983 (Federation of the Swiss Watch Industry, 2010a).
- With the creation and successful launch of the Swatch, the Swiss watch industry regained a limited foothold in the low price segment, represented by prices up to CHF 200 ex works. In 2007 cheap watches represented 72% of units exported. However, these watches only amounted to around 8% of the total value of exports (Federation of the Swiss Watch Industry, 2010a).

As **Figure 1.5** shows, the average unit price tripled between 1990 and 2007. As a result, the upper price segment and the luxury segment now dominate within the Swiss watch industry, as shown in **Figure 1.6.**

Figure 1.7 compares the four countries which, in 2007, achieved exports of at least a billion Swiss francs:

- In terms of value, Switzerland is well out in front as the leading exporter of watches in the world. More than 85% of these exports are within the upper price segment and the luxury segment.
- In terms of units sold, China dominates the world market with more than a billion watches. With an average price ex works of CHF 6, China is almost a hundred times cheaper than Switzerland and still ten times cheaper than Switzerland in the low price segment. Based on the average price, Germany too belongs to the low price segment. But German watches are 25% more expensive than Swiss watches in the low price segment.

Volume in Mio Swiss Francs

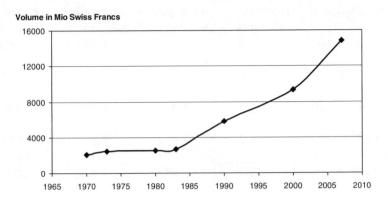

Volume in Mio units

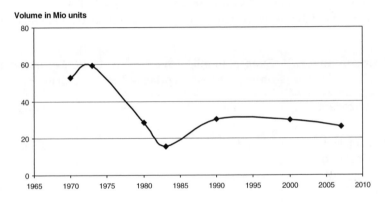

Average unit price in Swiss Francs

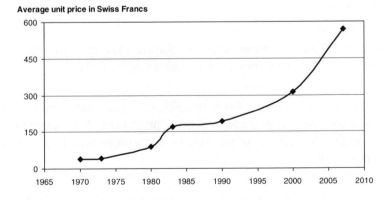

Figure 1.5: Watch exports from Switzerland 1970 to 2007
(data from Federation of the Swiss Watch Industry, 2010a)

Submarkets	Exports in mil. units	Av. export price in CHF	Exports in mil. CHF	Exports in %
CHF 0-200	18.7	64	1,200	8%
CHF 200-500	2.6	346	900	6%
CHF 500-3,000	3.7	1,324	4,900	33%
CHF 3,000+	1.0	7,800	7,800	53%
Total or average	26.0	569	14,800	100%

Figure 1.6: Submarkets of the Swiss watch exports 2007 (data from Federation of the Swiss Watch Industry, 2010a, rounded by the authors)

Countries	Exports in mil. units	Av. export price in CHF	Exports in mil. CHF
Switzerland	26	569	14,800
China incl. Hongkong	1,111	6	6,500
Germany	14	79	1,100
France	6	183	1,100

Figure 1.7: The four largest watch exporters 2007 (data from Federation of the Swiss Watch Industry, 2010a, rounded by the authors)

- The average price for French watches is just below the threshold between the low and medium price segments. This suggests that French exporters operate mainly in the low and medium price segments.

There are several reasons for the dominant position of Switzerland in the upper price segment and in the luxury class. The industry has a tradition of craftsmanship going back hundreds of years. This affords the expertise for the manufacture and design of watches which are technically and aesthetically outstanding. But it also brings prestige. And this prestige is not only associated with individual brands, but also embodied in the "Swiss made" label. The industry association sets out clear conditions which have to be fulfilled if products are to bear the "Swiss made" label: the movement and the watch have to be assembled in Switzerland and at least 50% of the value of the components of the movement must originate from Switzerland (Federation of the Swiss Watch Industry, 2010b).

2 Drivers of internationalization for companies

2.1 Framework for the internationalization of companies

The internationalization of companies is a very complex phenomenon. So complex, that there is no comprehensive theory available at this time with which we can begin this chapter. Instead, we must content ourselves with presenting the most important drivers and external conditions of internationalization.

We begin by establishing a framework showing how drivers, external conditions and explanatory models fit together. **Figure 2.1** displays this framework for the internationalization of companies.

For a company to risk moving into another country, with the difficulties and risks this can bring, there need to be strong reasons. Such drivers of internationalization are discussed in Section 2.2.

The external conditions are what determine whether internationalization is a step which is worth considering. Once the company has made that decision, the external conditions also determine whether it can be successfully implemented. As **Figure 2.1** shows, external conditions not only influence internationalization options, they can also create new reasons for internationalization. An example of this would be a free trade agreement which leads to more intense competition on the home market, thus bringing the necessity to open up new markets. External conditions are examined in Section 2.3.

As noted above, at present there is no full theory of the internationalization of companies. Indeed, the phenomenon is so complex that there may never be such a theory. There are, however, useful explanations of individual aspects of internationalization. Of these, the two most important are cost advantages and the experience curve. These ideas are outlined in Section 2.5.

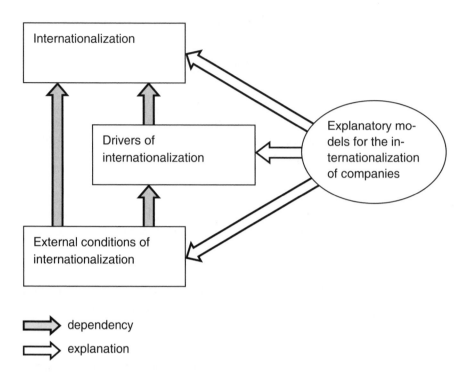

Figure 2.1: Framework for the internationalization of companies

2.2   Drivers of internationalization

There are many factors which can lead a company to go international. Here we set out seven drivers of internationalization. Each of these may take effect singly, or in combination with one or more of the others.

The most frequent factor driving a move into another country is the **need to find new customers** in order to create additional turnover and contribution margin (Barney/Hesterly, 2010, pp. 310 ff.; Hill/Jones, 2008, p. 270). Often when a company decides to go international for this reason, home markets are stagnating or even in decline. Or increasing customer concentration in the home market makes it difficult to hold existing customers and to gain new ones.

The second driver of internationalization is the **need to realize cost economies** (Grant, 2010, p. 386; Hill/Jones, 2008, p. 270 f.). Cost economies can be divided into two categories:

- As a result of new markets being opened up, fixed costs can be spread across more products. In this case, economies of scale will arise. In industries where development costs are high, this may be vital for survival. An example is the aircraft industry. Boeing and Airbus could not survive without recovering their high development costs by selling their aircraft beyond their home markets.
- Economies in the replication of knowledge-based assets often occur in the services sector. An example would be the creation of a new Disneyland theme park. In this case Disney gains considerably from what has been learned from the good and bad experiences the company has had with previous theme parks (Grant, 2010, p. 386).

Inset 2.1 illustrates these first two drivers of internationalization with the case of a Swiss food manufacturer.

Inset 2.1: Drivers of internationalization for the Swiss food manufacturer Narimpex (text based on Narimpex, 2010)

Narimpex is a family-owned company. In 2009 the company employed around 120 people and had total sales of some CHF 60 million. The company has two product groups. One of its facilities produces blended honeys, and the other dried fruits and nuts.

Up to 2000 almost all of the company's turnover came from the home market. As far as food is concerned, there are significant trade tariffs and non-tariff barriers between Switzerland and the European Union. As a result the company sells only a few niche products in the EU. However, as a result of a meeting at a trade fair the company was able to make contact with a retail chain in the Emirates. After their first samples of honey products sold well, Narimpex set up a sales office in Dubai. Now the company sells a range of honey products adapted to these markets through a number of different retail chains and achieves several million Swiss francs in sales each year in the Emirates and Saudi Arabia.

In Narimpex's home market, Switzerland, consumption of honey has been stagnating for many years. While the resident population has increased, the consumption per head has fallen. Narimpex has a large market share already and further growth could only be achieved by reducing the price and quality of products. The company has categorically rejected this option.   Since 1995 therefore, Narimpex has regularly attended international food fairs. Its attempts to open up a new export market have been successful in the Middle East and it is now looking to build a second export market.

Alongside the desire for growth, increases in fixed costs have played a critical role. As a result the company needs to augment the contribution margin by increasing sales.

A third driver of internationalization is **access to low cost raw materials and labor** (Barney/Hesterly, 2010, pp. 316 ff; Grant, 2010, p. 386; Hill/Jones, 2008, p. 271 f.). A good example of this was given in **Inset 2.1**: Japanese, Korean and Taiwanese textile manufacturers have constructed factories in Vietnam in order to take advantage of the much lower salaries.

Another reason for going international is **balancing risk**. By servicing a number of different geographical markets companies can sometimes compensate for a slump in demand in one region. For example, the financial crisis in 2008 led to dramatic falls in demand in the US. But the effect on demand in China and other Far Eastern markets was much less. Balancing risk is a driver that typically operates in combination with other drivers and does not constitute the sole motivation for going international.

A fifth driver of internationalization is the **desire to gain new competencies** (Barney/Hesterly, 2010, pp. 318 ff; Grant, 2010, p. 387; Hill/Jones, 2008, p. 272 f.). IKEA had more than one reason for entering the Japanese market. The company wanted to increase its sales and contribution margin, but also wanted to tackle the Japanese market's demand for high quality and to gain new competencies in quality management (Grant, 2010, p. 387). Empirical research confirms that expansion into other countries brings increased knowledge. According to this research, multi-national companies have a significant competitive advantage over national companies because they can generate knowledge in one country of operation and then apply this knowledge elsewhere (see for example Gupta/Govindarajan, 2000, pp. 473 ff.).

The Danish footwear company Ecco is influenced by all five of these drivers of internationalization. The company is described in **Inset 2.2**.

Inset 2.2: Drivers of internationalization for the Danish footwear company Ecco (text based on Ecco, 2010)

In 2009 this family-owned company had 15,000 employees and achieved sales of 5 billion Danish crowns. Of this turnover, 17% was from America, 9% from the Asia-Pacific region, and the remaining 72% from Europe. While many of the products are sold to wholesalers, Ecco is also active in the retail trade. By the end of 2009 the company had more than 900 dedicated shoe stores, 1,300 shop-in-shops and 1,600 shop points. The company produces in four factories located in Slovakia, China, Indonesia and Thailand. To assure quality, the company also has its own tanneries situated in the Netherlands, China, Indonesia and Thailand. Design and development of new models takes place in Denmark and Portugal, and since 2009, also in Thailand.

Selling their products worldwide produces increased turnover and contribution margin. This margin is further increased by vertical integration, with the company owning its own retail outlets. These stores also help to strengthen the brand. In addition, customers in these stores can be confident that they are not buying counterfeit goods.

In order to produce efficiently and at low cost, Ecco has concentrated product development, tannery operations and footwear production within a small number of locations. The tanneries and shoe factories have been established with costs in mind. While more than 70% of sales are in Europe, most of the production takes place in low-cost Asia.

The opening of a new design and development centre in Thailand in 2009 seems noteworthy. Until the end of 2008, Ecco had two such centres in Denmark and Portugal. But there is no production in these two countries. This third centre in Thailand is located alongside the company's largest factory. Ecco believes that this will strengthen coordination between design and production. In particular, it should significantly reduce the time taken to realise a new design as a prototype product.

A sixth driver of internationalization is **access to internationally active customers** (Grant, 2010, p. 386). For example firms offering advertising services and car part manufacturers are obliged to be international, because their most important customers are international themselves. The greatest demand for advertising services is from multinational corporations. Such corporations require a service provider which can support the company worldwide. Any supplier which is confined to a certain country or region has immediately given up a large slice of the potential demand. In the same way, international auto companies require suppliers who can serve them worldwide. If the car producers move to China, the car part manufacturers need to follow their customers so that they can supply auto-making operations in that country quickly and on favourable terms.

A seventh driver is **strategic power**. International activity and the associated size creates this power (Grant, 2010, p. 387 f). Power can be used to apply price pressure on locally-based competitors in particular countries. Beyond this, an international company may put pressure on suppliers, customers and even governments. From an ethical perspective, the pursuit of such power seems a somewhat doubtful reason for going international. Yet it is clearly the case that these considerations do play a role, though often alongside other drivers and not as the only reason to go international.

So far in this section we have identified seven drivers of internationalization. The first four of these can be grouped together under the heading "countermeasures against threats". With stagnating or declining markets at home and with cost pressures, companies are forced to look for new markets and/or to reduce production costs. In most cases, these four drivers can lead a company to take its first steps beyond its national borders.   The second set of three drivers is rather different. These could be grouped together as "opportunity seizing". In practice it is mostly companies which are already international that respond to these drivers and expand their international activity. **Figure 2.2** summarizes this argument.

Drivers of internationalization	Countermeasures against threats	Opportunity seizing
Access to new customers	***	**
Cost benefits of scale and replication	***	*
Access to low cost raw materials and labour	***	*
Balancing risks	***	**
Access to new competencies		***
Access to global customers	**	***
Gain strategic power		***

*** = very important link
** = important link
* = possible link

Figure 2.2: Linking the drivers of internationalization with opportunities and threats

2.3   External conditions for internationalization

The extent to which the various drivers presented above will actually lead to internationalization for particular companies depends greatly on the external conditions. From the practical point of view, the technical and legal conditions are the most relevant and these are described below.

Developments in telecommunications and in the transport of both goods and persons have contributed considerably to the internationalization of firms:

- The internet is clearly the most important factor. While it may be too early to pass a final judgement on the value of the web, we are in no doubt that the internet represents one of the most important inventions in the history of humanity, one which has not only changed the lives of individuals, but has also accelerated and simplified the management of international companies. For such companies, contact with partners and subsidiaries is now instantaneously possible and available around the clock, no matter where they are in the world.
- Mobile telephones, video conferencing, and other telecommunications developments have also added new instrumentalities for management.
- The air travel companies have a dense network of connections across the world, allowing executives to move quickly and comfortably to wherever they need to be.
- For the transport of goods, the container system allows sealed consignments to travel from their origin to their destination without the need for repacking and this has linked ships, trains, trucks and airplanes into a seamless system. Sanyal (2001, p. 20) offers an unusual example of this system at work: the British grouse season opens on 12th August each year. Tradition demands that London's top restaurants should have fresh grouse on the menu the same evening. But for some years now this has been extended to New York, where well-heeled diners may also feast on freshly slain British grouse on the evening of the 12th.

Alongside these technical developments in communications and logistics, legal conditions are also important for internationalization:

- Tariffs play a central role, adding to the cost of imported goods and thus protecting home products. Tariffs also bring in important revenues for governments. The impressive increases in international trade in both goods and services demonstrated in Chapter Two above are principally the result of lower tariffs brought about by more than 180 regional agreements (Gerber, 2005, p. 23 ff.) and innumerable bilateral trade agreements. But the key role is played by the World Trade Organization (WTO) based in Geneva. The WTO includes more than 150 countries and more than 97% of all world trade. The only important economic power which is still outside this group is Russia. **Inset 2.3** describes the work of this institution, which is central to internationalization.
- Non-tariff barriers are also important. They may be classified into three categories: restrictions, regulations and "buy local" campaigns (Morschett/Schramm-Klein/Zentes, 2010, p. 95). Restrictions typically take the form of quotas. Switzerland, for example, has import quotas for agricultural products like wine and fruit so that there will be less pressure on sales of home-produced products. But export quotas also exist: Japan limits sales of its automobiles to the US and this helps to reduce the US trade deficit. Regulations may take many different forms. In some cases companies have to obtain government permission to sell their products in a country. This is so in many countries, for example, for switchboards and for pharmaceuticals. Finally, it is important not to underestimate the power of buy local campaigns. NGOs, like trade unions, often launch such initiatives, and can usually rely on support from their governments, whether this is tacit or openly expressed.
- Foreign investment itself may be subject to far-reaching restrictions. In industries which are considered strategically important for the country, the government may allow joint ventures, but prohibit foreign companies from establishing fully owned subsidiaries. There may also be restrictive regulations concerning the composition of a company's board of directors. Finally, and not least in importance, laws limiting the transfer of profits may make foreign investments much less attractive.

Inset 2.3: The World Trade Organisation (text based on Gerber, 2005 and WTO, 2010)

In 1948 twenty-three countries signed up to the General Agreement on Tariffs and Trade (GATT). At the time GATT affected about one-fifth of world trade, reducing duties by a total of about 10 billion US dollars. Along with these customs reductions, GATT introduced measures to promote international trade. In the trade rounds which then followed, additional agreements were negotiated. These went beyond simple tariff reductions. They included problems like dumping and also addressed non-tariff barriers. The most intensive of these trade rounds was the Uruguay Round, which lasted from 1986 to 1994. In 1994 the new agreement that came out of the Uruguay Round was signed by 125 countries. One of its provisions was the creation of the WTO (Gerber, 2005, p. 21).

In 2008 the WTO had 153 members and was negotiating with a further 30 countries wishing to join the organization. More than 97% of world trade is now governed by WTO agreements (WTO, 2010).

The supreme decision-making body of the WTO is the ministerial conference, which takes place at least every two years. The general council, consisting of representatives of the member states, meets several times a year and oversees a number of more specialized councils and committees. Supporting all this activity is the WTO secretariat, which is located in Geneva (WTO, 2010).

Underlying all the various agreements on trade in goods and services which have been achieved under the auspices of the WTO are five basic principles:

- **Trade without discrimination:** This principle requires that each member country should grant all other member countries access to its markets on the same favorable terms. All the WTO members must be treated in the same way as the country's most favored trading partner (WTO, 2010). However, regional agreements, such as the North American Free Trade Area (NAFTA) and the European Union, are accepted exceptions. NAFTA members, like the members of the EU, grant each other more favorable trading terms than they allow for other WTO countries, thus discriminating against them (Gerber, 2005, p. 22). At the same time, this principle demands "national treatment". This means that imported goods are treated on the same terms as goods produced domestically, once they have entered the country. As a result, it is for instance not possible to set higher VAT rates for imports than for domestic goods (Gerber, 2005, p. 21 f.).

- **Freer trade through negotiation:** The objective of lowering trade barriers is reached through negotiations. Freedom of contract is respected. Each country is subject to regulations only if it signs and ratifies the relevant agreement. The WTO cannot dictate trade policies to its members (WTO, 2010).
- **Predictability through binding and transparency:** When countries agree to open their markets, they bind themselves. A country can change its bindings at a later time, but only after negotiating with its trading partners, which could mean compensating them for loss of trade. To improve transparency and build confidence, Trade Policy Reviews are regularly carried out by the WTO to examine its member countries' trade practices (WTO, 2010).
- **Promoting fair competition:** The rules of the WTO should allow fair and undistorted competition. To guarantee this, the WTO has a dispute settlement procedure for trade disputes between member countries. This is a means of protection for weaker countries against stronger nations (WTO, 2010).
- **Encouraging development and economic reform:** Over three quarters of WTO members are developing countries and countries in transition to market economies. To contribute to their development, the better-off countries have to improve the market access for goods exported by the least-developed countries and to offer increased technical assistance to them.

GATT has ushered in a period of rapid and effective liberalization of trade. The area in which the least progress has been made is perhaps agricultural produce. The negotiations in the Doha round have been going on for many years without yielding any significant result. Protectionist measures still impose a massive cost burden. "According to one calculation, consumers and governments in rich countries pay 350 billion US dollars a year to support agriculture – enough to fly their 41 million dairy cows first class around the world one and a half times" (WTO, 2010).

Regardless of whether the Doha round eventually proves successful in yielding an international agreement, it seems that the age of extensive worldwide agreements on tariff reductions is now over. A great deal of effort will be necessary to consolidate what has already been achieved and comparable effort will go into concluding focused agreements on special issues.

As we have seen, the external conditions play a key role in the internationalization of economies. Even the strongest drivers will not lead to internationalization if the external conditions are unfavourable. A good illustration of this is the effect of the North American Auto Pact of 1964, which quickly led to a considerable expansion of international trade. **Inset 2.4** explains the pact.

Inset 2.4: The North American Auto Pact of 1964
(text based on Krugman/Obstfeld, 2009, p. 134 f.)

In 1963, Canada's home auto industry was only about one tenth the size of its US counterpart. The reason for this was high import tariffs. US companies produced almost the same number of different car models in their facilities in Canada as they did in the US factories. But as a result of its much smaller volume of sales, Canada's facilities were less specialized and had higher costs per unit than in the US, leading in turn to higher prices.

The Auto Pact removed the tariffs. As a result US companies were able to create specialized facilities in Canada and the resulting economies of scale led to lower unit costs. These specialized production facilities in Canada could now serve the large US market as well as the Canadian market. On the other hand 90% of the car models were no longer produced in Canada after 1964 and had to be imported from the US.

2.4   Explanatory models for the internationalization of companies

There are a large number of explanatory models which can contribute to an understanding of economic globalization. It would be beyond the scope of this book to examine all of these. This section presents just two theoretical ideas which we believe are key concepts for under-standing the phenomenon: the theory of cost advantages, and the law of the experience curve.

Cost advantages explain many phenomena associated with economic internationalization:

- Absolute cost advantages of different countries will lead to interna-tional trade. Sri Lanka produces tea more cheaply than many other countries, including New Zealand, but New Zealand produces mut-ton more cheaply than Sri Lanka. Tea can be imported from Sri Lanka to be sold in New Zealand; mutton can be exported and sold in Sri Lanka. The foreign products will drive down the prices for home made mutton in Sri Lanka and tea produced in New Zealand. The trade also creates cost, particularly for transport. Nevertheless, if the original price difference is sufficiently large, companies in the two countries will engage in this trade, as will perhaps firms from other countries. But as Ricardo noted, the trade is worthwhile even if the cost advantages are only relative. New Zealand and Australia are both strong in sheep rearing and in producing wool and mutton. But even if New Zealand has an absolute cost advantage for both products, trade is possible. Trade is possible if there is a different rate of exchange between wool and mutton within each of the two countries. In this case each country can specialize in the product which it can produce relatively more cheaply (Sanyal, 2001, p. 13).
- Cost advantages provide an important explanation of international trade in goods and services. But they also account for a large pro-portion of FDI. The shifting of production facilities to Vietnam by Japanese, Korean and Taiwanese textile manufacturers described in **Inset 2.1** has its origin in cost advantages.
- The cost advantages of different countries for specific goods are of central importance in explaining comparative advantages. **Inset 2.5** shows how the OECD measures comparative advantages and offers

selected examples of comparative advantages in a number of countries.

Inset 2.5: Comparative advantages for individual countries and product groups (text based on OECD, 2010)

The OECD uses the following formula to measure the comparative advantage of a country for a particular product:

$$\frac{\text{Comparative advantage of country A for product a}}{} = \frac{\frac{\text{Exports of product a by country A}}{\text{Exports by country A}}}{\frac{\text{Exports of product a worldwide}}{\text{Export worldwide}}}$$

If the comparative advantage "takes a value less than 1, this implies that the country is not specialised in exporting this product ... The share of that category of goods ... within the total exports of goods of this country is less than the corresponding world share. Similarly

Countries / Products	Iceland	Switzerland	Turkey
Fish, crustaceans, molluscs and preparations thereof	**74.2**	0.0	0.5
Photographic apparatus, optical goods and watches	0.0	**8.5**	0.1
Textile yarn fabrics, made up articles and related products	0.1	0.6	**4.5**

Figure 2.3: Comparative advantages 2005 of Iceland, Switzerland and Turkey for selected products (data based on OECD, 2010)

if the index exceeds 1 this implies that the country is specialised in exporting this type of goods".

Figure 2.3 gives comparative advantages and disadvantages for Iceland, Switzerland and Turkey for three specific product groups. The data is striking. Each of the three countries has a clear comparative advantage in one of the product groups. The values are not only impressive in relation to the countries in the table. Even if other OECD members are included, the countries shown here remain clear leaders for one product group. Norway comes second for fish and sea food, but it scores only 6.6. Japan is in second place for optics and watches, but scores just 3.3. Portugal is second for textiles with 2.0.

A second approach which makes an important contribution to the explanation of economic internationalization is the law of the experience curve. It has been validated by empirical research in a number of very different industries:

- The law of the experience curve states that each time cumulative volume doubles for the production of a particular item then value added costs may fall by 20 - 30%. This law applies both to individual companies and to whole industries. However, this is not an automatic effect: cost reduction depends on cost-oriented management (Grant, 2010, p. 229 f; Hill/Jones, 2008, pp. 115 ff.). **Figure 2.4** displays this experience curve.
- There are two main reasons for the law (Grant, 2010, p. 231). As a result of learning or experience effects, production processes become ever more refined and the percentage of mistakes ever smaller. The experience curve also expresses economies of scale. This can be clearly observed in the air travel business. The constant increase in the volume of passengers and goods transported has led to a constant growth in the average dimensions of the airplanes in use. As the airplanes increase in size, the costs fall for each passenger mile and for each mile per ton of freight.

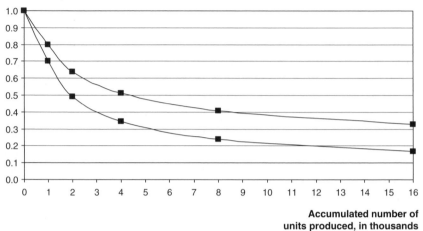

Index of real costs of added value per unit

Accumulated number of units produced, in thousands

Figure 2.4: Experience curve

End of year	1	2	3	4	5	6	7	8
Company A								
• Relative* market share	2	2	2	2	2	2	2	2
• Accumulated production	2,000	4,000	...	8,000	...	...	...	16,000
• Real unit cost	0.7 to 0.8	0.49 to 0.64	...	0.343 to 0.512	...	...	...	0.2401 to 0.4096
Company B								
• Relative* market share	0.5	0.5	0.5	0.5	0.5	0.5	0.5	0.5
• Accumulated production	1,000	2,000	...	4,000	...	...	...	8,000
• Real unit cost	1	0.7 to 0.8	...	0.49 to 0.64	...	...	...	0.343 to 0.512

* = Relative market share is one's own market share divided by the market share of the strongest competitor. A is No. 1 and has twice the size of B. B is No. 2.

Figure 2.5: Market share, accumulated production and unit cost

- The principal conclusion to be drawn from the experience curve is the following: companies with a large market share will double their cumulative volume more rapidly than those with a low market share. This allows them to achieve lower unit costs at a faster rate than competitors. **Figure 2.5** shows how this works. The cost advantage which ensues can be exploited in a number of different ways. The company might lower its product prices, but it could also use the effect to finance product development or to strengthen the image of the brand. A final possibility is to use the finance to diversify or to invest in new geographical markets.
- Clearly there is a link between the second driver of internationalization, realizing cost economies, and the experience curve. By building up foreign markets a company can increase its output and its market share. As Section 2.2 has shown, this leads both to economies of scale and/or economies of replication.

Part II

Strategic planning in general and in the international context

Part I explained internationalization and showed its relevance to social and economic developments and to business management. Part II now follows with an introduction to strategic planning.

Chapter 3 offers a general introduction to strategic planning. There are four sections:

- Section 3.1 explains what is meant by the term strategy and presents the four main characteristics of a strategy.
- Section 3.2 highlights the concept of success potentials. These constitute the central content of strategies. An inset shows an example: the success potentials of the thriving US airline Southwest.
- Section 3.3 sets out five classes of strategic document and outlines what each should contain.
- Finally in Section 3.4 the process of strategic planning is reviewed. The chapter begins by considering the most important requirements that must be met by any process for strategic planning. Next a standard process is presented. Finally an inset gives an account of how the standard process can be adapted to the specific needs of a particular planning project.

This introduction in Chapter 3 is general in focus and should be understood as applying to companies operating in domestic markets.

Chapter 4 moves towards the international context by showing how the strategic planning of a domestic company might lead it to consider going international:

- Section 4.1 explains portfolio analysis and displays the matrix of growth options. The use of these planning tools is often the starting point for a search for new markets. Examples of different forms of diversification are included in the first inset, and a second inset compares the varying performance of related diversification and unrelated diversification.

- Section 4.2 looks at reasons for going international for production and sourcing. It outlines value chain analysis and strategic cost analysis. The section concludes by revealing how the deployment of these analytic tools may lead a company to shift production and/or purchasing to a different country.

Finally in Part II, Chapter 5 provides an introduction to strategic planning in an international context. This offers a framework for the succeeding parts of the book:

- After a short introduction, Section 5.2 reports on the strategic documents required in an international context. This begins with documents for planning and carrying through an entry into new markets. Next come the documents needed to support the decision to shift production and/or supply to another country. The section ends with documents used for the strategic management of an international company.
- In Section 5.3 there is a brief review of the processes of strategic planning in an international context. Three processes are identified. The first is for planning entry into new markets, the second for planning production and/or supply from another country, and the third considers the strategic planning of an international company. At this stage only an outline of the processes is offered; a detailed statement of the processes together with the required methodological tools follows in Parts III, IV and V. Section 5.3 is thus a bridge between the general considerations with which this book begins and a detailed examination of the three key planning issues in an international context.

3   Strategic planning in general

3.1   Strategies

As **Figure 3.1** reveals, the term strategy can refer either to intended strategies or to realized strategies. Given that strategic plans are very rarely realized completely, intended strategies and realized strategies normally diverge to a greater or lesser extent. Accordingly, in the figure below, Case 2 is more probable than Case 1. Of course, it is also possible that a company has no intended strategy, and this is Case 3. Here, the realized strategy is the product of individual decisions and can be characterized as an emerged strategy (Grünig/Kühn, 2011, p. 7; Mintzberg, 1994, pp. 23 ff.).

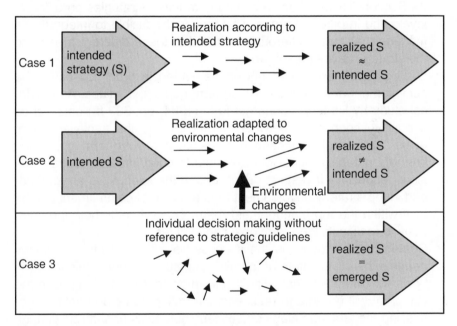

Figure 3.1: Intended and realized strategies (adapted from Mintzberg, 1994, p. 24)

Where the term strategy is used in this book without further qualification, it always means intended or planned strategy.

(Intended or planned) strategies have four key characteristics (Grünig/Kühn, 2011, p. 8):

- They provide a long-term guideline (Grünig/Kühn, 2011, p. 8). What long-term means will depend on the specific industry and company. To focus its investments strategically, a producer of electrical power will require guidelines for the next 25 years. In contrast, for a medium sized nationally-based consulting firm, three years should be sufficient to ensure the development of the company.
- Strategies should be shaped by the company's managers and fully supported by them. Usually this can only be made possible if the managers themselves are involved in strategy development, because otherwise they will not identify strongly enough with the strategies produced. The reason that this is so important is that the company leaders must be fully committed to the implementation process. As Section 3.3 will show, a company requires strategies on different levels and in different areas. This makes it possible to integrate the managers at these different levels and in these different areas into the strategy development process.
- Strategies are developed and implemented in order to secure the achievement of a company's long-term goals and values. An empirical study by Raffée/Effenberger/Fritz (1994, pp. 383 ff.) established a positive connection between strategies and the achievement of goals. This result is indeed a plausible one: long-term guidelines promote proactive behaviour and help to coordinate individual decisions, especially investment decisions. If the executives are embedded in the strategy development then a sense of commitment can be built within the top management team. These effects help the company to realise its long-term goals and values.
- Strategic plans focus on the success potentials which a company needs either to maintain or to build. The success potentials form the basis for future success. They guarantee that in the long term the company will be able to realize its overriding goals and values. Focussing the strategic plans on success potentials has the advantage that questions of detail are deliberately excluded. In general, the closer the focus on essentials, the smaller the differences between planned and realized strategies will be. Questions of detail are better left to operational planning or can be settled in individual decisions.

We have noted that the purpose of strategies is to preserve or construct success potentials. The concept of success potential is thus central to strategic planning. We now look at this concept in more detail.

3.2   Success potentials

The overriding goals and values of a company are central to its identity, forming its "raison d'être". Short-term optimization of a company's activities will not suffice to secure long-term achievement of these overriding objectives and values. What is required is investment for the long-term future. In this context Gälweiler (2005, pp. 26 ff.) introduced the concept of success potentials. As **Figure 3.2** shows, investments in the preservation of existing success potentials and in the construction of new ones are at the centre of strategy development and implementation. These investments guarantee future success both during and beyond the planning period.

The concept of success potential is an abstract one. Concretisation is therefore needed. This can be derived from the ROM model (Resources - Offer - Market positions) of success potentials (Grünig/Kühn, 2011, p. 10). **Figure 3.3** presents the model, which distinguishes three levels of success potentials as follows:

- Strong positions in attractive markets: "Strong positions mean substantial market shares in the served markets or market niches. The attractiveness of markets depends on their size, growth rate and intensity of competition" (Grünig/Kühn, 2011, p. 9 f.).
- Competitive advantages in offers: Competitive advantages in the market offers can be gained in three different ways. Products or services can be demonstrably higher in quality than those of competitors. Alternatively, they may have a better image than those of competitors as a result of a company's efforts in marketing communications. Finally, the products or services may be lower priced than those of competitors while maintaining an acceptable quality level.
- Competitive advantages in resources and processes: Here a wide variety of forms of competitive advantage may be constructed, ranging from better points of sale, through more productive factories to better qualified and motivated staff. This class of competitive ad-

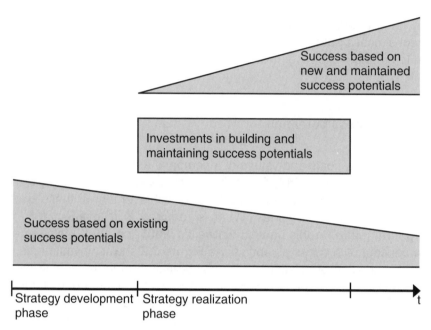

Figure 3.2: Building success potentials as the purpose of strategic management (Grünig/Kühn, 2011, p.10)

vantage would even include elements of company culture such as openness to change.

As **Figure 3.3** shows, each of the three levels builds on the preceding ones. Competitive advantages in the offer rarely arise by chance. They are typically the result of advantages in resources and processes. Maintaining low prices, for example, sets up a cost-aware culture leading to cheaper production processes. A strong market position too, is rarely the result of chance, but is produced by advantages on the two lower levels. To take an example, a high market share in the luxury watch segment is based on a strong brand (resources level) and on marketing communication which succeeds in attributing uniqueness and prestige (offers level).

Strategic planning can determine a company's offers and target market positions as a result of examining the company's resources. This is called the inside-out approach. The alternative is to begin with custom-

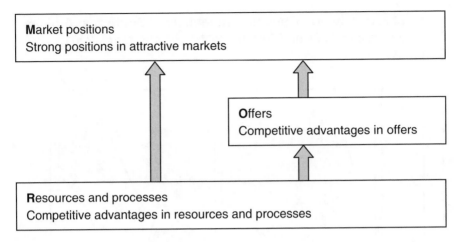

Market positions
Strong positions in attractive markets

Offers
Competitive advantages in offers

Resources and processes
Competitive advantages in resources and processes

⇒ = direction of influence

Figure 3.3: ROM model of success potentials (adapted from Grünig/Kühn, 2011, p. 11)

er needs and target market positions. The offers which the company wants to make and the resources it needs to construct are then specified on this basis. This is known as an outside-in approach (De Wit/Meyer, 2004, pp. 245 ff.; Grünig/Kühn, 2011, p. 285 f.). But whether strategic planning begins with resources or with market positions, there will always be loops in the process.

Inset 3.1 gives the success potentials for Southwest Airlines. The network of success potentials for this successful carrier provides a good illustration of what is important:

- Market position and competitive advantages need to be clear and understandable so that commitment can be won from the staff.
- For effective implementation, it is advisable to concentrate on a small number of key success potentials.
- Strong positive synergies among success potentials make the decisive difference from competitors.

Inset 3.1: Network of success potentials of Southwest Airlines
(text based on Coulter, 2010, pp. 284 ff.; Shah/Sterret, 2001, pp. 200 ff.)

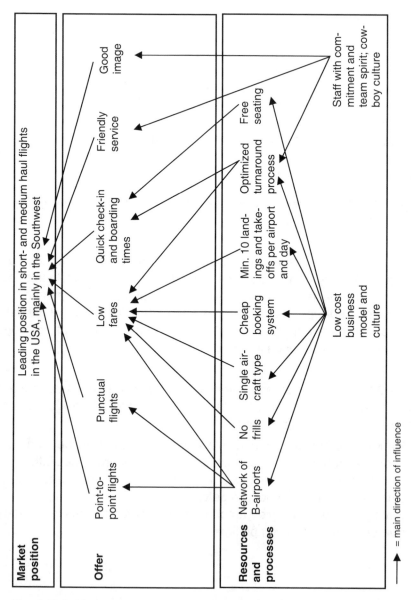

Figure 3.4: Network of success potentials of Southwest Airlines
(Grünig, 2011)

Southwest Airlines offers cheap short- and medium-haul flights within the US. Despite its low prices the company consistently achieves good end-of-year figures. Behind this financial success lies an impressive network of success potentials, summarized in **Figure 3.4.**

The description of the market position not only shows what Southwest Airlines offers, it also shows what is not offered. This airline does not fly international, nor does it offer commuter flights to international hubs. As a result, its customers are all travelling within the US and they do not need to begin or end their flight at a hub.

The customers receive an optimal offer, with punctual direct flights at low prices. Minimal check-in periods and accelerated boarding help to reduce waiting times. On-board service is very limited but this does not mean that it is of low quality as, in fact, the staff are highly motivated.

Resources and processes are based on by a low-cost business model. The willing staff have what the Americans call the cowboy spirit, a combination of hard work and integrity. Even the pilots will sometimes help to clean the aircraft or with the handling of luggage.

3.3   Types of strategies and other strategic documents

What all strategies have in common is that for a period of some years in the future they determine the success potentials which the company must either maintain or newly construct. However, differing planning levels within the company and different issues addressed mean that there are distinct types of strategy (see for instance Hill/Jones, 2008, p. 18 f.; Hofer/Schendel, 1978, pp. 27 ff.; Johnson/Scholes/Whittington, 2008, p. 14 f.; Miller/Dess, 1996, pp. 40 ff.).

The **corporate strategy** sets out future market positions (Hill/Jones, 2008, pp. 18 and 302 ff.; Hofer/Schendel, 1978, pp. 27 ff.; Johnson/ Scholes/Whittington, 2008, pp. 14 and 255 ff.; Miller/Dess, 1996, pp. 42

and 240 ff.). Such a strategy is required by a company, which is diversified in terms of products and/or geographical markets.

The principal content of a corporate strategy is as follows:

- It specifies future businesses. A business, in this sense, is a group of products or services which is clearly distinct from the other products and services of the corporation. To identify businesses, key characteristics of products and services can be used, such as quality and price. Alternatively, products and services can be separated into different businesses according to customer groups or geographical markets.
- The corporate strategy sets the target market position for each business. This is typically expressed as a target market share. But it may also include qualitative statements related to a target product image.
- To achieve these target market positions investment is required. This is especially so if the market position has to be improved or newly created. The corporate strategy, therefore, sets investment budgets for the businesses or at least specifies investment priorities.
- Setting future target market positions in the corporate strategy also involves decisions about diversification or focus. Diversification occurs when new geographical markets are entered or new product groups created. In contrast, a company may decide to abandon certain products or services or to withdraw from certain regions. In this case we speak of concentration (Johnson/Scholes/Whittington, 2008, p. 14).
- The corporate strategy must ensure that the combination of the various businesses achieves added value (Johnson/Scholes/Whittington, 2008, p. 14). The capital market can spread risk more efficiently than a diversified company can. So companies must create added value through synergies in marketing and/or production.

A **business strategy** determines target competitive advantages for a business (Hill/Jones, 2008, pp. 18 and 149 ff.; Hofer/Schendel, 1978, pp. 27 ff.; Johnson/Scholes/Whittington, 2008, pp. 14 and 221 ff.; Miller/Dess, 1996, pp. 40 f. and 146 ff.). In accordance with the criteria which have been used to define the different businesses within the corporate strategy, the individual business strategies are produced either for product groups, for customer groups, for regional markets or for different combinations of these three. For example, Nestlé could have a business strategy for chocolate products in the Swiss market.

The business strategy not only determines the generic competitive strategy (see Porter 1980, pp. 34 ff.) but also identifies the competitive advantages for the offer. This serves to make the chosen generic strategy more detailed so that it can be used to position the company amongst its market competitors. The business strategy further specifies competitive advantages at the level of resources and processes. This creates the basis for advantages in the offer which are sustainable. For example, low prices can only be maintained long-term if resources and processes produce low costs.

What are known as **functional strategies** constitute a third sub-type of strategy (Hill/Jones, 2008, pp. 18 and 109 ff.; Hofer/Schendel, 1978, pp. 27 ff.). Functional strategies set out success potentials which need to be maintained or constructed for specific tasks or functions within the company. Examples are marketing, human resources management, operations and sourcing.

As the reader will note, the authors take a broad view as to what the content of a business strategy might be. In this view, business strategies specify both target competitive advantages in the offer and also the corresponding competitive advantages in resources and processes. As a result, success potentials for functions like marketing, human resources management, operations and sourcing are frequently defined within business strategies. This can lead to duplication, with business strategies and functional strategies containing the same provisions. To avoid this, functional strategies should be used sparingly. Our view is that functional strategies are only required in two cases, as follows:

- In cases where functions are perceived as affecting more than one business, a functional strategy will define a common framework. An example would be a common marketing strategy, in order to create a shared brand image and appearance for products and services which different businesses sell under the same brand name.
- Complexity can also justify the use of a functional strategy, and this is so whether the function concerned affects a single business or applies to more than one business. For example, in cases where production is spread across a number of specialized facilities it makes sense to have an operations strategy, even if it only concerns a single business.

The principal documents required for strategic management are these three types of strategy. But there are two further types of strategic document:

- A **mission statement** sets out a company's overriding objectives and values. It thus provides the normative basis for strategic management (Carpenter/Sanders, 2009, pp. 46 ff.; Grünig/Kühn, 2011, p. 32). Nevertheless, in the course of strategic analysis issues may arise which challenge these goals and values and can lead to a revision of the mission statement.
- Once strategies have been defined, **implementation programs** are required to ensure their realization (Grünig/Kühn, 2011, pp. 31 ff.; Wheelen/Hunger, 2010, pp. 322 ff.). These programs ensure that the concrete activities required to implement strategic goals and measures actually take place. To this end, it is particularly important to appoint program leaders who report to the board and who take responsibility for the implementation programs.

Figure 3.5 summarizes the essential content of these five types of strategic documents.

3.4   Process of strategic planning

Strategic planning is the process by which strategies and other strategic documents are produced. If the mission statement, the strategies, and the implementation programs are to advance the company towards long-term success, then the process must satisfy three requirements:

- The process must be oriented towards issues within the company. In other words, the process must be tailored to company needs. What follows here is an account of a standard process which needs to be adapted to specific needs. Later, in Chapters 8, 11 and 17 three processes will be presented. They deal with specific issues in internationalization and to this extent are already tailored processes.
- The process has to be precisely defined and carried out systematically. This brings the advantage that the working group is not constantly confronted with process issues and can thus concentrate on the central content.

Content \ Types	Mission statement	Corporate strategy	Business strategy	Functional strategy	Implementation programs
Overriding objectives and values	***				
Market positions	*	***	*	*	*
Competitive advantages in offers		*	***	*	*
Competitive advantages in resources and processes		*	***	***	*
Implementation measures					***

*** = main content
* = complementary content

Figure 3.5: Types of strategic documents (adapted from Grünig/Kühn, 2011, p. 32)

- The company's executives must be embedded within the strategy development process. As we have already noted in Section 3.1, this is an absolute requirement in order that strategies are produced which enjoy support and will therefore be implemented. If the management is not involved there is a grave danger that the required commitment will not be produced and there may even be resistance. They need to be deployed in planning tasks related to their areas of responsibility. For example, the strategy for a division needs to be developed by the leaders of that division. Where possible, the project leader should be the divisional chief.

Figure 3.6 presents one possible process for strategic planning. This is a standard process which allows a diversified company to produce or revise the various strategic documents presented in 3.3 above.

We now describe this process which has one preliminary step and eight main steps (Grünig/Kühn, 2011, pp. 50 ff.).

Preparing the strategy planning project in **Step 0** involves tackling a number of practical tasks. The issues must be clearly identified. Project organization and schedule must be fixed. The question of whether to bring in outside consultants has to be answered. Finally the project costs must be budgeted.

As most researchers and consultants agree, the planning of strategies must be preceded by a phase of strategic analysis. The main emphasis of this **Step 1** is on data collection and analyses in three fields:
- Global environment
- Relevant industries
- The company itself

Strategic analysis ends with problem diagnosis. This is restricted to an approximate evaluation of strategic opportunities and threats, because detailed assessment of current strategies is only carried out in Steps 3 to 5.

The mission statement defining the company's overriding objectives and values forms the basis for the determination of future strategies. However, these objectives and values cannot be fixed without relation to reality. For this reason the company mission statement has to be checked in **Step 2** against the findings of strategic analysis and, if needed, either revised or replaced.

Step 3 is the development of the corporate strategy. This involves first of all the definition of strategic businesses in order to provide a strategic view of the diversified company. Step 3 then requires an assessment of the company's current market positions. These are evaluated according to the criteria of industry attractiveness and competitive strength. Finally, Step 3 also includes developing and assessing strategic options.

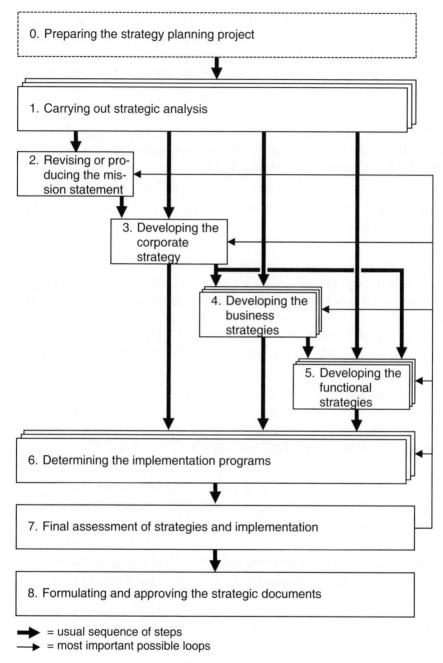

Figure 3.6: Process of strategic planning (adapted from Grünig/Kühn, 2011, p. 47)

Step 4 consists of developing the business strategies. Elaborating a business strategy first involves evaluating the current competitive position. Based on this, the future generic competitive strategy can be chosen and the target competitive advantages can be determined both at the level of the offer and at the level of resources and processes.

In **Step 5** the necessary functional strategies are developed. They coordinate activities shared by more than one business and guarantee the effective execution of complex tasks.

Step 6 involves the planning of the implementation measures, especially the creation of strategic programs.

Step 7 is the final assessment of both strategies and programs. Having progressed through the various steps, with staff sometimes working in parallel on different strategies, it is essential to achieve a global view once more before the strategies and programs are finally approved and realized. Step 7 might, for example, uncover the accumulation of too many high risks or reveal the impossibility of financing all the programs.

Step 8 involves the formulation and approval of strategic documents. To serve as effective guidelines for managers during the phase of implementation, the mission statement, the strategies and the program plans must be formulated both concisely and very precisely.

The process described here is a standard process which needs to be adapted to the specific issues of the company and to its context and structure. **Inset 3.2** provides an example of how this might be done.

> **Inset 3.2: Strategy planning process of the car parts dealer Swiss Automotive Group** (text based on Swiss Automotive Group, 2011)
>
> **1. The company**
>
> Swiss Automotive Group trades in car spares in three European countries. The company has 1500 staff and a turnover of 500 million

CHF. The company supplies original manufacturers' parts to regional dealers as well as to garages. These garages mostly do not represent a particular car maker and they carry out repairs and servicing on a wide range of car models.

2. The strategic planning process

A board committee initiated the strategic planning process four months ahead of the strategy workshop. Two key questions were formulated:

- How can the company strengthen its competitive position in the car parts trade in the three countries where it operates?
- Can opportunities for diversification be found which would have strong synergies with the current activities?

Starting from these two questions, executives analysed the three different country markets for car parts and then put forward suggestions as to how to strengthen the company's market positions. They each used the same methods and structured their reports in the same way, so that the three reports could be compared easily against each other. At the same time young executives examined four specific diversification proposals previously put forward by the board committee. Here too the work was structured according to a pre-designed analytic scheme. In parallel, the company owners fixed the goals for the next years and critically reviewed the company's mission statement.

Figure 3.7 presents the program for the two and a half day workshop which was attended by the board of directors, the CEO and the CFO.

After the workshop, business strategies were formulated for the three country markets. These were presented at the next board meeting for formal approval. The business strategies were based on goals and conditions approved at the workshop. At the same time two of the diversification proposals were further researched. Busi-

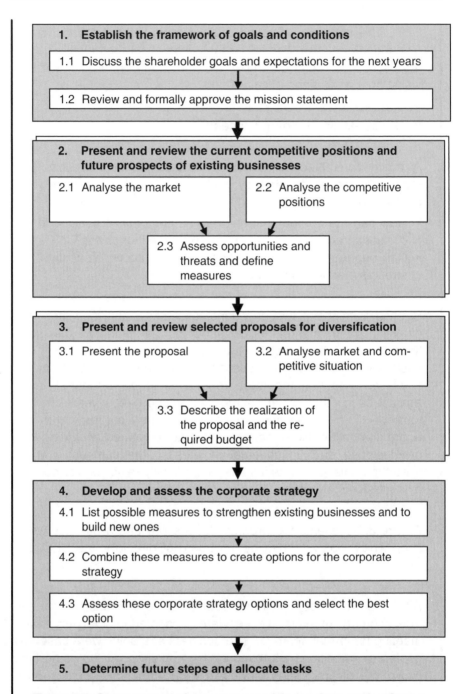

Figure 3.7: Strategy workshop program of Swiss Automotive Group
(adapted from Swiss Automotive Group, 2011)

ness plans were drawn up and presented to the Board. Once business strategies and new business plans were approved by the Board, they were implemented step by step.

3. Comparison with standard process

A comparison with the standard process reveals many similarities. As in the standard process, this process begins with project planning. This not only determines the process, but also formulates the questions which should be the focus of analysis and planning.

Next comes the analysis and fixing of the normative framework of goals and conditions. In fact, the workshop begins with these questions, though it treats them in the reverse order.

Next the process follows the standard process by first developing the corporate strategy in the workshop, and then, after the workshop, developing the business strategies. Functional strategies are not required as the necessary decisions will be taken when developing the business strategies.

The implementation of the two selected diversification proposals begins with the formulation of business plans. This is an intermediate step which is not part of the standard process. Once the strategies and business plans have been approved by the board, projects will be set up in order to implement them.

The final two steps in the standard process are missing here. The strategies and business plans are evaluated and implemented separately. This is a result of the workshop, which is central to the strategic planning process. The workshop serves not only to produce and assess corporate strategy options, but also makes a decision about the future corporate strategy.

4 Strategic planning of a domestic company as the starting point for going international

4.1 Strategic planning as the starting point for going international for new markets

4.1.1 Preliminary remarks

As Section 2.2 shows, internationalization is often the result of unsatisfactory prospects in the home market. Portfolio analysis and the Ansoff matrix of growth options are two tools used in strategic analysis which can help a domestically based company to investigate the possibilities of entering new markets. We now present each in turn.

Going international for new markets can also be the result of opportunities in new markets. This will not be considered here, but only in Part III below.

4.1.2 Portfolio analysis

Portfolio methods for strategic planning were first developed by consulting companies in the 1970s. As the term suggests, a diversified company can be compared to an investment portfolio (Wheelen/ Hunger, 2010, p. 268). Portfolio methods for strategic planning can be characterized as follows:

- A portfolio analysis provides an overview of the market positions of the various businesses in a diversified company or division (Miller/Dess, 1996, p. 275 f.).
- Portfolios are usually set up with two dimensions, one of which represents market attractiveness and the other the competitive strength of the business. While the company cannot greatly influence the first dimension, it can take measures to improve its market position.
- Portfolio analysis reveals whether the portfolio of businesses is balanced. A balanced portfolio has businesses in both mature and growing markets. Businesses in mature markets need relatively little ongoing investment and can thus provide free cash flow. Normally,

however, their long-term prospects are limited: as the market life cycle progresses, turnover and contribution margins tend to decline. In contrast, businesses in growing markets require investment so that they can grow as the market grows. Such investment normally produces a negative cash flow. If a company wishes to strengthen its market position, the financial resources required will be even greater. But of course growing markets promise positive perspectives for many years to come.

The Boston Consulting Group portfolio method is a well-known example of the portfolio approach (Hedley, 1977, pp. 9 ff.; Wheelen/Hunger, 2010, pp. 269 ff.):

- In accordance with the law of the market life cycle, the method takes real market growth, that is market growth adjusted for inflation, as its indicator of market attractiveness.
- The competitive strength of a business is represented by its relative market share. To calculate this, the market share of the business is divided by that of its most important competitor. If the business has a market share of 20% and its closest competitor has 10%, the relative market share is 2.0. If the closest competitor had 25% of the market, then the relative market share of our business would be 0.8. The relative market share as a measure of the competitive strength of a business is based on the law of the experience curve, presented in Section 2.4 above.

  Figure 4.1 shows a Boston Consulting Group portfolio, with its matrix divided into four squares. The average real growth of the relevant market is used to divide the vertical axis into two halves. In the upper half the market is growing faster than average, in the lower more slowly. In this example the average rate of growth for the food market in Switzerland is used. For Unilever, the average growth of the worldwide market in consumer goods would be used. Southwest Airlines would use the figure for growth in air traffic in the US. The horizontal axis is also divided into two. As mid-point a relative market share of 1 is used. To the right of this point are businesses which have a market leader position. A logarithmic scale is preferred for the horizontal axis, as this provides a more realistic measure of business strength than a numerical scale. The size of the circles representing the businesses reflects turnover or contribution margin. The intention is to show their relative importance for the company as a whole.

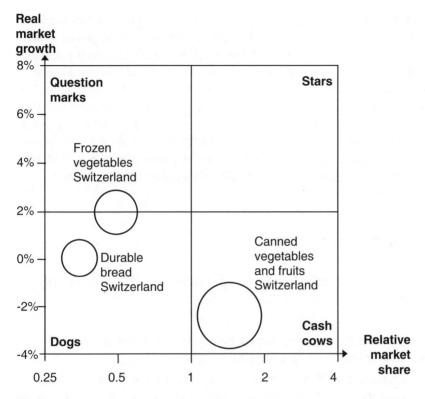

Figure 4.1: Boston Consulting Group portfolio of a purely domestic company

- Different strategic approaches are recommended for businesses in each of the four squares, as the names given to the quadrants make clear. However, these norm strategies should not be applied unthinkingly: apart from the position in the portfolio, the future strategy to be adopted for a business should take account of the specific competitive context and of its specific strengths and weaknesses.
- The BCG portfolio method is straightforward. There is a clear connection between the position of a business in the portfolio matrix and its free cash flow. Perhaps the main disadvantage of the method is its simplicity. It uses only one variable as indicator of market attractiveness and one to measure business strength. However, there is no doubt that these two variables represent very important criteria for assessing market attractiveness and competitive strength.

Figure 4.1 shows a portfolio without future prospects. Most of the businesses are in markets and submarkets with low or negative growth rates. This means that current levels of turnover can only be maintained if market share can be wrested from competitors. But in view of how unattractive the future is for these markets and submarkets, it is doubtful if this would be a sensible strategy. Improved market penetration as a result of investment to raise market share usually only brings a reasonable return if the market is growing. So in this situation, growth options must be sought elsewhere than in current activities, that is in diversification. Section 4.1.3 now examines diversification options.

4.1.3   Growth options matrix

Figure 4.2 presents the four basic options for growth in Ansoff's growth options matrix.

However, Ansoff's scheme can be extended to provide a more differentiated account of the possibilities for growth:

- With new products and services it is important to make a distinction between new products and services at the same level in the value creation process and new products and services at a different level in the value creation process. This leads us to distinguish horizontal diversification, vertical backward diversification and vertical forward diversification.
- As regards new markets, we distinguish between new customers in existing geographical markets, similar customers in new geographical markets and new customers in new geographical markets. This allows distinctions to be made between customer diversification, geographical diversification and geographical and customer diversification.
- Finally, lateral diversification is divided into related lateral diversification and unrelated lateral diversification. In related diversification there will be synergies between existing activities and the planned new activities.

Markets	Existing markets	New markets
Products and services		
Existing products	Improved market penetration	Market diversification
New products	Product diversification	Lateral diversification

Figure 4.2: Growth options matrix (adapted from Ansoff, 1965, p. 109)

Figure 4.3 presents the extended version of Ansoff's matrix. Two further comments must be made:

- All the various growth options in the first line and in the first column are related diversifications. The first line displays options which all build on existing products and services, while in the first column the activities are all directed at existing customer groups in current geographical markets. With lateral diversifications each case must be considered separately to determine whether or not it counts as a related diversification or an unrelated one.
- While this matrix offers a differentiated overview of the various growth options, it offers no help as regards the development and comparison of specific diversification projects. It is a purely descriptive approach, not a prescriptive one (Lynch, 2000, p. 581).

Before moving on to an assessment of the different growth options, we present in **Inset 4.1** a number of examples of the different forms of diversification.

Markets / Products and services	Existing customers in existing geographical markets	New customers in existing geographical markets	Similar customers in new geographical markets	New customers in new geographical markets
Existing products and services	Improved market penetration	Customer diversification	Geographical diversification	Geographical and customer diversification
New products and services at the same level	Horizontal diversification			
New products and services at a different level in the value creation system	Vertical forward diversification			
	Vertical backward diversification			

Related lateral diversification

Unrelated lateral diversification

Figure 4.3: Enlarged growth options matrix

Inset 4.1: Examples of the different forms of diversification

The different forms of diversification presented in **Figure 4.3** are not mere hypothetical constructs but are easily recognizable as distinct types in real businesses, as the examples here will show.

Adidas and Nike are two companies which **diversified horizontally** by extending their product ranges from sports shoes to sports clothing, in the first instance, and then to sports equipment. These extensions of the product range targeted existing customers, whether trade customers or end consumers.

The Richemont Group decided to open Montblanc stores. This is an example of **vertical forward diversification**. The shops were intended to strengthen the Montblanc brand while also affording direct access to customers.

Vinamilk is a Vietnamese dairy food producer. The company provides an example of **vertical backward diversification**. It built up its own milk production facilities to guarantee the supply of high quality raw milk which had been properly cooled after milking and was not contaminated.

Migros, one of the largest retailers in Switzerland, acquired Scana, a company specializing in the supply and delivery of food and near food products to hotels, restaurants and canteens. This was a **customer diversification** option, since the acquisition gave Migros access to a customer group that was growing more rapidly than retail trade.

Heineken and Carlsberg represent good examples of **geographical diversification**. Both these beer producers have systematically built a worldwide network of subsidiaries. Today their brands are better known across the world than, for example, Budweiser, even though Budweiser continues to produce more beer than either of them. However, Budweiser is firmly focussed on the US market.

Geographical expansion often means that companies target a new customer group (**geographical and customer diversification**). Examples include many medium-sized machine manufacturing companies in Germany and Switzerland. They sell their products directly to the end users in their home markets while in their export markets, they distribute them by selling to agents. A different example of geographical and customer diversification is provided by a large number of Swiss food companies which cover all segments in the domestic market but concentrate their exports on the premium segment.

Canon offers an example of **related lateral diversification**. Although cameras, photocopiers, printers and calculators are different products, addressed to different customers, their production is based on the same areas of competence: most importantly, know-how in fine optics, precision mechanics and micro electronics. Thus there are important synergies through shared basic technologies.

In contrast, **unrelated lateral diversification** brings no synergies, or at best only weak synergistic effects. One example is a producer of cigars which diversified into cycle manufacture. Another, a chain of retail kiosks which acquired a manufacturer of beds and mattresses. In these examples there are no obvious synergies and, in fact, both diversification projects failed. But conglomerates like General Electrics and Tyco are also built on unrelated lateral diversifications. The histories of these two companies show constant changes in their portfolios of businesses. And this is not surprising: with only weak synergies between the businesses, the portfolio of businesses can be managed like an investment portfolio.

Three principal criteria are used to assess growth options:

- **Growth potential** is the most important criterion. This is because a domestic company with stagnating businesses needs new activities which promise growth.
- Also crucial is the potential for **synergistic effects**. As **Inset 4.2** shows, the relationship between the new activities and the existing ones is decisive for success. Related diversifications will bring improved performance in comparison with a focussed company, while unrelated diversifications lower performance.
- The third criterion is **risk**. The closer the diversification is to existing activities, the lower the risk.

Inset 4.2: The performance of related and unrelated diversifications (text based on Palich/Cardinal/Miller, 2000, pp. 155 ff.)

Determining the optimal breadth of activity of a company has been an important research area for more than three decades. Palich, Cardinal and Miller have produced a meta-analysis which summarizes this research.

The result of this analysis is clear: regardless of which measure of performance is adopted – ROI, ROS or others – the inverted U model shown in **Figure 4.4** is validated. For company managers, the finding is that neither a very narrow nor a very wide field of activity is optimal for success. The optimal degree of diversification may well be hard to identify, but it is located where businesses use the same resources and where genuine economies of scope can be found.

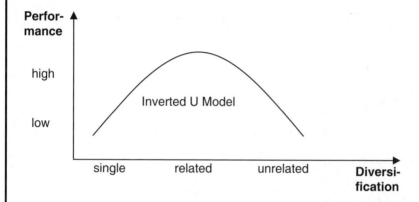

Figure 4.4: Inverted U model (adapted from Palich/Cardinal/Miller, 2000, p. 157)

Figure 4.5 gives an overview of the assessments of the various growth options, based on the professional experience of the authors:

- While improved market penetration is an optimal choice as regards synergies, there is a clear risk that the resources invested in a saturated or degenerating market will not produce a return. This option also performs poorly on the growth potential criterion.
- Even in the slowly growing economies of Western Europe, North America and Japan, there are still products and services for which demand is increasing. Horizontal diversification into one of these areas is certainly an option in order to add to the portfolio a business which has growth potential. But horizontal diversification is only successful if the company has the required competences and resources to produce products or services which are competitive.

Criteria / Growth options	Growth potential	Synergy effects	Risk
Improved market penetration	+	+ + +	- -
Horizontal diversification	++	+	- -
Vertical forward diversification	+	+ +	- -
Vertical backward diversification	+	+	- -
Customer diversification	+ +	+ +	-
Geographical diversification	+ + +	+ +	-
Geographical and customer diversification	+ + +	+ (+)	-
Related lateral diversification	+ + +	+ (+)	- -
Unrelated lateral diversification	+ + +	+	- - -

+	= small	-	= low
+ +	= large	- -	= high
+++	= very large	- - -	= very high

Figure 4.5: Evaluation of the growth options

- Vertical forward integration is not generally seen as a promising option for growth. If demand for a product or service is stagnating, then this is likely to be equally so at the subsequent stage in the value creation process. For example, if demand for hi-fi and audio systems is declining, this will also have a negative effect on the turnover of specialist stores retailing this equipment. However, vertical forward integration will help to establish products with consumers. It also allows businesses to enjoy the combined margins of two stages in the value creation system.
- Vertical backward diversification will also not lead to growth if the market is stagnating. If demand for automobiles is falling, then the same will largely be true for car parts. Only the trade in replacement parts is unaffected by the numbers of new automobiles sold.
- Opening up to customer segments which are growing can be a successful option. As the basic retail market has become stagnant, many food producers have moved into the growing business serving restaurants and hotels. A different example is the systematic development of the growing customer segment of public administration and public companies by consulting firms.
- Geographical diversification into growing markets is an attractive option to strengthen the portfolio. In Eastern Europe, the Asia Pacific and South America there are numerous countries where the real growth rates of the economies are almost 10%. It is mainly the emergence of a middle class which makes these markets attractive for European and US companies. Well educated singles and dual income married couples increasingly have sufficient income to afford to buy their own house and to pay for a car, insurances, foreign holidays and so on.
- Geographical diversification remains an attractive option for growth, even if this means moving into new customer segments. Although there will generally be fewer synergies, the advantage remains that markets can be chosen which are growing much faster than average.
- Lateral diversification offers the advantage too, that growth markets can be targeted and that this will add an effective growth element to a portfolio of stagnating businesses. The level of risk involved depends essentially on how closely the new activities are linked to existing ones. The level of risk is normally significantly higher for unrelated lateral diversification.

To sum up, it seems that geographical diversification is always a strong option, and this remains so whether or not it means serving a new customer segment.

4.2   Strategic planning as the starting point for going international for production and sourcing

4.2.1   Preliminary remarks

Section 4.1 has shown how portfolio analysis and the resulting examination of growth options can impel a domestic company to plan to move into new markets. However, strategic analysis can also lead to a decision to move beyond domestic borders for purchasing or for production. The following section deals with this.

In particular, a domestically based company can be driven to shift purchasing and production abroad as a result of value chain analysis (Porter, 1985, pp. 34 ff.) and an ensuing strategic cost analysis (Thompson/Strickland, 2003, pp. 128 ff.). We now explain these two approaches and then examine the basic options open to companies who wish to reduce their costs.

4.2.2   Value chain analysis

The meeting of customer needs and the resulting creation of economic goods takes place according to value creation processes or, to use Porter's term, value systems (Porter, 1985, pp. 59 ff.). Typically a single company only accounts for a part of the process. **Figure 4.6** shows two companies within their value creation processes. The first is a leather goods wholesaler. The company purchases goods from a number of different suppliers and resells these goods to retailers. The contribution of this company is principally to assemble a range of products which is attractive to retailers and also to carry out a number of logistical functions. The second example is a drinks company. This firm has

Value creation process of a leather wholesaler

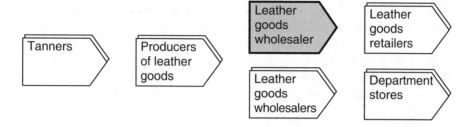

Value creation process of a beverage company

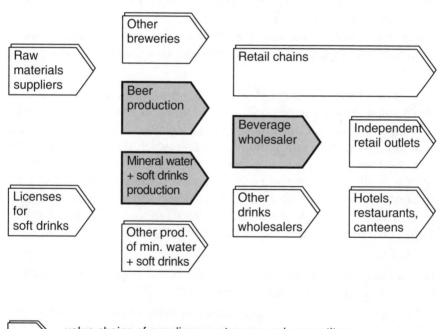

Figure 4.6: Two companies in their value creation processes
(adapted from Grünig/Kühn, 2011, p. 272)

three businesses. With regard to production, the company owns and runs a brewery, as well as a second facility for bottling mineral water. This second facility also produces soft drinks under a licence agreement. But the company is also a wholesaler, distributing beer, mineral water, and soft drinks from a variety of producers, including the products of their direct competitors. At the same time, the company's own drinks products are distributed not only by the company's wholesale business but also by other wholesalers.

Competition takes place within the different stages of the value creation processes. The leather goods wholesaler is in competition with other wholesalers of leather goods. Some of these will also be focussed companies, but if a diversified company has a leather goods wholesale business as one of its business activities, then it will also be a competitor. In contrast, the drinks business occupies three different competitive arenas or industries. And in each of these three it will be in competition both with focused companies and with diversified companies.

The value chain is a concept which allows a closer examination of a firm's value creation within one part of the value creation system. **Figure 4.7** shows the proposed value chain. This divides activities into ten categories: six represent primary activities which contribute directly to output. Three categories are support activities which sustain the primary activities by procuring and organizing the necessary resources. One category includes the management activities. The value chain produces a margin. "Margin is the difference between total value and the collective cost of performing the value activities" (Porter, 1985, p. 38).

In this book we propose a modified form of the original value chain of Porter. There are two reasons motivating this:

- Primary activities and support activities need to be coordinated and in the long term, they need to be developed and kept up to date. This presupposes a broad spectrum of management activities, from personal leadership through planning, monitoring and organization to information management. For this reason management activities has been added as a category (Zentes/Swoboda/Morschett, 2004, p. 222).

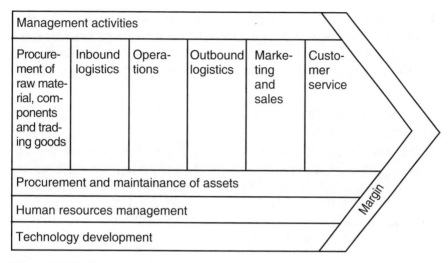

Management activities					
Procurement of raw material, components and trading goods	Inbound logistics	Operations	Outbound logistics	Marketing and sales	Customer service
Procurement and maintainance of assets					
Human resources management					
Technology development					

Figure 4.7: Value chain (adapted from Porter, 1985, p. 37)

- Procurement of raw material and components for production or of finished goods for trading is a central task. It must therefore be classified as a primary activity (Zentes/Swoboda/Morschett, 2004, p. 221).

The categories presented here are part of the value creation process of nearly all industries. However, the labels may stand for entirely different forms of activity, according to the industry concerned. Technology development in the pharmaceutical industry, for example, means developing new active ingredients and new pharmaceutical formulations. Research and development would be an appropriate name for this activity. But in retail banking, technology development means the development of new financial products, new processes, and new forms of marketing, which is some way from the common understanding of R&D. This is why Porter (1985, p. 42) prefers the term technology development.

The value chain varies from industry to industry, and also from company to company. Differences in value activities and in the interfaces between these activities can be the source of decisive competitive advantages. Production in workshops, for example, offers far greater flexibility than a conveyor belt production line. Typically, a much greater range of different variations of a basic product can be produced, as can limited series or unique one-off products, since no set-up times have to be factored into costs. Although production in workshops requires more complicated planning, this presents little difficulty if the company has an effective computer-supported production planning process in place.

Two important questions must be answered when determining the value chain of a business:

- The first concerns the level of detail required when defining the various activities. It is important to identify and list separately those activities with a high potential for differentiation, those with high or rising costs and those with different cost drivers. Unless this is done, the value chain analysis will not be able to identify possible areas for differentiation from competitors and for cost reductions (Porter, 1985, p. 45).
- Sometimes it may be difficult to decide which category to assign an activity to. What counts is the value of the activity within the system as a whole. The processing of orders, for example, can be seen as part of marketing and sales or alternatively as part of operations and logistics. If the order processing system has the potential to develop customer relationships then it should be classified under marketing und sales. If it is merely a system for delivering products on time and as cheaply as possible, then it is better placed within operations and logistics (Porter, 1985, pp. 45 ff.).

Inset 4.3 shows the value chain for the production of airplane seat coverings.

> **Inset 4.3: Value chain for the production of airplane seat coverings**
>
> Lantal Textiles (Lantal) produces fabrics for international air, road and rail transport and for cruise ships (Lantal, 2011). The textiles produced include carpets, seating covers, curtains, wall coverings, and head cushion covers. Lantal further produces pneumatic systems, which are made up of pneumatic cushions and associated components including pumps, valves, motors and hoses. Lantal also offers services such as advice on interior design and cleaning of textiles (Thahabi, 2010, p. 213 f.).

Figure 4.8 displays the most important activities in the value chain for airplane seat coverings manufactured by Lantal Textiles.

While Lantal staff is under the management of their immediate line managers, the company also has an order planning system which prescribes the work to be done. Management is also responsible for financial control and for maintaining the ISO certificate.

In order to produce seat coverings for aircraft, the company needs to buy in wool, polyester and dyes.

Inbound logistics is responsible for quality control, for warehousing and for supplying production with raw materials and components.

The wool and polyester is made into yarn which is then dyed. The fabrics are carefully checked for quality and flaws are corrected by hand-sewing. These are mostly tiny knots which result from the yarn-spinning process. The next stages are producing the fabrics and treating them in order to make them fire-resistant. A final quality control stage checks once more for flaws and incorporates laboratory tests to check the flammability.

After packing, the fabrics are either delivered directly to the customer or stored ready for transport. As these fabrics are destined for airlines, the upholstery fabrics are delivered to the closest airport used by the particular airline. The airline then uses its own freight capacity to deliver the fabrics to the companies making the seats.

In sales and marketing Lantal employs both personal and non-personal communication. Personal communication includes contact through Lantal salesmen and through local representatives. The representatives operate in a country market and are familiar with the language and customs. They work only circa 30-40% for Lantal, also representing other suppliers to airlines. As a result they are in constant close contact with the airline companies. The company also uses trade fairs to find customers. Non-personal communication includes printed advertisements in specialist publications, the company website, and mass mailshots.

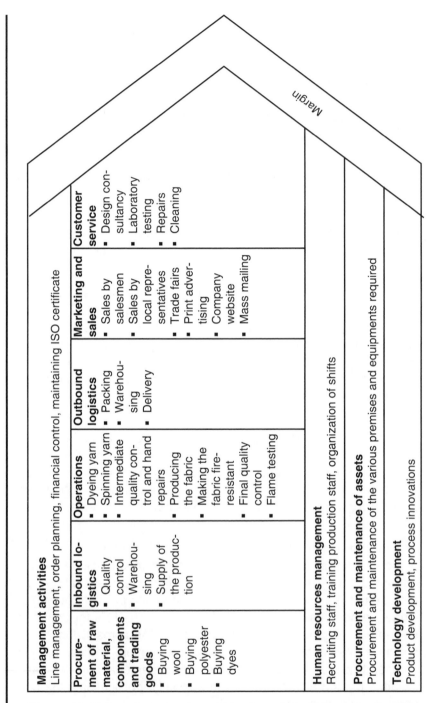

Figure 4.8: Value chain for the production of airplane seat coverings

Lantal offers a large number of extra services. These include advice on design, warehousing, laboratory testing, repairs and cleaning. For important customers, these services are provided free of charge.

The human resources department recruits the company staff. For production, the human resources department trains many of the staff. This is because many of the trades required for the textile production can no longer be studied in Switzerland. Production is organized in shifts. Shift planning is also looked after by the human resources department.

Lantal possesses a dyeing facility for its textile production together with a specialist laboratory for mixing and testing the dyes. The company also has spinning machines, industrial looms, flame-test facilities, and IT systems including an internal network and SAP software. All these assets must be sourced and maintained.

Lantal has its own product development department. Innovation may be either a response to market demands or a result of technical developments. Lantal is also constantly trying to improve production efficiency. This leads to innovations in the production process.

The value chain provides a solid basis on which to assess possibilities for differentiation from competitors and for cost reductions. Here we are principally interested in costs. The following section shows how the value chain can be amplified with cost information.

4.2.3   Strategic cost analysis

Strategic cost analysis includes calculating the costs of the activities in the value chain and comparing them with the costs of competitors.

The determination of the **costs of the value activities** must take place in an appropriate way. The costs of a business or of a value chain are generally arranged according to cost categories. Depending on how sophisticated the cost accounting system is, cost centres and cost objects information may also be available. This form of cost accounting provides a good basis for daily business. But as Thompson/Strickland (2003, p. 134 f.) rightly emphasize, it is not appropriate for strategic planning. Decisions of a strategic nature, such as shifting to outsourcing or moving production to another country must be based on the costs of the value activities concerned. This requires what is known as activity based costing (Cooper/Kaplan, 1988, pp. 96 ff.; Horngren et al., 2009, pp. 162 ff. and 412 ff.). This form of cost accounting identifies one or more cost drivers for each activity and then allocates to each activity the costs which it directly causes. As it does not distribute indirect costs, it avoids the danger of assuming too large cost saving potentials.

The **evaluation of own costs** requires an estimation of the costs of one or more close competitors. Thompson/Strickland characterize this as "an advanced art in competitive intelligence" (2003, p. 133):

- If the competitor is a focussed company, then the total costs of its value chain can be estimated by referring to the company's profit and loss statements. Diversified companies which are listed are required to report separately on their operating segments. This also usually allows a rough estimate of the costs of the different businesses or value chains. But diversified companies which are unlisted are not required to provide these details and so it is impossible to determine the costs for each value chain.
- More detailed information would of course be desirable. The costs of the different value activities of a competitor would directly indicate the areas in which the company's value creation process is competitive and those in which it is not. But it is doubtful that such information can be obtained by legal means.

4.2.4   Options for achieving cost competitiveness

If comparison with competitors shows that unit costs are too high, a number of possibilities offer themselves. The various options are shown in **Figure 4.9** and explained below.

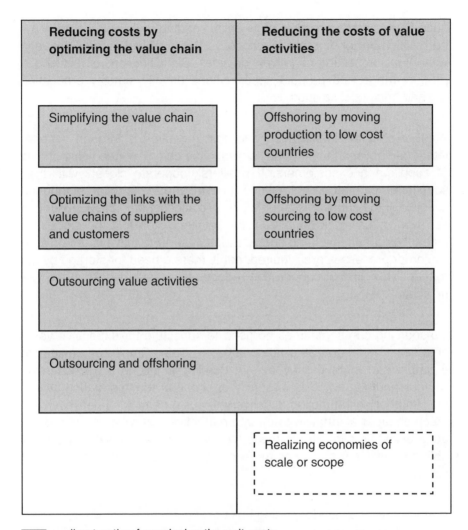

Reducing costs by optimizing the value chain	Reducing the costs of value activities
Simplifying the value chain	Offshoring by moving production to low cost countries
Optimizing the links with the value chains of suppliers and customers	Offshoring by moving sourcing to low cost countries
Outsourcing value activities	
Outsourcing and offshoring	
	Realizing economies of scale or scope

◻ = direct option for reducing the unit costs

⌐ ¬ = indirect option for reducing the unit costs, needing diversification
└ ┘   and growth according to section 4.1

Figure 4.9: Important options for achieving cost competitiveness

Usually unit costs can be brought down if the value chain is simplified by reducing the number of different activities (Thompson/Strickland, 2003, p. 139). Drastic simplifications of the value chain are typically only possible by simplifying products or reducing the variety in the product range. For example, a manufacturer of electric tools might produce fewer different models of its drills, sanding tools, and so on. Maybe the number of different functions on the machines can be reduced without this impacting negatively on sales. Simplifications of this kind in product range and product specifications usually simplify production too and bring cost savings.

Another path to simplification and cost reduction is through a better interface between the company's own value chain and the value chains of suppliers and customers. If retailers cooperate closely with their suppliers they may be able almost to eliminate the function of inbound logistics. If the supplier is given electronic access, then the supplier can see how much stock remains in the retailer's stores. If the stock falls below an agreed level, the supplier tops it up. With this system no special order processes are required, nor is there a need for storage by the retailer. This form of cooperation reduces the overall stocks in the value chain.

Outsourcing can sometimes be used to substitute for expensive value activities (Thompson/Strickland, 2003, p. 139). Small companies for example can save money by outsourcing functions like accounting without incurring any loss of quality or scope of the information available. Another such function is delivery to customers. A carrier may be a much cheaper alternative to an internal delivery service which is operating below its capacity. In these two cases the specialist company is able to carry out the work more cheaply because of economies of scale.

A more radical option for cutting unit costs than those considered so far is to shift high cost value activities to a low cost country (Thompson/Strickland, 2003, p. 139). Typically this means that production is moved to a low wage country. But costs can be reduced by moving other value activities too. For example, many companies have moved their call centers to India.

The identification of new suppliers in low cost countries can also bring significant cost reductions (Thompson/Strickland, 2003, p. 138). Many European retail chains now buy their furniture abroad, in Eastern Europe or East Asia, rather than in their home market.

Companies often lower costs by combining outsourcing and offshoring. Production in the home country is abandoned and finished goods are procured in a low wage country. This path has been followed by numerous European textile companies. Having given up production, these companies are transformed into private label distributors. With the fierce competition between the manufacturers in far-eastern countries, collections can be purchased on very favourable terms.

As a final point, costs can be reduced by economies of scale and of scope. These effects depend on an increase in turnover, so this is an indirect path to cost reduction. On the question of increasing sales the reader is directed to Section 4.1 above.

5 Introduction to strategic planning in the international context

5.1 Preliminary remarks

Chapter 3 provided a general introduction to strategic planning oriented towards the context of a domestic company. Chapter 4 demonstrated how the strategic planning carried out by such a company might suggest the need to internationalize one or more of its activities. Chapter 5 now examines how such internationalization might be strategically planned. This chapter also considers strategic planning for companies which have already successfully managed to internationalize.

The present chapter thus takes up the main theme of the book. It provides an introduction to strategic planning in the international context and sets out a framework for Parts III, IV and V of the book, which follow this introduction with a detailed discussion of the individual issues.

5.2 Types of strategies and other strategic documents in the international context

For strategic planning in a domestic context, Section 3.3 has proposed three types of strategies: corporate strategies, business strategies and functional strategies. But to what extent does this scheme apply to strategic planning in the international context? Are there further types of strategies, or do we need to provide a different classification?

In the literature there is frequent mention of international strategies (Barney/Hesterly, 2010, p. 308 f.; Carpenter/Sanders, 2009, pp. 256 ff.; Haberberg/Rieple, 2008, p. 197 f.; Johnson/Scholes/Whittington, 2008, p. 14). But while there is general agreement on the concepts of corporate, business and functional strategies, there are competing views as to what an international strategy is:

- For Johnson/Scholes/Whittington an international strategy is a document supporting the opening up of new geographical markets: "International strategy is a form of diversification into new geographical markets. It is often at least as challenging as diversification" (2008, p. 14). For Haberberg/Rieple (2008, p. 197) too a central issue of an international strategy is the selection of markets to serve and the associated question of whether products and services need to be adapted to the needs of this market or whether standardized products can be sold.

- Haberberg/Rieple also include a second issue which can be part of an international strategy: "International firms must also consider where to locate their various value chain activities" (2008, p. 197).
- These first two approaches assume a context in which a company is going international. In contrast, Barney/Hesterly start from a company which is already international. "Firms that operate in multiple countries simultaneously are implementing international strategies. International strategies are actually a special case of the corporate strategies" (2010, p. 308).
- Carpenter/Sanders also see international strategies as supporting the planning of an internationally active firm. But unlike Barney/Hesterly they assume that an international strategy can be either a business strategy or a corporate strategy. "A firm's international strategy is how it approaches the cross-border activities. ... In the narrowest sense, a firm's managers need only think about international strategy when they conduct ... their business across national borders. ... Other international activities represent key elements of the firm's corporate strategy" (2009, p. 256).

Our own account of the types of strategy required in an international context is based on the following two considerations:

- The various differing views of international strategy are all valid, but it seems important to give each of the four distinct views a different name in order to avoid confusion.
- In line with the statements by Barney/Hesterly (2010, p. 308) and Carpenter/Sanders (2009, p. 256) strategies in an international context should be linked with those in the domestic context. The different types of strategies which we propose for the international context should therefore be characterized in terms of corporate strategies, business strategies and functional strategies.

With these aims in mind, we present our own suggestion in **Figure 5.1**. We will now comment on each of the categories in this scheme.

All companies, whether already international, or going international, need a normative basis, that is a statement of the objectives and values on which to base their activities. For this reason a careful critical review of the **mission statement** is just as important in an international context as in a domestic one. Section 3.3 has already outlined the content of a mission statement and this requires no special adaptation, remaining the same for a domestic and for an international context.

An **internationalization strategy for new markets** is a document which supports the planning of geographical diversification. Following on from an analysis of the various options for expansion into other countries, the document determines which markets are to be entered and sets a timetable and priorities. In order to function as a specific guiding framework for entry into new markets, the strategy must also indicate which products will be marketed and how the market entry will be achieved. In terms of content, the first set of considerations – the identification of markets and the setting of priorities – are part of corporate strategy. In contrast, the specification of the products and the form of market entry belong to business strategy. To this extent the internationalization strategy for new markets is a combination of corporate and business strategy.

To realize the internationalization strategy for new markets consists in entering new geographical markets. To prepare for this and carry it through, a detailed plan of action is required. We call this a **market entry program**.

The shifting of production or purchasing to another country also has to be based on strategic analysis and planning. Such activity ends with the development of an **internationalization strategy for production and sourcing**. The content of this type of strategy reveals it to be a special type of functional strategy. It determines what is to be purchased and where and/or what is to be produced and where. In order to link the various purchasing and production activities together, the strategy also has to deal with logistics.

Like an internationalization strategy for new markets, an internationalization strategy for production and sourcing also requires implementation planning. Programs must be created to build up an infrastructure and to plan the commencement of production or sourcing in a new country. These are **production and sourcing relocation programs**.

Purposes and types / Content	Defining the norma-tive bases	Going international for new markets	
	Mission statement	Internatio-nalization strategy for new markets	Market entry programs
Overriding objectives and values	✳✳✳		
Market positions	✳	✳✳✳	✳
Competitive advantages in offers		✳✳	✳
Competitive advantages in resources and processes		✳✳	
Implementation measures			✳✳✳

✳✳✳ = very important content
✳✳ = important content
✳   = complementary content

Figure 5.1: Types of strategic documents in the international context

The strategic planning of an internationally active company is based on the same documents presented in Section 3.3 for a domestic company: alongside the mission statement, a **corporate strategy** is required, together with a number of **business strategies**. Also **functional strategies** may be needed. As Section 3.3 makes clear, the authors advise restraint with regard to functional strategies. Often operations strategies are needed. They cover sourcing, inbound logistics, production and outbound logistics. Because these strategies are so vital, they have been emphasized in the figure. Finally, for an international company too, **implementation programs** will be necessary.

Going international for production and sourcing		Being international			
Internationalization strategy for production and sourcing	Production and sourcing relocation programs	(International) corporate strategy	(International) business strategies	(International) functional, especially operations strategies	(International) implementation programs
*		***	*	*	*
*		**	***	*	*
***	*	**	***	***	*
	***				***

*** = very important content
** = important content
* = complementary content

Figure 5.1: Types of strategic documents in the international context
(continued)

The difference between an international and a national company is not in the documents and their names but in the content. In particular, the corporate strategy of an international company will be considerably more complex than one of a domestic company:

- The corporate strategy must determine the level of integration and responsiveness.
- When defining strategic businesses and setting strategic objectives we have to specify along with products and customer groups the various served geographical markets and the decentralized operation units.

- In addition a product standardization and an operations policy have to be determined. These policies create a framework for the business strategies and the operations strategies.

We can summarise what has been said in this section in two main points:
- The planning of internationalization and the strategic management of an international company are contexts which require specific sets of strategic management documents.
- Although strategic management in the international context requires specific documents, these can be directly associated with the generic strategic document types presented in Section 3.3. The fundamental strategic questions remain the same. Whether a company is domestic, is going international or is already international, what the strategic documents must determine are the normative basis, the target market positions, the offers, the resources and the implementation measures.

5.3   Strategic planning processes in the international context

In Section 3.4 we presented a standardized strategic planning process. At the same time we emphasized that this standard process needs to be adapted to specific issues and to the specific context and structure of the company.

Going international for new markets is a specific issue of this kind and requires an adaptation of the strategic planning process. Part III of this book looks at this question in detail. Chapter 6 and 7 present the foundations for a successful resolution of this problem. Building on these foundations, Chapter 8 outlines the process we recommend for developing an internationalization strategy for new markets.

Going international for production and sourcing also requires an adapted planning process. This is addressed in Part IV: Chapters 9 and 10 set out the bases and Chapter 11 presents the tailored process for developing an internationalization strategy for production and sourcing.

Strategic planning is concerned with the same issues, whether it is for a domestic company or an international one. In this sense, the international context is not a special issue and does not require an adaptation of the process. However, as will be explained in Part V, the high complexity and specific structure of international companies makes the strategy development process more difficult. Based on foundations outlined in Chapters 12 to 16, Chapter 17 explains the strategic planning process in an international company.

Part III

Strategies for going international for new markets

Part III focuses on how to build up new markets.

Chapter 6 first explains how to identify attractive foreign markets. There are three sections:

- After preliminary remarks in Section 6.1, Section 6.2 proposes decision criteria for selecting new markets.
- Section 6.3 then offers a process for evaluating markets. After an overview, the three steps of the process are explained in detail. An inset introduces the BERI index, which can be used as the basis for determining the risks of country markets. In another inset, an approach known as industry segment analysis is described. We recommend this approach as a valuable way to gain an overview of a market. When assessing markets, one important factor is access to distribution channels. A third inset shows how increasing concentration makes it more and more difficult to gain access to retail chains for food and near food.

Chapter 7 deals with the evaluation of the various forms of entry:

- The opening section offers an overview of the various forms of entry while Section 7.2 reviews the various possibilities for export. For small and medium-sized businesses desiring to enter a foreign market, export is the most obvious choice and the one most often made. A first inset gives an account of a case of export through a distributor. A second inset explains how companies can choose a suitable distributor or agent in a foreign market.
- Entry modes for production in the host country are presented in Section 7.3. There are a number of insets with examples illustrating different approaches to setting up production in a new market.
- Section 7.4 describes franchising, a method of opening up new markets which is popular in service industries and in retailing.
- In section 7.5 recommendations for evaluating market entry modes are presented. First evaluation criteria are presented. Then external

and internal conditions influencing the evaluation are discussed. Finally, an evaluation process is proposed.

Chapter 8 focuses on the process for developing an internationalization strategy for new markets together with the required market entry programs:

- Section 8.1 gives an overview of the recommended process. The succeeding sections describe the individual steps in this process.
- Section 8.2 explains why there is a need to prepare the strategy planning project, and also what needs to be done.
- Sections 8.3 and 8.4 briefly pick up the ideas presented in Chapters 6 and 7 concerning the selection of the most attractive markets and the choice of the most suitable market entry mode.
- Next Section 8.5 reveals that it is necessary to produce a feasibility study for each market which is selected as attractive. These studies should reveal how the markets would be opened up and what the costs would be.
- Section 8.6 is concerned with the development of the internationalization strategy. Based on the feasibility studies, the internationalization strategy specifies the country markets to be entered and the order in which they will be tackled. The decision for or against any particular country market will depend not only on available finance but crucially on the profitability of entry into the new market. To clarify this, an inset shows how the net present value can be used to estimate the profitability of each potential country market entry.
- If market entries are realized in collaboration with partners, agreements must be negotiated and signed. This is explained in Section 8.7.
- Where new market positions have to be constructed, market entry programs will be required. Section 8.8 shows how to develop these programs.

6 Evaluating new markets

6.1 Preliminary remarks

The analysis of potential new markets and the ensuing selection of the attractive ones are tasks which make great demands, both in terms of content and methodology:

- The complexity in content arises because entry into a new market may mean two things at the same time: entry into a new geographical market and entry into a new industry market. This means that there are many relevant areas which need to be brought into the decision making.
- The methodological difficulty arises from a dilemma. The collection of data for a new potential market is on the one hand expensive and time-consuming: this would seem to suggest that a selection should be made quickly and that the analysis should be confined to a small number of potential markets. But while this approach may seem to make sense in financial terms, it brings on the other hand the danger with it that attractive markets may be eliminated at an early stage of the selection process because the available information about them is not sufficiently fine-grained.

The identification of attractive markets may proceed in one of three ways:

- The company is open to every possibility and makes a broad survey of potential markets. In this case a procedure in three steps is recommended. First a broad initial list is drawn up. Next, a relatively straightforward analysis eliminates the less attractive markets on this initial list. Finally a detailed analysis is carried out of the remaining candidates which allows the most attractive to be identified.
- The company relies on personal contacts or the experiences of other firms and therefore focuses from the very beginning on a limited number of candidate markets. In this case, the company can directly begin with the detailed analysis and the selection of the best candidates. There will be no need for an initial list and an elimination of less attractive markets.
- The company knows from the outset which market or markets it wishes to enter. In this case no selection process is required. But we must point out, however, that the selection has been an intuitive one

which may turn out to be less than optimal. Given the huge investments required for constructing a new market position we strongly recommend companies to carry out a formal comparison of their preferred target market(s) with one or two alternative options. For example, if the company has determined it would like to enter the Lithuanian market, it would seem reasonable to compare this market with those of Estonia and Latvia.

6.2   Criteria for evaluating new markets

This chapter is concerned with the selection of attractive markets. To identify the best candidate markets, formal decision criteria are required which reflect parameters of market attractiveness.

We see a market as having two dimensions. First there is the geographical boundary (e.g. Germany) and then there is the industry dimension (e.g. motor vehicle production). What this means is that we need two kinds of criteria: criteria related to each country market as a whole and then criteria relating to specific industry markets within that country.

Figure 6.1 presents our key criteria for assessing and selecting country and industry markets.

6.3   Process for evaluating new markets

6.3.1   Overview of the process

Figure 6.2 gives an overview of our recommended process for the evaluation of new geographical markets.

This process is based on two heuristic principles: factorization and subgoal reduction (Grünig/Kühn, 2009, p. 71):

Criteria for evaluating the geographical market in general	Criteria for evaluating industry markets inside the geographical market
Key figures • Development of population • Development of GDP • Development of GDP per capita	**Key figures** • Development of quantities in total and per sub-market • Development of prices in total and per sub-market ■ Development of market volume in total und per sub-market
Legal restrictions for foreign economic activities • Possible legal forms • Conditions for profit repatriation • Conditions for sales (e.g. local production) • Operations risks	**Market system** • Players • Flows of products and services • Flows of information
Society • Political system • Ethnic and religious groups • Languages • Demographic structure • Cultural distance • Political risks	**Producers and traders** • Sub-markets • National and international competitors • Wholesalers and retailers • Competitive intensity
Infrastructure • Traffic infrastrucure • Telecommunications infrastructure • Health care system	**Customers** • Customer segments • Link between customer segments and sub-markets; industry segments • Demand similarity

Figure 6.1: Criteria for evaluating new markets

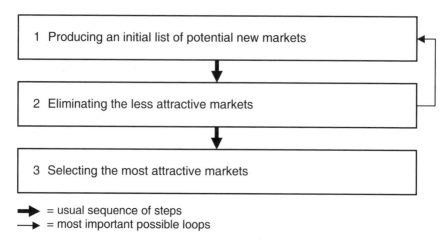

➡ = usual sequence of steps
→ = most important possible loops

Figure 6.2: Process for evaluating new markets

- The heuristic rule of factorization means that the original, overly complex problem is disassembled into a series of manageable sub-problems.
- The principle of sub-goal reduction proposes that a complex goal can be attained by completing a series of simpler goals. In Step 2 the sub-goal of eliminating less attractive markets is addressed. Then, in Step 3 the most attractive markets are selected from those remaining on the list.

As with any heuristic process, loops may occur within this process. For example, after Step 2 there may be too few candidate markets remaining. In this case it is necessary to go back to Step 1 in order to generate a new initial list.

We now describe each of the steps in detail.

6.3.2   Step 1: Producing an initial list of potential new markets

6.3.2.1 General considerations

The initial list of potential new markets must have two dimensions:

- The first dimension is geographical markets, which are typically country markets. However, it is also possible to include a group of countries on the list for evaluation, such as the Maghreb countries or the Emirates. Similarly, a larger country may be divided into separate regional markets. An example would be to evaluate the South of Germany - the federal states of Bavaria and Baden-Würtenberg - separately from the rest of the country.
- The second dimension is the industry markets. When embarking on internationalization, a company will typically consider all the industry markets which the company already serves in the home market. While in principle it is always possible to set up completely new activities in unknown industry markets abroad, for practical reasons it is wise to begin with a related diversification into industry markets where synergies can be used.

There will nearly always be a very large number of potential markets which could theoretically be considered. To keep the process within sensible limits, there should be criteria for inclusion within or elimination from the initial list of potential markets. These appear in Section 6.2.2.

6.3.2.2 Initial elimination criteria

Often the statutes, the mission statement or company policy will limit the field of activity of a company.

- To take an example, a kiosk group may have a mission statement specifying that the group aims at a strong position in this form of retailing in Europe. Here the focus is clearly on expansion within Europe. Movement to countries outside Europe should only be considered if growth within Europe is not possible. It would, of course, require a revision of the mission statement.
- Company policy may also impose limitations. A company may exclude a priori any activities in countries with high risks. **Inset 6.1** describes the BERI Index which determines the country risks and which many companies use as a basis for decision-making.

Inset 6.1: The BERI Index (text based on BERI, 2007; BERI, 2009; BERI, 2011)

Since 1966 BERI (= Business Environment Risk Intelligence) has published risk estimates for countries of economic and political importance. Three times a year, at the beginning of April, August and December, BERI publishes an index with four different values for each of 50 countries included on the list: the value for the previous year, the current value, an estimation for the following year and an estimation for five years into the future.

The BERI Index has three sub-indices:
- The Political Risk Index reflects socio-political conditions and may point to possible political changes.
- The Operations Risk Index rates conditions for economic activities in the country concerned.
- The Remittance and Repatriation Factor shows conditions relating to the export of capital and profits from the country concerned.

The BERI Index and the three sub-indices are based on a multitude of facts and figures, including expert opinion as well as quantitative data. The methods for producing the current index rating and the values for the future are subject to continuous validation and development.

The values of the BERI Index and the three sub-indices can vary between 0 and 100. Values of 70 and more indicate a stable business environment and low political risk. Values of 39 or less reflect unacceptable business conditions and prohibitive political risk.

Figure 6.3 shows the BERI index and the three sub-indices for China for the years 2001 to 2007.

A company can use the BERI Index according to its needs and there are companies which routinely only use one aspect of the index.

Year	Combined score	Political risk index	Operations risk index	Remittance and repatriation factor
2001	57	56	49	66
2002	58	56	50	67
2003	58	56	50	69
2004	59	56	51	70
2005	60	56	52	71
2006	61	57	53	72
2007	61	57	53	73

Figure 6.3: China's ratings 2001 to 2007 (BERI, 2009)

The resources available may make it impossible for a company to serve a particular market. Take the example of a producer of mobile phones. If the company cannot offer a certain frequency range, whether because of missing know-how or production infrastructure, this makes it impossible to gain access to any of the markets using this frequency range.

Country	Holcim	Lafarge	Cemex	Total
Argentina	38%	11%	0%	49%
Canada	19%	33%	0%	52%
France	13%	34%	0%	47%
Indonesia	0%	3%	44%	47%
Mexico	19%	4%	65%	88%
Philippines	38%	21%	22%	81%
South Africa	36%	26%	0%	62%
Spain	10%	19%	27%	56%
Venezuela	25%	24%	41%	90%

Figure 6.4: Capacity shares of Holcim, Lafarge and Cemex in selected markets in 1999 (adapted from Bartlett/Beamish, 2011, p. 151)

To keep the list within reasonable bounds, other initial criteria may be used. One possibility is to stipulate a minimum rate of growth in the target market in recent years. Another would be to exclude all those countries in which competitors already enjoy a dominant position. As **Figure 6.4** shows, the three cement producers with the greatest production capacities – Holcim, Lafarge and Cemex – together enjoy a dominant position in a number of markets. It would not be reasonable for a different cement manufacturer to even consider entering one of these markets.

6.3.2.3 The resulting initial list

The resulting initial list has two dimensions, as can be seen in **Figure 6.5.** The vertical axis lists the various countries (or parts of countries or country groups) while the horizontal one is divided according to the different industry markets.

Industries / Geo-graphical market	Industry market I	Industry market II	Industry market III
Country A			
Country B	✕		
Region C1 in Country C			
Rest of country C		✕	
Country D			
Country group E, F and G			✕
Country H			✕

☐ = potential new markets   ✕ = no potential new market

Figure 6.5: Initial list of potential new markets

The figure demonstrates how the use of initial elimination criteria leads to a manageable number of rows and columns, and also allows some cells in the grid to be eliminated. These could be cells with low growth rates or markets with unassailable competition.

6.3.3   Step 2: Eliminating the less attractive markets

6.3.3.1 Planning and carrying out the market search

The relatively large number of potential markets included in the first round means that the time spent on researching each separate market must be kept within limits. For this reason, we recommend using the internet to access secondary data.

6.3.3.2 Analyzing the data

"Getting the information is only half the job. Analysis and interpretation of that information must also be provided to decision makers" (Cateora/Gilly/Graham, 2009, p. 238).

Figure 6.6 presents the form of table needed to display the data which will be used to eliminate the least attractive country markets. On the left hand side are the countries included in the initial list as a result of Step 1. The table primarily presents quantitative information about the country markets as a whole and also for each of the relevant industry markets. To some extent this information may consist of estimates. This will often be the case for the relevant sub-markets.

The table provides a summary that can be supplemented by visual material and graphic representations. **Figure 6.7** for instance, summarizes the situation in three markets for a producer of automobile spare parts, like brake pads, exhausts, bulbs and so on. For this company the number of vehicles on the road and their average age will be important when assessing a potential market. For each potential market these

Geographical market	General information for the geographical market						Information for industry market I			Information for industry market II			Information for industry market III		
	GDP per capita	Real annual GDP growth	Political Risk Index	Operations Risk Index	Profit, repatriation factor	...	Market size	Size of relevant sub-market	...	Market size	Size of relevant sub-market	...	Market size	Size of relevant sub-market	...
Country A															
Country B							⊠	⊠	⊠						
Region C1 in country C															
Rest of country C															
Country D										⊠	⊠	⊠			
Country group E, F and G													⊠	⊠	⊠
Country H													⊠	⊠	⊠

☐ = Potential new market   ⊠ = No potential new market

Figure 6.6: Summary of market data

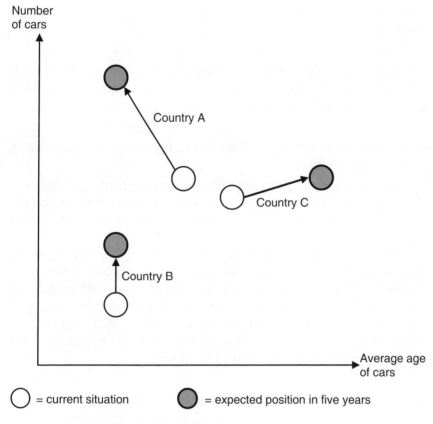

Figure 6.7: Comparison of three car part markets

two key parameters can be displayed visually on a graph with two ax-es. The figure is an effective example of this: Market C would be much more attractive to car part manufacturers than the others, despite the fact that the rate of growth in the overall number of vehicles is greater in A and B. In C the age of the vehicles will increase, making for above-average growth in the market for replaceable parts.

6.3.3.3 Evaluating the markets and eliminating the less attractive ones

In the first round the objective is to reduce the size of the initial list of potential markets. This is essential because the detailed analysis to be carried out later in the second round will consume a great deal of time and money.

As a basis for the elimination of the less attractive markets, **Figure 6.6** contains the essential facts and figures for the countries on the initial list, together with data for the industry markets under consideration.

The best way to eliminate candidates is to set minimum requirements for specific parameters:

- One condition could be the possibility to move capital and profits out of the country without restriction. Any country not meeting this condition would be eliminated, along with the industry markets in that country.
- It is also possible to have conditions which only concern a single industry market. For example, for industry market I there could be a minimum volume in the relevant sub-market set at $200 million. If the relevant part of an industry market in any specific country is clearly below this level, then that market is eliminated. The country itself, however, can remain in the list if there are other industry markets there which meet the required conditions.

Figure 6.8 shows the result of this first round of the elimination process.

- Four industry markets have been eliminated as they do not meet the minimum requirements.
- Country B now no longer has any potential industry markets, because both of its candidate markets have been eliminated. So country B will be removed from the list entirely.
- Country D also disappears from the list of potential new markets, but unlike country B, this is not because of its industry markets, but because the country as a whole does not meet the minimum requirements.

This process is simple. The difficulty lies in setting the requirements. If the requirements are too strict, attractive markets may be eliminated in the first round. If, on the other hand, they are too lax, then the initial list will not be much reduced, and the detailed analysis required in the se-

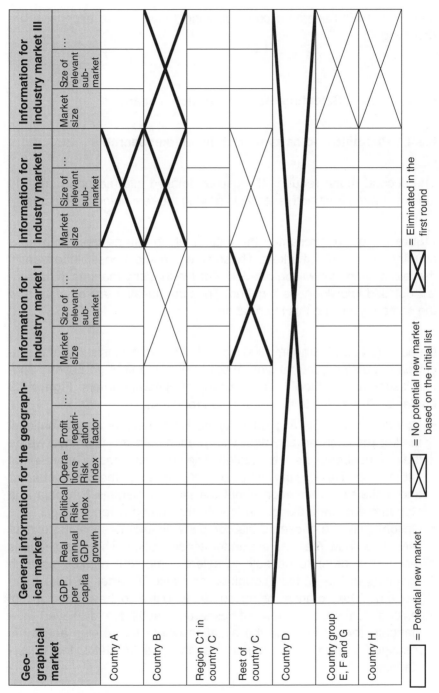

Figure 6.8: Remaining markets after the first round

cond round will become a correspondingly much more expensive un-
dertaking.

6.3.4   Step 3: Selecting the most attractive markets

6.3.4.1 Planning and carrying out the market search

The second round requires the use of detailed information in order to
identify the most attractive markets among the remaining candidates.

Figure 6.1 above presented the criteria which can be used to assess
country and industry markets. These criteria make it possible to identify
the information that will be needed. For the industry markets in particular, detailed knowledge is required. Thus the question arises as to how
the company will get this information.

Cateora, Gilly and Graham (2009, pp. 237 ff.) rightly insist that the difficulties in obtaining information about foreign markets go beyond content issues and include the overcoming of cultural barriers. **Figure 6.9**
presents three paths to the information required:

- Option B usually is a good solution. Here there is an international
  market research organization with branches in the countries where
  the potential markets are situated. They have access to the relevant
  information. This organization can also overcome the cultural barrier
  and make the information about the various markets available in a
  standard and understandable form to the company requesting it.
- Option C can be chosen if the company already has leading executives who know the markets under consideration. This knowledge is
  required in order to be able to select competent market research
  agencies in the various countries and also in order to brief them
  properly. The commissioning company will also have the task of
  making sure that the market research results are displayed in a
  standard form. Similar is the situation where the foreign agency is
  managed by the home country nation. This facilitates the understanding.

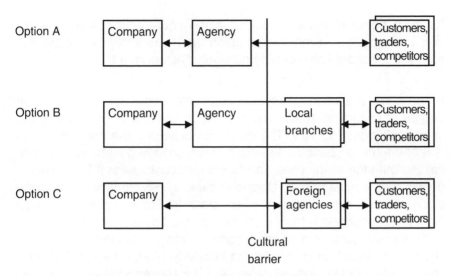

Figure 6.9: Managing the cultural barrier in international market research (adapted from Cateora/Gilly/Graham, 2009, p. 239)

- Option A is not a wise choice. Using an agency in the home country with no branches in the foreign countries being examined may produce only rather general information. It would be risky to select countries on information which is not sufficiently detailed.

The cooperation with market research agencies in each of the potential markets undoubtedly costs a great deal of time and money. Despite this, we find it essential. Irrespective of the entry mode which may be chosen, the opening up of a new country market always requires very significant investment. For this reason, all necessary measures must be taken to prevent the company choosing the wrong market in which to invest.

6.3.4.2 Analyzing the data

In the first round the reduction of the data results essentially in a table presenting quantitative information, but for the second round, a written report on each country is required. These reports will each include a section looking at the country as a whole and then separate sections for each potential industry market in the country. These reports will present a great deal more information than was available for the first round. They should also include qualitative assessments.

In the general section on each country attention must be paid to the degree of cultural distance between the potential new market and the company's home country. The closer the culture of the host country to that of the home country, the simpler it will be to negotiate with authorities, to manage employees and to contact customers. It is no coincidence that companies in German-speaking Switzerland often have close contacts with Germany while those in French-speaking Suisse Romande cooperate with French companies. The reason for this is not just geographical proximity and a common tongue, but includes cultural closeness. Based on Hofstede and Hofstede (2005), **Figure 6.10** presents values for five cultural dimensions for German-speaking Switzerland, Suisse Romande, Germany, France and China. **Figure 6.11** extends this to show the cultural differences between the two main language areas of Switzerland and the other three countries. The sum of the differences between Germany and German-speaking Switerland

Indices / Countries	Power distance index	Individual-ism index	Masculini-ty index	Uncertain-ty avoid-ance index	Long term orientation index
French-speaking Switzerland	70	64	58	70	40
German-speaking Switzerland	26	69	72	56	40
Germany	35	67	66	65	31
France	68	71	43	86	39
China	80	20	66	30	118

Figure 6.10: The five cultural indices of Hofstede for Switzerland, Germany, France and China (Hofstede/Hofstede, 2005, p. 43 f., p. 78 f., p. 120 f., p. 168 f., p. 211 f.)

Indices differences / Countries differences	Differences in power distance index	Differences in individualism index	Differences in masculinity index	Differences in un-certainty avoidance index	Differences in long term orientation index	Total differences
Difference German and French Switzerland	44	5	14	14	0	77
Difference German Switzerland – Germany	9	2	6	9	9	35
Difference French Switzerland – Germany	35	3	8	5	9	60
Difference German Switzerland – France	42	2	29	30	1	104
Difference French Switzerland – France	2	7	15	16	1	41
Difference German Switzerland – China	54	49	6	26	78	213
Difference French Switzerland – China	10	44	8	40	78	180

Figure 6.11: Cultural differences between regions of Switzerland, Germany, France and China

is only 35. For France and French-speaking Switzerland the figure is 41, almost as low. Measured in this way, the cultural difference be-tween German-speaking and French-speaking citizens of Switzerland, 77, is considerably greater. But compare this with the differences between either part of Switzerland and China. These are much higher figures, 213 for German speakers and 180 for French speakers.

For each industry market under consideration, the data which has been collected should be summarized by using methods from strategic analysis:

- Market system analysis can be used to reveal the market players and the market structure (Grünig/Kühn, 2011, pp. 93 ff.).
- To represent the competitive situation, we recommend Porter's five forces model and also his strategic groups model (1980, pp. 3 ff. and 126 ff.). In addition, there should be strengths and weaknesses profiles for each important competitor (Grünig/Kühn, 2011, pp. 98 ff.).
- Porter's industry segment analysis (1985, pp. 231 ff.) allows an overview of customer segments and their demand behaviour. **Inset 6.2** explains this method.
- Finally, the situation should be shown for wholesale and for retail. For a company producing goods for consumption, entry into a foreign market is only possible if that company can gain access to distribution channels. Increasingly, this is becoming a particular problem for SMEs in food and near-food. As **Inset 6.3** shows, concentration has greatly progressed in the retailing of food and near-food. Large retail chains privilege large suppliers like Nestlé and Unilever. In many markets SMEs can gain access only to specialised retailers with low market shares.

Inset 6.2: Industry segment analysis (text based on Grünig/Kühn, 2011, pp. 230 ff.; Porter, 1985, pp. 231 ff.)

Industry segment analysis consists of three steps:

1. First the customers in the industry must be classified into customer segments: groups with similar needs and requirements. The different types of products and services available in the market are also divided into categories, known as submarkets. A matrix is drawn up on the basis of these categories.
2. Next, each square in the matrix is considered and a certain number of these eliminated because they are not relevant. To do this it is necessary to estimate market volume and market growth for each square: if the estimation shows low volume plus below av-

Customers / Products	Families with low income	Young people buying their first car	Purchasers of a second car	Retired persons	Companies providing company cars	Craftsmen etc.	Car rental and car sharing companies	Farmers
Micro cars			X	X				
Sub-compacts		X	X	X	X	X	X	
Compacts	X	X	X	X	X	X	X	
4-wheel sub-compacts		X	X	X	X	X	X	
4-wheel compacts	X	X	X	X	X	X	X	X
Cheap mini-vans	X						X	
Cheap cabriolets		X	X	X				
Second hand cars	X	X						X

X = important in terms of volume
☐ = Industry segments

Figure 6.12: Industry segments in the European market for low budget cars

erage growth, then that square can be eliminated from further consideration. At this stage too, we must consider whether certain squares can be combined into single industry segments, which is possible if the resources used for serving these areas are the same. Applying these two considerations will usually mean that the number of industry segments remaining is now much smaller than the total number of squares in the matrix.

3. The third step is to analyze each of the industry segments. For each of them the customer requirements must be identified, together with the most important suppliers in the market and their market positions.

Figure 6.12 shows industry segments in the market for low budget cars in Europe. For most European countries, figures for the different sub-markets can be obtained from industry statistics. Estimations by those who know the industry can be used to allocate these totals to the various customer segments. An industry segment analysis quantified in this way is an ideal basis on which to assess a European market for low budget cars and to determine whether or not to enter the market.

Inset 6.3: Concentration in food and near food retailing (text based on Deloitte, 2011; Dicken, 2007, pp. 367 ff.; ETC group, 2005, pp. 6 ff.)

In 2004 the world market for food and near food retailing was worth 3,500 billion USD. Up to 2009 the market was growing at an average of 6.5% per annum and by 2009 had achieved a total of 4,800 billion USD. While growth rates in Europe and North America have fallen back, there has been above average growth in Latin America, Africa-Middle East and Asia-Pacific.

Figure 6.13 provides an impressive summary of the concentration in retail for food and near food:

- The three largest competitors accounted for 13% of retail sales worldwide in 2004. They have been able to maintain this share of the market, despite being relatively weak in the growth regions of Asia-Pacific, Africa-Middle East and Latin America: even in 2009, none of the top three world companies were in the top ten companies for each of these regions.
- In 2004 the top ten worldwide had 24% of world sales. In 2009 this had fallen by 1% to 23%. But in these five years the list of companies making up the top ten changed considerably. Only five of the top ten of 2004 held their place for 2009. Yet in both 2004 and 2009 all top ten companies were US-based or Europe

Company	Country of origin	Revenue from food and near food 2004	Revenue from food and near food 2009
Wal-Mart	USA	288	405
Carrefour	France	99	120
Tesco	UK	65	90
Total for top ten	-	839	1,087
Total world market	-	3,500	4,800

Figures in billion USD

Figure 6.13: The largest retailers for food and near food (Deloitte, 2011, p. 26; ETC group, 2005, p. 6)

an. However, none of these world top ten figure in the top tens for the three growth regions of the world. This is why they have lost market share.

While the world market has advanced steadily, the concentration process within many country markets has progressed much faster, especially in the mature markets of North America and Western Europe. In the US, France and the UK Wal-Mart, Carrefour and Tesco are clear national market leaders. In smaller countries too, there are usually a small number of dominant companies. For example, in Switzerland Migros and Coop together have more than 50% of retail sales.

This process of concentration is set to continue, most notably by spreading to countries in the regions enjoying rapid growth. The large international retail chains are present in these markets and this is likely to contribute to the worldwide concentration. In future, companies from the Asia-Pacific, the Middle East and Latin America may make it into the elite of worldwide retailers.

The ongoing concentration process will increase the bargaining power of the remaining retail chains for food and near food. This will weaken the bargaining power of the producers of food and near food, principally affecting the SMEs.

6.3.4.3 Evaluating the markets and selecting the most attractive ones

The country reports produced in Step 4 form the basis for the assessment of the markets. These reports provide a view of the country – in some cases of a region of that country, or of a group of countries - and of the potentially attractive industry markets there. These will be detailed and comprehensive reports with qualitative information, including, for example, descriptions of consumer habits. Because the reports are very detailed, it is not easy to make an evaluation just by reading them: to formally evaluate each market and select the most attractive ones we recommend using a scoring model.

Figure 6.14 shows what a scoring model looks like:

- The vertical axis has the different options. These are the country and industry markets which survived the first round and were examined in detailed reports in the second round.
- The horizontal axis shows specific criteria and the importance of each criterion together with the overall evaluation.
- Separate assessments are made on each criterion of each industry market in each country. An assessment of the country market as a whole can be derived by averaging the values for the industry markets in that country.
- Predetermined scales are used for the assessments and also for the weightings of the criteria. The scale for assessing the options has an even number of levels. This helps to deter any tendency for evaluations to hug the middle ground.
- In our example, a score of 30 is required to justify further pursuit of market entry. The table shows that four different options achieve that score. Because of the fixed costs that occur with entry into a new country market, it is advisable, if at all possible, to try to enter more than one industry market in the same new country. This would justify entering industry market III in country A despite the fact that this market did not achieve the required total score of 30. With industry market I and the country as a whole achieving high scores, it makes sense to go into that market too. Country H poses more of a difficulty. While one industry market looks attractive, the other is markedly less so. Here we would depart from our general recommendation and not enter both markets in that country.

Options		Criteria						Overall evaluation	
Geographi-cal market	Industry market	Cultural distance	Size of the target sub-markets	Growth of the target sub-markets	Competitive intensity	Access to distribution channels		Industry market	Geographi-cal market
		Importance of the criteria							
		2	3	2	2	3			
A	I	2	4	3	4	3		39	32
	III	2	2	2	3	3		25	
C1	I	3	2	2	1	2		26	24
	II	3	3	1	2	1		24	
	III	3	1	3	2	1		22	
Rest of C	III	3	2	2	3	1		25	25
E, F + G	I	2	4	2	4	3		37	35.5
	II	2	3	3	3	3		34	
H	I	2	1	2	2	2		21	29.5
	II	2	4	3	2	4		38	

Scores: 4 = very positive   3 = positive   2 = negative   1 = very negative
Importance of the criterion: 3 = high   2 = medium   1 = low

Figure 6.14: Scoring model for selecting the most attractive markets

- The assessment represented in **Figure 6.14** suggests entry into five industry markets in three countries: industry markets I and III in country A, industry markets I and II in country group E, F and G and finally industry market II in country H.

7 Evaluating market entry modes

7.1 Preliminary remarks and overview of the entry modes

When a company has decided to go international for new markets, it also has to decide on an adequate entry mode. It can choose from a wide range of options, which range from export entry modes to investment modes. In this chapter the different available market entry modes are described and practical tools are presented which can help companies to choose between them.

Entry modes can be broadly categorized into three groups:

- The first group comprises export entry modes, in which a company's final product is manufactured in the home country and then transported to the target country. For most companies, exporting is the initial step into internationalization (Hollensen, 2011, p. 335).
- The common attribute of the second group of entry modes is that production takes place in the target country itself, either in cooperation with a local company (as with licensing) or by the company itself.
- As a specific cooperative mode, franchising is also a viable option. This is an attractive alternative in the service industry. Restaurant chains, retailing chains and other service providers can franchise their business concept and their brand name to independent companies in the target country who provide the service to the final customer and pay the franchisor a running fee for the right to do so.

While all of these modes may be selected for a number of different reasons, there seems to be a single dominant reason for selecting each one, in particular from the perspective of an SME. In this chapter, we will focus on the modes that are used primarily with a market-seeking motive. Modes that are chosen mainly with an efficiency-seeking motive, like contract manufacturing, are described in chapter 10.

Combinations between entry modes are possible and common. For example, a company could manufacture components in the home country and send them to an affiliate in the target market, where final assembly takes place. Or it could produce in the host country and sell via a chain of franchised outlets. Since there are very many possible combinations, we do not discuss them here. However, the evaluation of any combination can be based on evaluation of the basic modes of which it is composed.

7.2   Export

7.2.1   Overview

The different forms of export are illustrated in **Figure 7.1**. Here, the first distinction to make is between indirect export and direct export. The options are explained in the following sections.

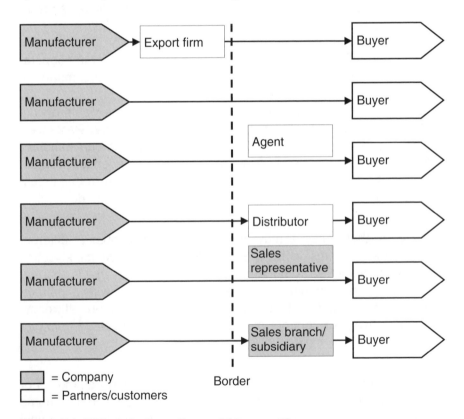

Figure 7.1: Different alternatives within exporting

7.2.2   Indirect export

A first option for internationalization, and one with very low resource commitment, is indirect exporting. Indirect exporting occurs when the exporting manufacturer uses independent middlemen located in its home country (Root, 1994, p. 57). Usually, these export specialists or trading companies act as merchants, buying the product from the manufacturer and selling it in foreign markets. For the manufacturer, this turns the sale into a domestic sale; all cross-border activities are undertaken by the intermediary.

In Switzerland, as in other countries, a large number of export intermediaries are ready to carry out the export process for other companies. The benefits are evident: the manufacturer does not need to develop international know-how, the sales department can follow their normal domestic processes, and no resources need be devoted to internationalization. And for each attractive foreign market, one can find a specialized trading company that has business relationships and know-how in this market. On the other hand, there are disadvantages. The firm has almost no control over the way the product is marketed in the foreign country. Products may be sold through inappropriate channels, with poor service or sales support, and be under- or over-priced. This can damage the reputation of the manufacturing company. Furthermore, the company has no exposure to the foreign market(s) so it cannot learn from experience and does not develop any relationships in the foreign market (Hollensen, 2011, p. 337).

Nevertheless, indirect exporting may be an option for SMEs if the company only sporadically sells products abroad and/or if the international sales are spread over a large number of different countries where it would be difficult to build up specific knowledge.

7.2.3   Direct export to the final customer

Direct exporting means that the manufacturer sells directly to any type of customer in a foreign country. This buyer may be either the final customer for a product or intermediaries located in the foreign market.

Exporting is an easy way to tap the potential of a market. It avoids the substantial cost of establishing manufacturing operations in a foreign country and if it uses previously unused production capacity in the home country factory, it will even help to achieve economies of scale, thus rendering existing sales in the home country more profitable.

In some industries, e.g. in very large machinery, there may be a direct contact between the manufacturer in the home country and the buyer in the host country. The deal may be negotiated while the buyer is on a visit to the manufacturer in its headquarters or factory in the home country. In the case of a standardized product, the purchase may even take place as an unsolicited order by e-mail. However, it is much more common for exporting to occur as a result of marketing and sales efforts in the country of the customer.

7.2.4   Direct export via a distributor

A distributor acts as sales organization for the company in the foreign market. Distributors are independent merchants who buy the products from the company and sell them to customers. Their profit stems from the margin they make in this process. Distributors have substantial freedom to choose their own customers and to set the conditions for sales, including prices. Distributors may sell directly to final customers in the foreign market. Usually, though, they sell to other resellers in the country, e.g. wholesalers or retailers. Often distributors own and operate wholesale and/or retail channels, warehouses and/or service organizations (Hollensen, 2011, p. 342). They maintain stock in the target country which increases the company's ability to deliver. Because they are merchants, the stock is financed by the distributor.

Distributors usually seek exclusive rights for a specific sales territory. Manufacturers often use an exclusive distributor for a specific country who represents the manufacturer in all aspects of sales and service in that country, as the example in **Inset 7.1** shows.

Inset 7.1: Armaka AG as distributor for Tulikivi in the Swiss market (text based on Armaka, 2011; Tulikivi, 2011)

Armaka AG was established in 1975 in Switzerland. It is a trading company which specializes in products for building fireplaces and stoves. For the Swiss market, it is the exclusive distributor for the products of Tulikivi, a Finnish company.

Tulikivi is the world's largest manufacturer of heat-retaining fireplaces. The group is known for its soapstone fireplaces and natural stone products. To sell its products in foreign markets, Tulikivi uses various strategies. In a few markets, it has its own sales subsidiaries. In other countries, it uses a number of distributors with fixed sales territories. But in many countries, the company relies on a sole importer which acts as distributor and resells the fireplaces to final customers or to specialized trade.

Armaka AG carries out this task for Switzerland. As the sole distributor for Tulikivi in Switzerland, the company sells to specialized trade and to builders, who then sell the products to the final customer and install them. Armaka carries inventory and has three large showrooms for Tulikivi products across Switzerland. Its employees provide the customers with advice and technical expertise on the products throughout the entire process of choosing, installing and using Tulikivi products.

As is typical for distributors, apart from Tulikivi products, Armaka also sells those of Mondex (Finland), NIVE (Sweden), and Varde Ovne (Denmark). These product ranges are complementary. For the distributor, the advantage is that it can offer its customers a broader choice. But it is also a cost-efficient way for the distributor to cover its fixed costs, as the contribution margins of different suppliers bring economies of scale and scope. Of course, from the perspective of Tulikivi, Armaka's efforts to sell Tulikivi products may be less intensive because it may also be beneficial for Armaka to sell any of the other products. Here, there is an evident trade-off between the benefits of a distributor exclusively selling one company's products and one that can distribute costs, but may also distribute sales effort.

Distributors are used because they are familiar with the local market and customs. They also have existing customer contacts and access to a sales network. However they represent an additional stage between a company and its final customers in a foreign country. Market information and feedback on the exporter's product may be limited. Often, after a number of years, a company will seek to change the entry mode and establish its own sales subsidiary in a country to replace the distributor.

National laws regarding export intermediaries differ strongly from region to region. It is important to be well-informed about the legal situation in the target country. In particular, companies should inform themselves about ways to terminate a contract with the intermediary and the costs associated with such termination. In many countries, compensation has to be paid to the intermediary in the case of contract termination because, among other things, the intermediary has usually invested money to establish the market for the exporter.

7.2.5   Direct export via an agent

Alternatively, an agent can represent a company in a foreign market. But unlike a distributor, an agent is an independent company that sells to customers in the name of and on behalf of the exporter. An agent does not take title to the goods and will not usually hold the products in stock. Instead, the exporter ships the products directly to the customers, and all arrangements regarding financing, credit, promotion, etc., are made directly between the exporter and the buyer. Since the agent acts on behalf of the exporting company, its room for maneuver is limited. The exporting company remains in control of the most important parameters, including sales price. The agent makes its revenues from the commissions paid by the exporter (Hollensen, 2011, p. 342).

Like distributors, agents often have exclusive rights for a specific country or region. They become involved because they are familiar with the local market and have business relationships in this market. They have an incentive to sell the products because their commission is tied to sales. However, agents may handle the exporter's products alongside products from other companies, even competing products. As a result, they may devote more time to a competitor's products if this will enhance their own profit. After all, an agent is an independent company which will primarily strive to maximize its own success.

Inset 7.2 explains how to choose a partner in the foreign market.

Inset 7.2: Choosing a distributor or agent in the foreign market

The selection of a suitable distributor or agent is crucial for success in the foreign market. There are several ways to identify such partners:

- Frequently, a company already has business contacts or personal relations with prospective distributors from third countries.
- A company could try to use specialized institutions like OSEC in Switzerland or the Bundesstelle für Außenhandelsinformationen in Germany.
- Chambers of commerce and foreign trade institutions organize field trips to interesting regions and provide contacts with prospective business partners in these regions.
- Trade fairs in the target region are also an important opportunity to meet potential trade partners who can act as agents or distributors in a specific country.

The key characteristics of the intermediary will greatly depend on the specific tasks it needs to fulfill for the manufacturer. The company must first determine what the channel is intended to accomplish (Root, 1994, p. 59):

- What geographical market coverage should the channel have in the target country?
- What logistical services need to be carried out in the target country?
- What specific selling and promotion efforts need to be undertaken in the target country?
- What pre- or post-sales service does the channel need to provide?

Among other criteria, it is useful to analyze the size of the company, the financial situation, the existing infrastructure (warehouses, transport fleet), the market coverage, the position in the market, the number and quality of employees, in particular their knowledge of the specific industry, sales expertise, the reputation in the local market, the ability to provide after-sales service, the existing customer base, and finally their relationships with local sales channels and local officials.

7.2.6   Direct export with sales representatives

Instead of using a local partner, exporting companies can use their own sales force to contact the customers in the foreign market. Sometimes it will be important for the customer to have a direct relationship with the manufacturer. In this case, the company has control and can give clear orders to its employees in the foreign market (e.g. which customers to visit, how often, etc.). When a company uses distributors or agents, it has little influence on the attention that is being paid to its products. But with its own employees, it can fully determine the commitment towards a specific market, for example by deciding how many sales representatives will service the market. There are two basic types of sales representatives:

- **Resident sales representatives** in foreign countries signal a strong commitment to a specific market.
- **Domestically-based sales representatives** travel to the target country to perform the sales function. This involves a rather high operating cost, in particular travel costs. However, they are more flexible than resident reps and are usually responsible for more than one market. As they are not tied to a specific country, they can devote their time to the market which is currently the most attractive.

In any event, sales representatives are employees on the company's payroll. Having one's own sales force for a foreign market brings an operating cost for this market. This cost occurs, at least partly, independently of the extent of sales success in the foreign market. In contrast, an agent is paid on a commission. This creates variable costs which are low when sales are low. A distributor may even create income for the company before sales in the foreign market have taken off, since the distributor buys stock so that he can deliver in case of a sale. But a sales representative creates fixed costs. Thus, a certain sales volume is required before a sales representative can become a profitable choice.

The higher fixed cost of sales representatives, relative to agents or distributors, combined with a lower (variable) cost per unit sold, leads to the traditional recommendation that one's own sales representatives should only be employed beyond a certain sales volume. A break-even analysis clearly shows that below a certain sales level, it is more efficient to use agents (or distributors).

7.2.7   Direct export with a sales branch or a sales subsidiary

Beyond using single sales representatives in the foreign market, a company may consider it beneficial to establish a formal branch office. A **sales branch** or branch office is an organizational unit in the host country that is merely an extension of the parent company and therefore is not a separate legal entity in the host country. Usually, a branch is governed by the national law of the parent company. The parent company remains directly liable regarding its customers and its employees. Branch offices are entitled to run businesses within a specified scope in the host country. This distinguishes them from **representative offices** which are by law prohibited from engaging in direct, profit-making business activities. Representative offices serve more as liaison offices, establishing contacts with local government or handling market research (Shenkar/Luo, 2008, p. 297).

In contrast to a foreign branch office, a **foreign sales subsidiary** is a local company that is owned by the exporting company. The foreign subsidiary is a separate legal entity and is governed by the laws of the host country. Usually, the foreign subsidiary will be the official contract partner for foreign customers. Thus, the subsidiary will act as a merchant, buying products from the parent company and selling them to its local customers.

The branch office and the sales subsidiary provide a strong foothold in the foreign market. For example, if a product needs intensive servicing, a travelling salesperson may not be able to provide that service. In this case, a more permanent foreign base is needed (Hollensen, 2011, p. 388). Customers may prefer to receive sales advice and, especially, service from the manufacturer itself, since the exporting manufacturer usually has the greatest product competence.

Sales subsidiaries usually take over the full selling process and, in addition, often at least some of the marketing functions for the foreign market. Compared to a branch office, they often enjoy more autonomy and can adapt better to local customer needs.

The decision between a branch office and a sales subsidiary is driven by a number of factors. First, there may be legal considerations. In some countries, entities beyond a certain size have to be organized as a separate legal entity. Furthermore, with a sales subsidiary, legal disputes are regulated within the foreign country. This may not always be beneficial for a foreign company but it is usually cheaper and less complex than international law cases. And in addition, foreign subsidiaries create their own income statements and may incur profits. These profits are taxed in the host country and can be used most easily in the host country, to expand business there. In the case of a branch office, profits are automatically part of the parent company's profits since the office has no separate legal identity. On the other hand, profits generated in sales subsidiaries may be more difficult to transfer to the home market.

7.3   Entry modes with production in the host country

7.3.1   Preliminary remarks and overview

Export may not be the most efficient choice. But under certain circumstances, producing in the home country and then transferring products to the target country may lead to prohibitively high costs. If, for example, customs duties on imports are very high in the target market, then exporting accumulates costs that may make the product lose its competitiveness in the foreign market. Some countries may even prohibit the sale of foreign products. Even with rather low trade barriers, customs duties of a few percent increase the price of the exported good or reduce the profit margins.

In these cases, a company should look for options to circumvent these trade barriers. Producing in the target market may become necessary. In this chapter, we focus primarily on the option of licensing, since this is an option that does not require substantial resources, making it suitable for SMEs. We will also briefly describe wholly-owned production subsidiaries and production joint ventures. However, more space is devoted to these options in Part IV in the presentation of going international for production and sourcing.

The major disadvantage of all entry modes with production in the host country is the loss of a potential country-of-origin effect. For example, "Swissness" has developed into a major sales advantage worldwide. Prestigious watches are manufactured in Switzerland and would be likely to lose their appeal if they were "made in Taiwan". Similarly, for machinery and cars the label "made in Germany", and for fashion items the label "made in Italy" may improve the image of a product so much that there is an absolute need to produce in the home country. The price premium can be used to cover additional expenses such as costs created by trade barriers. Yet, past experience has shown that "made-in" images may not be as powerful as one might wish. German cars are now made in the USA and in China; Victorinox offers clothing that is not produced in Switzerland. Final products and components of Austrian and US-American sporting goods are now manufactured in Asia without these goods being less valued by customers.

7.3.2 Licensing agreements

Licensing is a strategy with which a company can use production in a foreign country without major capital investment. It leads to production by a licensee without any requirement for the licensor to create a new operation abroad (Hollensen, 2011, pp. 358 ff.; Morschett/Schramm-Klein/Zentes, 2010, p. 283 f.).

In licensing agreements the licensor grants the rights to intellectual property to the licensee for a defined period. In return, the licensee pays royalty fees. The nature of licensing agreements varies depending on the position of the activity in the value chain, e.g. production and/or distribution and marketing (see e.g. Hill, 2008, p. 407 f.):

- In **process licenses** the licensor grants the licensee the right to use a specific production technology, often based on a patent.
- In the case of a **product license**, the licensor grants the right to manufacture a product or certain products in accordance with specific procedures, processes or formulas.
- If, in addition, a **distribution license** is granted, the licensee has the right to market the products in a specific territory. If not, the licensor (i.e. the home country company) may take over the sales function itself. If that is the case, then the licensee is similar to a contract manufacturer.

In any case, licensing is an option for companies that have an attractive process or product technology but may lack the financial resources or managerial capacity to exploit this in a foreign country. With licensing, this task is mainly shifted to the licensee, usually a local company in the specific foreign market. Licensing brings a number of benefits (Bradley, 2005, p. 244). It gives a company access to a foreign market with low capital investment and, thus, low capital risk. It can give access even to a difficult market because the market access is granted by the local partner. The local partner is interested in selling the product and usually also provides the necessary services. Due to the local presence, customer service by the licensee may improve service levels and delivery speed in the foreign country.

Investment barriers can be disregarded since the company is not investing its own money. Trade barriers are largely irrelevant since the product is produced in the target market. Moreover, production costs in most host countries are lower than in Western European countries like Switzerland or Germany. This supports the negotiation process with potential licensees since it usually helps to raise margins. Examples of international licensing agreements are presented in **Inset 7.3** and **Inset 7.4**.

Inset 7.3: MAN Diesel & Turbo enters foreign markets via licensing (text based on MAN Diesel & Turbo, 2011; Burr/Herstatt/Marquardt/Walch, 2011)

MAN Diesel & Turbo SE, based in Augsburg, Germany, is the world's leading provider of large-bore diesel engines and turbomachinery for marine and stationary applications. It designs two-stroke and four-stroke engines. In the mid-1980s the company recognized that production in Europe had become too expensive and that the markets for ship construction had shifted towards Asia.

MAN Diesel & Turbo responded to these developments by changing the business model. Instead of manufacturing in Europe, many products were no longer manufactured in-house. Instead, licences were given to Asian companies with manufacturing facilities in the relevant target markets. Asian companies (e.g. Hyunday Heavy Industries) began to use the technology of MAN to manufacture diesel ship engines and to pay royalties to MAN for the right to do so. The local companies sold their output to shipbuilders in Asia. With this approach, MAN remains world market leader but now produces less than 10% of its engines itself.

On the other hand, a licensee is an independent company with its own interests. The licensor needs to disclose its technology to a foreign partner, and regularly discloses business knowledge beyond the technology because the licensor usually provides support to the licensee within a long-term relationship. The risk of creating a future competitor is significant. Furthermore, the company has only a passive interaction with the market, since sales are usually realized by the licensee. The licensee has to inform the licensor company about the sales volume since this determines the royalties, but the company may still have very little information about the market. In addition, if the products are sold under the licensor's brand, the local licensee has a strong influence on the home country company's reputation.

Inset 7.4: BMW's local assembly to overcome trade barriers
(text based on BMW, 2011)

The BMW Group strategy of ensuring that production is tuned to market demands around the world also applies to smaller markets with worthwhile potential, in which customs regulations may, for example, complicate the import of complete automobiles. In such areas, the BMW Group manufactures automobiles from parts kits in assembly plants.

This is known as the "Completely Knocked Down" (CKD) production process. In the CKD process, certain parts and components are packaged as kits and exported for assembly in the countries concerned. These kits are then supplemented with locally manufactured parts in the partner countries. Assembly takes place in the foreign market with adherence to the BMW Group's global quality standards. Currently, the BMW Group uses CKD assembly to manufacture automobiles with partners in six countries: Egypt, India, Indonesia, Malaysia, Russia, and Thailand.

It has to be kept in mind that the licensee is an independent company that strives to maximize its own profits. For example, selling the licensor's products at very expensive prices may lead to attractive margins and maximize the profit of the licensee, while royalties, if they are determined per unit, would remain low. This means that the licensor not only needs to check the quality of the licensee's production but also to monitor its sales efforts and price policy. These issues should be included in the licensing contract.

Furthermore, licensing limits the flexibility of the company, at least during the duration of the licensing contract. If the company wishes to change the strategy and use another entry mode, it cannot usually do so without the agreement of the licensee. Thus, licensing binds a company for a certain number of years.

7.3.3   Wholly-owned production subsidiary

Instead of having products produced by a licensee, a company can **set up an own factory** in the target market. This option has all of the benefits of local production that have already been listed for licensing (e.g. circumvention of trade barriers). In addition, it has the benefit of full control over operations, including production output and quality. A wholly-owned production subsidiary has a number of benefits with regard to selling in the foreign market which is illustrated by the example in **Inset 7.5**:

- First, it signals commitment to the market. This is appreciated by local customers and by local governments. Producing in a country makes the company an insider and a local employer.
- Second, subsidies are often paid by local governments as an incentive to local investment.
- Third, local production (by local employees) is usually quick to adapt to changing market needs in the target market. In a wholly-owned subsidiary, the company is in full control but its employees are socialized in the target country. This helps the company to adapt to local tastes.
- Fourth, local production improves the service level. For example, delivery times are shorter and supply shortages are less likely to occur.
- Fifth, local production reduces transportation costs for the final products.

Inset 7.5 VW sets up production in the US to conquer the market (text based on Ewing, 2011)

In the USA, Volkswagen has lost market share in the last few decades and it dropped to only 2 percent in the mid-2000s. Problems in the USA market included the neglect of features that US customers demanded (including simple things like cup holders) but also slow adaptation to new trends that were relevant to the US market. For instance, VW was late to market with an SUV and with a modern minivan. And while some drivers appreciated VW's European-style handling and interior controls, many found the suspension too stiff and the dashboard too complicated. Such buyers were more likely to choose a less expensive Honda or Toyota, which were more tuned to American tastes.

But now Volkswagen, which has often declared its intention to achieve the same stature in the United States that it boasts elsewhere, is mounting its first serious effort in decades to compete with the Japanese and Korean manufacturers that have nearly driven it out of the U.S. market. In early 2011, it introduced the Jetta which VW designed specifically for American consumers and which will be made at a new $1 billion factory in Chattanooga, Tennessee. It will be the first car that Volkswagen has built in the United States since the 1980s. By starting to build cars in the United States from 2011 on, Volkswagen intends to adapt better and faster to US demand. What is more, it can avoid the high labor costs in Germany and the strong euro, and compete better on price with the Toyota Camry and Honda Accord.

On the other hand, with wholly-owned production in the target market, the company commits resources to a specific country. This bears substantial risk. And the capital investment creates fixed costs which can only be covered in the case of sufficient output. The company must reach the minimum size of a cost-efficient factory in the target country. While exporting and licensing do not bind substantial resources to one market, establishing one's own production does. So the decision to do so is a very long-term one with a strategic impact on the entire company. But if a specific market is expected to become very attractive in the future and the sales volume is already sufficiently high, then local production will be a good way to fully exploit the potential of this market.

When considering market entry with a wholly-owned production subsidiary, there is an additional option: the **acquisition of a local company** that already has a product range that can be sold in the host country (Hill, 2008). Acquiring a company has different objectives from exporting or establishing a greenfield investment, since in this case the main focus usually is not on finding a means to sell the company's existing products in an additional market but on exploiting the market potential in the target market with a new product range, one that the company initially did not manufacture.

This option requires substantial financial resources. But for large SMEs and MNEs, it is an option which gives quick access to a new market. The company immediately gains local resources, such as products, brands, distribution networks, and often local management expertise and market knowledge. The company buys into a market position and a running operation. This leads to quick cash-flow generation from the beginning. Cash-flow can be used immediately to finance the acquisition. The newly-acquired operation will already have a certain size, and consequently may realize economies of scale that a newly-established operation could take years to achieve.

Obviously, a suitable take-over object needs to be available. Compared to a greenfield establishment, an acquisition is a high-risk option and evaluating a foreign company is a complex task. Buying a company leads to substantial integration costs and synergy effects are often lower than initially expected. Experience shows that the acquirer often overpays for take-over objects since it does not have fully transparent information with which to evaluate it. Mergers and acquisitions have often been shown not to deliver the expected results. Hostile take-overs bear additional risks, since the local management is likely to leave the company after the acquisition.

Overall, an acquisition is a risky option that must be very carefully considered. For SMEs in particular, a slow organic expansion is usually preferable to the high-risk alternative of an acquisition. However, there are many examples of successful acquisitions. Each case must be carefully analyzed on its own merits.

7.3.4   Production joint venture

Another option for production in the target country is a joint venture with a local company. As regards market access, working with a joint venture partner may have some benefits. The local partner may facilitate the adaptation of products to local tastes. Usually, the local partner company is more familiar with local market conditions. Furthermore, a local joint venture partner not only shares the risk of setting up operations in the target country, it can also speed up the process.

Often, a production joint venture in a target market uses the production facilities of the local partner and the product technology and/or the brand name and/or the financial resources for investment of the internationalizing company. As in the case of a take-over, the local partner may also have a product range that is of interest. Production can often start very quickly. Like the licensee, the local company can also give the joint venture access to necessary local resources, e.g. a distribution network.

Similar to a production joint venture is the case where a stake in the foreign company is acquired to enter the market. This can be a production company or a service operation, for example in the field of retailing or banking, as **Inset 7.6** illustrates.

> **Inset 7.6: Migros acquires 49% of the German retailer Gries Deco Holding** (text based on Migros, 2009)
>
> In January 2009, Swiss retailer Migros acquired 49% of the German retail company Gries Deco Holding (GDH) which sells furnishing accessories, home decoration and small furniture under the name "Depot". In early 2009, Depot operated 148 stores in Germany and Austria. In the coming years, the company intends to expand strongly by opening 30 outlets per year and a number of shop-in-shops in furniture stores. As a side effect, Migros will benefit from synergies for its own store chain "Interio". Migros has announced that the stake in GDH will be enhanced over time.
>
> For Migros, acquiring this stake gives it quick access to the German market and the potential to expand its sales with this additional store format. Migros has also gained management know-how, since the co-owner of the successful chain, Christian Gries, will stay in charge as Managing Director of the store chain.

7.4   Franchising

While franchising is generally a potential entry mode in all sectors and industries, it has its main relevance in retailing (including restaurants) and other parts of the service industry. It is usually used in outlet-based business models, such as retail stores, car rentals, cosmetics studios, hotels and restaurants.

Franchising is defined as a contractual agreement between two legally and financially separate companies, the franchisor and the franchisee (Morschett/Schramm-Klein/Zentes, 2010, p. 283 f.). The franchisor, who has established a market-tested business concept, enters into a relationship with a number of franchisees, typically small business owners, who are allowed to use the franchisor's brand and must operate their business according to the franchisor's specified format and processes. The franchisor provides ongoing commercial and technical assistance. In return, the franchisees typically pay an initial fee as well as royalties, which average about 5 % of gross sales, plus some advertising fees (Inma, 2005, p. 29).

A fundamental characteristic of franchising is that it always involves two separate and independent companies which assume distinct roles and a strict division of tasks in order to achieve a joint objective. Since the franchisee owns his business, he is entitled to all profits that are generated. Franchising thus combines the benefits of a large, efficient system, including economies of scale in procurement, logistics, advertising, IT systems, and central administration, with the strength of an independent entrepreneur who manages the outlet, including customer contact and supervision of store employees. The common brand enables all participants in the franchising system to benefit from the advertising and goodwill generated by each outlet. From the consumer perspective, it is often impossible to detect the difference between franchises and wholly-owned branches.

For the franchisor, franchising has considerable benefits (Berman/ Evans, 2010, pp. 108 ff.; Kutschker/Schmid, 2011, p. 879):
- Franchising allows for rapid growth of a business concept. If the success of a concept depends upon rapid market coverage, then franchising is an especially good way to achieve this market coverage. The usual financial constraints are circumvented because franchisees finance the investment for new sites.
- The motivation of franchisees is high, because they manage their own stores.

- Franchisees have knowledge of the local markets and their customer and employee contact is direct and personal.
- Written franchise agreements require the franchisee to keep to stringent operating rules set by the franchisor.

One major disadvantage for a franchisor is that he has no hierarchical control over the franchisee. The franchisee is an independent contractor, not an employee. Franchisees can harm the overall reputation of the franchise system if they do not maintain company standards. Changes in the franchisors' strategy may be slow to implement, because franchise contracts usually run for three to five years, and substantial changes are only possible by changing the contracts. Another drawback is that under European law, the franchisor is not allowed to set the prices to the final consumer. Accordingly, marketing and management is more complex for a franchise system than for a truly uniform and hierarchically managed system of company-owned outlets.

If a company wishes to use franchising as its international market entry mode, it has a number of different options (Morschett/Schramm-Klein/Zentes, 2010, p. 285). A franchisor may sign individual contracts with partners in the different countries. The signing entities can be the company in the home country and different franchisees in their own countries. This direct foreign franchising is based on a set of international contracts. Usually, though, it is better to establish a legal entity in the target country which then acts as franchisor. In this case, the franchising contracts are within the target country. The legal entity can be a wholly-owned subsidiary of the parent company or it can be a joint venture. In the latter case, franchising is combined with a joint venture to benefit from the local market knowledge of a strong partner. Normally the partner then selects the local franchisees. As another alternative, a company can also use master franchising. In this case, the franchisor signs a single contract with one master franchisee in the target market who can then grant franchises in that market.

7.5   Recommendations for evaluating market entry modes

7.5.1   Evaluation criteria

The market entry modes described above differ in many aspects. They can be characterized along a number of dimensions. However, the six most important aspects are as follows (Morschett, 2007):

- **Control**: Different entry modes offer different degrees of control. In direct exporting via one's own sales subsidiary or modes with full ownership, the company can take important decisions on its own while cooperative arrangements, like selling via a distributor, reduce decision autonomy. Control is usually seen as the main benefit of fully-owned modes, since "maintaining decision-making control allows the firm to determine its own destiny" (Driscoll/Paliwoda, 1997, p. 64).
- **Resource commitment**: Resource commitment refers to assets that have to be dedicated to the target market and that lose part of their value when shifted to an alternative use. For example, exporting via an agent requires a rather low resource commitment. If the target market turns less attractive, a company can easily shift its exports to other markets. Setting up production sites in the target market has the opposite effect: substantial assets are tied to the market and cannot easily be used for other destinations. Partnership modes often have the advantage that the partner takes over part or all of the investment required. Resource commitment is directly associated with investment risk. The more assets a company has to invest in a specific market, the more assets are risk-exposed. In countries with high political risk (e.g. some countries in Latin America and North Africa), it may be wise to keep investments low.
- **Costs and profit potential**: Different market entry modes lead to different costs of serving the selected market. Producing in the host country may reduce production costs and the costs of distribution logistics. It may help to overcome substantial custom tariffs. But there is also the possibility that it reduces economies of scale and thereby leads to higher unit costs. With partner strategies, the revenue is shared with partners but it may be higher due to better market knowledge. With licensing, a company does get its income from royalties, not directly from sales. All of these aspects have to be considered when evaluating different market entry modes.

- **Flexibility**: Resource commitment is closely related to flexibility. The more resources are tied to a specific market, the less flexibly a company can usually react and change its strategy. However, partnership modes may also be inflexible, since they tie a company to long-term contracts. From this perspective, export modes offer the highest flexibility.
- **Partner resources**: Local partners can have valuable resources, not only financial assets but also local market knowledge, access to distribution networks, and relations with local customers and the host country government.
- **Knowledge dissemination**: Entry modes also differ in the potential dissemination risk. This is the risk that knowledge is transferred to a partner who might use it against the interest of the firm (Hill/Hwang/Kim, 1990). This risk is particularly high in cooperative strategies. Licensing out production to another company leads to a substantial knowledge transfer to this partner. While the knowledge may be protected by contract (depending on the enforcement of intellectual property rights in the target country), the partner company still learns over time. Often new competitors emerge from former licensing partners. From this perspective, producing alone in the foreign country is preferable to outsourcing production. Knowledge can usually be best protected by centralizing production in the home country.

The challenge in choosing an optimal entry mode is that these six factors tend to be conflicting forces. More control is usually linked to more resource commitment, and, consequently, more risk exposure. Sharing the investment with a partner automatically brings the risk of knowledge dissemination. So, the choice of a market entry mode will always have to evaluate the trade-off between the benefits of more internal modes (mainly more control) and their higher costs (resource commitment) (Malhotra/Agarwal/Ulgado, 2004, p. 6).

7.5.2   Conditions influencing the evaluation

Given the advantages and disadvantages of each entry mode, there is no single optimal market entry mode for each situation. Rather, the decision will always depend on a number of factors. For example, a

SME may simply not have the necessary financial assets to build or acquire a production plant in a foreign country. Or it may not have the necessary market knowledge to sell without the help of a local intermediary. Various aspects need to be considered (Root, 1994, p. 9):

- company-specific attributes (e.g. the financial resources of the company)
- product-specific attributes (e.g. the requirement for technical customer service, complexity, perishability or transportability)
- host country environmental attributes (e.g. the political risk in the country, legal restrictions, availability of skilled labor, labor cost)
- target market attributes (e.g. present and projected size of the market, competitive structure, availability of potential business partners)
- home country attributes (e.g. the country image, the cost level).

In addition to this, a number of attributes of the host country have to be evaluated in relation to the home country, for example, the similarity of the two markets, the cultural distance between the countries and also the geographical distance, which influences transport time and costs. In particular, the existence of trade barriers between the home country and the host country will influence the choice of entry mode. If both countries are in the same regional agreement (e.g. the EU or the EF-TA) or have free trade agreements in force, trade barriers are low and this may make exports more favorable.

7.5.3   Evaluation process

Market entry modes are multi-dimensional concepts. And the specific situation of a company that wants to sell a specific product in a specific market is unique. Management literature on the choice of market entry mode is complex and does not provide clear and consistent recommendations (e.g. Morschett/Schramm-Klein/Swoboda, 2010; Kutschker/Schmid, 2011, p. 932). Despite this, there are practical methods available to support a company in its evaluation of possible market entry modes (Zentes/Swoboda/Schramm-Klein, 2010, pp. 252 ff.) and these can be combined into a systematic evaluation process.

The proposed evaluation process is shown in **Figure 7.2**:

1. Eliminate the less suitable entry modes based on external and internal conditions

2. Select the best suitable entry modes based on a detailed evaluation

Figure 7.2: Process for evaluating market entry modes

A decision heuristic appropriate for **Step 1** would first require companies to identify the most important external and internal determinants of entry mode choice in a particular situation. **Figure 7.3** provides two grids which illustrate the fit between specific market entry modes and market characteristics (left hand grid) and between market entry modes and market attractiveness and competitive strength (right hand side). These can be used as rules of thumb. For example, in a market that is attractive but characterized by rather high barriers, a company should use the support of a local partner and engage in a joint venture. If the market is less attractive, commitment of one's own resources to the market is not necessary and licensing may be sufficient. If the company has a strong competitive advantage over local competitors, it can set

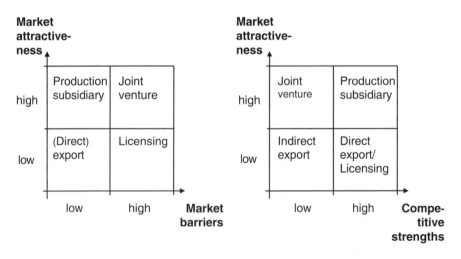

Figure 7.3: Matching market attributes, internal attributes and entry modes (Zentes, 1993, p. 70)

up a wholly-owned production subsidiary in an attractive market. If the competitive strength is rather low, the complementary advantages of a local partner may be necessary which would suggest a joint venture.

For the more detailed analysis in **Step 2,** a scoring model will help to structure the decision. **Figure 7.4** gives an example. Since many different criteria have to be considered simultaneously, this model involves listing the criteria, discussing the relevance of each criterion for the company (which results in a specific weight) and determining the

Criteria	Importance of the criteria	Options		
		Export via distributor	Export via sales subsidiary	Licensing
Control over marketing	2	1	4	2
Control over after-sales service	2	2	4	2
Required financial resources	3	4	2	4
Required management resources	1	4	2	3
Production costs	3	1	1	4
Custom duties to be paid	2	1	1	4
Flexibility to switch entry modes	1	2	3	2
Access to distribution channels	3	4	2	4
Risk of knowledge dissemination	2	2	4	1
Overall evaluation		**45**	**46**	**59**

Scores: 4 = very positive   3 = positive 2 = negative 1 = very negative
Importance of the criteria: 3 = high   2 = medium   1 = low

Figure 7.4: Scoring model for selecting the market entry mode (adapted from Mühlbacher/Dahringer/Leihs, 2006, p. 435)

score of each market entry mode with regard to each criterion. This not only provides an "aggregate weighted score" for each entry mode but – more importantly – leads to structured and rational discussion.

8 Developing an internationalization strategy for new markets

8.1 Overview of the process

Chapter 8 sets out a process which can be used when developing an internationalization strategy for new markets together with the associated market entry programs. This proposal is based on our earlier discussion of how to select markets in Chapter 6 and also on the presentation of market entry modes in Chapter 7.

Figure 8.1 provides an overview of the proposal:

- The process begins with a preliminary step in which the framework conditions are established, together with the organization and timetable for the project.
- The next two steps are first, to select attractive markets and then, to determine the corresponding market entry modes.
- Following on from this, in the third step feasibility studies are carried out for each market. It is these feasibility studies which will form the basis for the development of the internationalization strategy in Step 4.
- Finally, the feasibility studies and the internationalization strategy will be used as a basis for establishing entry programs for the target markets.

The process put forward here is based on the heuristic principles of factorization and adjustment to tools (Grünig/Kühn, 2009, p. 71):

- The heuristic rule of factorization means that the original, overly complex problem is disassembled into a series of manageable sub-problems.
- The second heuristic principle is to set up the sub-problems in such a way that proven tools can be applied to them. This principle is applied in Steps 1 and 2, where the work is based on the methods introduced in Chapters 6 and 7.

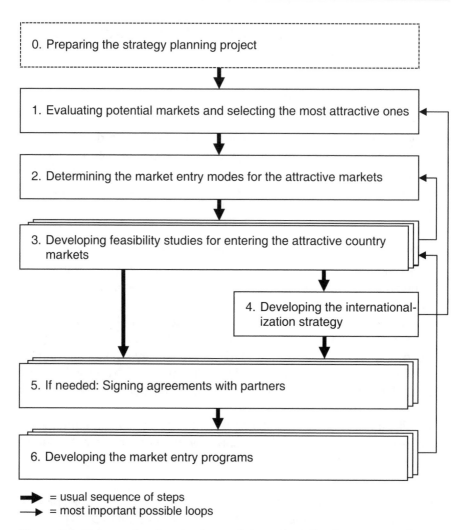

= usual sequence of steps
= most important possible loops

Figure 8.1: Process for developing an internationalization strategy for new markets

As well as giving the sequence of steps, the figure also includes the most important heuristic loops. With heuristic procedures like this one, other loops may occur too, not shown in this chart.

Each step in the process will now be briefly described.

8.2   Step 0: Preparing the strategy planning project

There are two general points to make about the work required for developing an internationalization strategy together with the associated market entry programs:

- This is a very **complex task**. As will be clear from the preceding Chapters 6 and 7, there are very many factors to consider. As a result it is not easy to achieve a coherent and practical result.
- Internationalization typically becomes an option when there are threats on the home market or perceived opportunities abroad. This means that there are **unique circumstances**, which lead to the development of an internationalization strategy.

The development of an internationalization strategy thus meets the two most important qualifying criteria for a project. Like any project, the work should begin with a phase of project preparation.

Project preparation must answer five questions:

- What conditions must be respected when developing the strategy?
- How will the project be organized?
- Should external consultants be brought in? If so, what tasks will they be given?
- What is the timetable for the project?
- How much will the project to develop an internationalization strategy for new markets cost?

Two kinds of **conditions** must be fixed:

- The first concerns internationalization itself. Should the internationalization focus on particular countries or continents? Alternatively, are there territories which are to be completely excluded? For example, a company may wish to avoid the US because of legal liability for products. And are there also market entry forms which must be excluded? There might be a basic company policy that for quality reasons and/or from a desire to protect the company's knowledge base and know-how, any form of partnership is excluded. As a result, market entry modes with agents, distributors, licensed partners, joint ventures or franchising would not even be considered.
- The second type of condition concerns the financial aspects. The project should not come up with plans which turn out to be un-

financeable. So it is better to fix the framework from the beginning. This can be in the form of a total sum for a period of some years, or an annual budget. The first of these two options is the more flexible. Managing the budgets for a number of years as a single sum is certainly preferable when attempting to set up a new subsidiary with its own production.

Success in any project demands effective **project organisation,** which means that for the various persons and groups involved in the project there is clarity about their tasks, their areas of competence and their responsibilities. The complexity of the project organization depends on how large the company is and on how many different markets are to be examined:

- There is always a need for a group which has the competence to take binding decisions. It is this group which defines the mandates and then reviews and formally approves the findings at each stage in the process. This decision-making group could be the board of directors, the executive board, or a group constituted ad hoc for the purpose.
- In small companies, or when there are few potential markets to examine, a single working group alongside the decision-making group is all that is necessary. This working group, supported by external consultants, carries out all the required analysis and planning and submits the results of this work to the decision-makers. A project manager will be appointed to lead the working group. The group should be made up of staff who will later play an important part in actually building up the new markets and of employees who may have knowledge of the markets under consideration.
- In larger companies, and whenever a large number of potential markets is to be examined, a more extensive structure will be needed. A steering committee must be set up which reports to the decision-making group. The project manager will lead the steering committee, and should be assisted by a project administrator. The steering committee will also include all the leaders of the individual working groups, which each focus on one or more specific geographical markets and carry out the analysis and planning required for those markets. The steering committee is responsible for crucial tasks: it allocates work to the working groups, coordinates their work, and subsequently combines and reduces the data they submit. It also has to prepare presentations to the decision-making group.

As the two preceding chapters have shown, detailed information about the potential markets is needed in order to select the most attractive ones and to determine the optimal market entry mode. If the company itself does not have this information, then it must bring in **consultants** who do have the required knowledge. The company may also need help in coordinating the project, if experience in this area is not available within the company.

A clearly structured **project procedure** is of vital importance. **Figure 8.1** offers our suggestion, which can either be applied as it stands, or can be adapted to specific requirements. This procedure provides a useful overview and helps everyone to deal with the complexity of the tasks. The procedure must also be fitted to a project timetable. The simplest way to do this is to schedule milestones for the completion of the different steps.

Developing an internationalization strategy for new markets requires a great deal of effort and has high costs, especially, as often happens, when one or more consultants are brought into the team. A **budget** should be set for the analysis and planning. In the interests of cost control and to provide a good overview of what is being spent, the budget should include work done on company time as well as work done by outsiders and also material costs, including travel costs.

8.3   Step 1: Evaluating potential markets and selecting the most attractive ones

Step 1 requires the identification of markets which could be attractive. Chapter 6 has described how such markets are analyzed and selected, and what the evaluation criteria are. We add nothing more here.

The outcome of Step 1 is a limited number of combinations of industry and country markets which look particularly promising. From this point on, the work focuses on these potential markets. But we have seen that heuristic processes include the possibility of loops in the process. This means that new markets may be added later. Here it may be helpful to consider an example. Let us suppose that on the list of the potential markets is the market for construction machines in Argentina. This idea takes on concrete form as the discussions progress: the company decides to create a sales subsidiary with a decentralized network of sales and after sales points. Once the decision has been made to create a decentralized infrastructure in Argentina, it becomes sensible to examine too the possibility of entering the market for agricultural machinery. Note that even if the contribution margin of agricultural machinery is lower than that of construction machinery, entry to this market might still be profitable, since the costs of the service points are already covered by the construction machinery.

8.4   Step 2: Determining the market entry modes for the attractive markets

Step 2 requires the market entry mode to be determined for each of the potential markets. Where the market entry requires one or more partners, a list of candidates as potential partners must be drawn up.

Chapter 7 outlines the various market entry modes, together with their advantages and disadvantages. The chapter also discusses the requirements partners need to meet, so again, we need say little more on these subjects here.

The markets under consideration are combinations of industry and country markets. **Figure 8.2** returns to the example used in Chapter 6 and presents the five industry markets, in three geographical markets, which were identified as the most attractive by the selection process.

When determining market entry modes in Step 2 there are two points to emphasize:

- Conditions of the company, of the market and of the products often greatly reduce the range of possible market entry modes. In practice, it mostly happens that only two or three market entry modes are considered. If, for instance, the capital available is limited and the company does not want to involve partners for quality reasons, the only remaining possibilities are direct export to the final customer, sales representatives or a sales branch.

Most attractive markets		Entry modes		
Geographical markets	Industry markets	Production subsidiary	Sales subsidiary	Distributor
A	I	■		
	III	■		
E, F + G	I		■	
	II		■	⌐ ⌐
H	II		■	

■ = selected entry mode
⌐ ⌐ = entry mode which would fit best

Figure 8.2: Market - entry mode combinations as result of Step 2

- The market entry mode must be determined separately for each industry market. This means that in a country market two or three different entry modes may be used at the same time, though in different industry markets. Combining them can be beneficial, both for the sake of simplicity and to optimize cost levels. So if a sales branch or even a sales subsidiary is opened in a new country, then if possible, this could be responsible for all the products sold into that country.

These two points are evident in **Figure 8.2.** Here only three of the ten market entry modes presented in Chapter 7 have been considered. In addition, for each geographical market a single market entry mode is used. In the geographical market E, F + G the products for industry market II will be distributed via a sales subsidiary and not by an independent distributor.

The result of Step 2 is a clear decision about which industry and country markets are preferred and how the potential market entry will be accomplished. The next step consists in the production of a feasibility study for each combination of market and entry mode. With reference to **Figure 8.2**, three such studies are needed.

8.5   Step 3: Developing feasibility studies for entering the attractive country markets

Step 3 requires the detailed planning of market entry into each of the preferred new markets. Although at this stage a final decision has not yet been made, these detailed plans are required in order to furnish the information required for a soundly based decision. Thus the market entry plans can be seen as feasibility studies.

Two important decisions have already been made in Steps 1 and 2:

- Step 1 determined the potential industry markets to be served.
- Step 2 determined the optimal market entry form and also established a list of potential partners, in cases where a partner is required.

These two decisions are core elements for the feasibility study. As **Figure 8.3** shows, other factors must also be included:

- When a selected market entry mode requires a partner, contact must be made with potential partners. These discussions will be evaluated and the most suitable partner identified. But at this stage contractual agreements cannot be made, as the final decision for market entry has not yet been taken.
- Marketing plans must be drawn up which determine the marketing mix to be used in each target industry market (Root, 1994, p. 20). This requires at the very least that the four Ps be addressed: product, place, promotion and price (McCarthy, 1960).

  A further important component in a market entry plan is the resources required. What exactly is included here will depend on the market entry mode. Direct export, for example, requires virtually no resources. Contrast this with setting up a wholly-owned subsidiary with production, which will often require the investment of very large sums of money.

1. Served industry markets
2. Market entry mode(s)
3. If needed: Partner(s)
4. Marketing plans for the served industry markets

    4.1 Industry market A

    4.2 Industry market B
5. Resources needed

    5.1 Human resources

    5.2 Assets

    5.3 Working capital
6. Quantitative objectives

    6.1 Industry market A

    6.2 Industry market B
7. Measures

    7.1 Order of entering the industry markets

    7.2 Steps and time needed for building up activities in industry market A

    7.3 Steps and time needed for building up activities in industry market B
8. Responsibilities
9. Budget

    9.1 Expenses including investments

    9.2 Revenues
10. Economic evaluation

Figure 8.3: Table of contents of a feasibility study for entering a country market

- On the basis of these reflections, quantitative objectives can be defined. Financial planning requires quantitative targets in terms of units sold and sales revenue. From these figures it is possible to derive target market shares. The figures will provide a stronger basis if it is possible to set targets not only for the whole industry market, but also for the served industry segments (see **Inset 6.2**).
- Yet another element in a feasibility study is the planning of necessary measures and the setting of a timetable. It needs to be clear

how the market entry will proceed and how long it will take to achieve the targets for the market. However, the feasibility study will not set dates. This will be done after the decision in Step 4.

- The feasibility study should indicate how responsibilities will be divided during the market entry phase. How will the project be integrated within the mother company? Can an employee be identified who could be project leader?

- The feasibility study needs to demonstrate the financial consequences of market entry. Rough estimates are required for annual expenses and revenues so that the profitability of the market entry can be evaluated. This may be a difficult task, and it is better to be cautious by giving somewhat higher estimates for expenses and lower ones for revenues. Within expenses, both one time expenses when setting up and also ongoing running costs for raw materials, staff etc. must be included.

- The final section of the feasibility study must be an evaluation of the profitability of the market entry. This requires an investment appraisal. Often the net present value method is used for this. It is explained in **Inset 8.1.**

Figure 8.3 lists the various elements required in a market entry feasibility study presented as a logical sequence of different points to consider. However, producing the study is unlikely to be a strictly linear process. As Root emphasizes, "The design of a market entry is actually iterative with many feedback loops" (Root, 1994, p. 3).

8.6   Step 4: Developing the internationalization strategy

The feasibility studies provide a basis for the work of Step 4, which is to determine the internationalization strategy. The first task is to decide which markets will be entered and in what order. Once the decision has been taken, a brief and clear formulation of the internationalization strategy for new markets must be set down in writing.

The decision to enter or not to enter a new market will depend on several criteria:

- An important criterion is profitability: The investments required must bring a positive return. This can be judged according to the investment appraisals which appear at the end of each feasibility study. **Inset 8.1** describes the Net Present Value (NPV) method, a method frequently used in investment appraisals. The inset shows net present values for three different market entry options.
- A second important decision criteron is financeability. Financeability can set upper limits on investments. This could mean that a company will have to enter markets one by one, rather than all at once. Sometimes financeability constraints may prevent a company from entering a market at all.
- Other criteria are possible. For instance the presence of an important customer in a country market can be an important factor in the decision to enter a market.

To get an overview of the different consequences of each option and for determining the overall consequences of the options, a scoring model can be useful (see **Inset 6.1**).

Inset 8.1: The Net Present Value as an approach to assessing market entry options

The NPV method discounts the free cash flows of different years to present values (Horngren et al., 2009, pp. 762 ff.). The net present value then represents the total profit or total loss from an investment in present-day values.

The discount rate is calculated by adding a risk premium to a percentage rate of return on capital. The risk premium is intended to take account of specific risks in the market. As a result, it will vary from case to case.

To show how NPV can be used to assess the profitability of a market entry option, we return to the example used earlier in Chapters 6 and 8. **Figure 8.2** shows the situation after market entry modes have been determined. Under review is the proposal that market A will be entered with a production subsidiary, while market E, F + G and market H will be entered by a sales subsidiary.

Market entry options	Free cash flows									Discount rate	Net Present Value
	Year 0	Year 1	Year 2	Year 3	Year 4	Year 5	Year 6	Year 7	Year 8		
Market A with wholly owned production subsidiary	- 1,500	+ 150	+ 200	+ 250	+ 250	+ 250	+ 250	+ 250	+ 750	10%	- 58
Market E, F + G with sales subsidiary	- 600	+ 90	+ 120	+ 150	+ 150	+ 150	+ 150	+ 150	+ 150	9%	+ 160
Market H with sales subsidiary	- 400	+ 60	+ 80	+ 100	+ 100	+ 100	+ 100	+ 100	+ 100	8%	+ 131

Figures in 1,000 EUR

Figure 8.4: Net Present Values of market entry options

Figure 8.4 gives net present values for the three options. Note the following points:

- The relatively much higher initial investment in Market A compared to the other two markets is a consequence of the difference in entry mode.
- The differences in the discount rates can be traced to differences in risk. The influence of the discount rate is considerable. If, for example, "Market H with a sales subsidiary" had 9% instead of 8% the net present value would fall by 18%. This is because of the compounding of interest.
- For all three options the free cash flows rise until year three, after which they remain level. This is the result of building up the market, which, in this example, is a process taking three years. The high free cash flow in Year 8 for Market A can be attributed to the fact that a fictional payment has been added for this year. This is because the investment of 1,500 is amortized over 12 years, which means that at the end of Year 8 the factory has a value of 500. This value has been added to the calculation.
- The result is clear. Market entry with a sales subsidiary leads to positive net present values ranging between a quarter and a third of the initial investment. Therefore, market entry with a sales subsidiary appears a positive move. In contrast, setting up production in Market A does not. If the laws in that country specify local production, then the company should abstain from entering that market. But if alternative entry modes are possible, then a feasibility study based on a more cost-advantageous entry mode should be carried out and this can then be used to assess profitability a second time.

The internationalization strategy for new markets brings together in a single document the various decisions which have been made and gives an overview of what must happen and when and what the financial consequences of these decisions are. Usually a few pages are sufficient. Although there are many details which need to be fixed, these can be included in the market entry programs and do not need to be reproduced in the internationalization strategy.

Figure 8.5 proposes a structure for the document setting out an internationalization strategy for new markets:

- The first point contains the decision made.
- Points 2 and 3 summarize the key points from the feasibility studies for the markets in question.
- Point 4 gives the timing for each market entry. Whether these market entries are to take place simultaneously or in a staged sequence will depend on available staff and financial resources. This is true both for entry into new geographical markets and for entry into different industry markets in these countries.
- Points 5 and 6 also go back to the feasibility studies for the markets selected, listing responsibilities and providing a financial summary.

---

1. Country and industry markets to build up

2. Entry modes and, if needed, partners

3. Quantitative market objectives

4. Timetable

5. Responsibilities

6. Investment budgets and free cash flow targets

Figure 8.5: Table of contents of an internationalization strategy for new markets

8.7   Step 5: Signing agreements with partners

Step 4 leads to a decision to enter specific markets. This may require the company to commit itself to partners and sign contracts with them. Step Five consists of the negotiation and signing of agreements with future partners.

8.8   Step 6: Developing the market entry programs

The final step is the formulation of market entry programs for each of the markets selected. The basis for these programs will be the feasibility studies produced in Step 3. They will need to be reviewed in line with the decisions made in Step 4 and then turned into concrete programs of action.

The most important adaptation will be in the planning of deadlines. In the internationalization strategy for new markets time windows are given for the entry to each country and industry market. Within these time windows, detailed plans must fix the timing and set milestones.

Whenever Step 5 leads to a decision to work with a partner, the partner needs to be closely involved in determining the market entry program. It is important that the partner identifies with the content of the program, since the partner will be involved in implementing it.

Part IV

Strategies for going international for production and sourcing

Part IV describes the relocation of production or sourcing activities to foreign countries.

Chapter 9 explains how attractive sourcing locations abroad are identified. The chapter consists of three sections:

- After a brief introduction in Section 9.1, Section 9.2 provides an extensive account of decision criteria for the evaluation and selection of countries for production or sourcing. Insets on selected regions and companies illustrate the relevance of the criteria. An inset discusses divestment decisions, as there are lessons to learn from the negative experiences of other companies.
- In Section 9.3, a three-step process for the evaluation of new production and sourcing locations is introduced. After an initial list of potential sourcing locations has been produced, less attractive locations are eliminated on the basis of a coarse-grained analysis. The most attractive sourcing or production countries are then evaluated, based on a detailed analysis.

Chapter 10 explains the evaluation of different operation modes when sourcing from foreign countries:

- After an overview of the different operation modes in Section 10.1, the following sections describe four groups of operation modes.
- Section 10.2 focuses on sourcing from trade companies, while in Section 10.3 sourcing from foreign manufacturers is highlighted.
- Section 10.4 describes contract manufacturing, one of the most common operation modes for sourcing abroad. This section includes a detailed discussion of the advantages and disadvantages of outsourcing. Two insets present examples of contract manufacturing.
- Section 10.5 explains the establishment of own production abroad, either independently or in the form of a joint venture. An inset describes how a Norwegian company relocated its production to low-cost countries.

- After the presentation of the available operation modes in Sections 10.2 to 10.5, Section 10.6 explains how to evaluate operation modes with respect to a specific country. Evaluation criteria are presented, together with internal and external conditions influencing the evaluation. The chapter concludes by proposing a two-step evaluation process.

Chapter 11 describes a process for the development of an internationalization strategy for production and sourcing:

- After an overview of the process in Section 11.1, the following sections explain the steps in the process. Step 0 is project planning, explained in Section 11.2.
- Step 1, described in Section 11.3, includes the evaluation of potential sourcing countries and the evaluation of potential operation modes. It is emphasized that country selection and operation mode selection have to be carried out in an iterative process.
- In Section 11.4, Step 2 is described. In this step suitable "location-operation mode" combinations are determined.
- Step 3, the production of feasibility studies for the selected location-operation mode combinations, is described in the following section. An inset explains how the method of net present value calculation can be used to determine the profitability of an option.
- Section 11.6 explains how the internationalization strategy is developed. Based on the feasibility studies, a combination of sourcing and production options abroad is selected. After this, the sequence and time frame for the relocation activities are fixed.
- After a brief description of final negotiations with a partner in Section 11.7, Section 11.8 explains how to develop relocation programs for the various sourcing intentions.

9 Evaluating new production and sourcing locations

9.1 Preliminary remarks

In this chapter we adopt the perspective of a company assessing a foreign location for production or sourcing while the target market into which the output will be sold remains the home country. In such cases, the relocation is mainly driven by cost considerations. Not explicitly discussed here is the constellation in which sourcing is offshored to one foreign country and the target market is a third country.

The selection of sourcing locations is a different matter from the selection of foreign markets, where the company looks at the two dimensions of "country" and "industry" simultaneously. There is usually already a clear idea about which production stage of which product group is to be relocated to another country. The output from the country evaluation is simply a country short-list with country descriptions.

The choice of a concrete location within a country – which is closely associated with the choice of a potential supplier or partner – is discussed in Chapter 11.

9.2 Criteria for evaluating new production and sourcing locations

9.2.1 Overview

The criteria applied in the selection process will vary. The rough selection in the first round uses coarser, macro-level decision criteria, while in the second round, a finer grained analysis is required, with more detailed information and a larger number of criteria.

The assessment of countries as sourcing locations has to consider three levels of information:

- **Information about the country in general:** Macro-level data have to be considered, such as labor cost, economic freedom in the country, and distance from the home country.
- **Information about the specific industry in the country:** A given country may be obviously more or less attractive as a location for high-tech products like pharmaceuticals or for simpler products like textiles. Information on the industry has to be analyzed, including competitiveness, industry structure and players, and the development of costs.
- **Information about the particular production stage** in the value chain which may take place in the foreign country: Even within a single industry, the attractiveness of a country may differ according to the stage in production. A country may be attractive for the initial transformation of raw materials into parts, less attractive for building complex components, but again more attractive for the final assembly stage.

In both rounds of the process and on all three levels of information, the criteria for assessing prospective sourcing countries can be categorized into four groups (cf. Shenkar/Luo, 2008, p. 277):

- cost factors, e.g. labor costs
- strategic factors, e.g. the availability of skilled labor
- political factors, e.g. the FDI policy
- demand factors. These are less relevant for the selection of a purely sourcing country. But they may influence the decision if the sourcing country is linked to a potential market entry, which could also be under consideration at the same time.

If the intention is to source from independent suppliers, there is a more fundamental criterion: Are the products to be sourced available in that country or are there at least suppliers that could start manufacturing the required products? If not, the country can be eliminated from the list immediately.

Norway	43.64		South Korea	11.49
Belgium	38.59		Malta	10.27
Switzerland	37.14		Portugal	10.03
West. Germany	36.05		Czech Rep.	8.86
Denmark	35.08		Croatia	7.89
Finland	33.76		Slovakia	7.80
France	33.31		Estonia	7.30
Austria	33.20		Hungary	6.94
Luxembourg	33.09		Poland	6.04
Sweden	32.88		Lithuania	5.45
Netherlands	32.75		Latvia	5.25
Ireland	29.62		Turkey	4.33
Italy	27.40		Russia	3.61
USA	22.95		Romania	3.39
Japan	22.86		Belarus	2.67
United Kingdom	22.21		Bulgaria	2.44
Spain	21.87		China	2.25
East. Germany	21.11		Ukraine	1.81
Canada	21.01		Moldavia	1.74
Greece	16.44		Georgia	1.65
Slovenia	13.18		Philippines	1.33

Data in EUR per hour, 2009

Figure 9.1: Labor costs in manufacturing industries in different countries
(adapted from Institut der Deutschen Wirtschaft, 2010)

9.2.2   Cost factors

Among the cost factors, **labor costs** are usually the dominant variable. In many industries, these constitute a substantial proportion of total production costs. And labor costs differ substantially between different countries, as **Figure 9.1** demonstrates. In some countries, even within Europe, labor cost per hour is ten times lower than in Switzerland or Germany.

It has to be noted, however, that the relative cost advantages of a sourcing country are dynamic, not static. This becomes evident in **Inset 9.1**.

Inset 9.1: China is becoming too expensive
(text based on Textilwirtschaft, 2010; Appel/Hein, 2010)

With rising labor costs in China, clothing manufacturers have started to shift their sourcing and production to countries like Bangladesh, Cambodia, India, Indonesia and Vietnam, even though this may result in higher transportation costs. In 2010, wages in China rose between 5 % and 20 % after the introduction of minimum wage levels. This increased production costs for clothing by between 2% and 5 %.

In addition to this, the demand on the domestic market in China is growing rapidly, making production capacity hard to find. While the factories in China have been suffering from increasing labor costs, the growing demand from domestic customers has compensated for this trend. As a result, Chinese producers no longer depend on their foreign customers. Many of them, in fact, prefer domestic customers as an alternative to complying with the high ecological and social standards that foreign customers demand.

Contributing to the uncomfortable situation for Western textile companies is the rise in cotton prices and scarcity on the cotton market. Some countries, such as India, have reacted by prohibiting cotton exports to China in order to secure the supply to their own industry.

This situation reveals the importance of good supplier relationships. As E. Bezner, executive of Olymp, one of the leading shirt manufacturers in Europe, points out: "It is only thanks to our long-established relationships with Chinese suppliers that we can still get our products manufactured there at acceptable prices."

But it is not enough only to analyze labor cost. Too often, companies underestimate **logistics costs**. Frequently, these make up a third of overall procurement costs. Products have to be transported from the production location in the foreign country to the home market. Often, product parts or components are produced in the home country, transported to the processing country and re-transported, leading to double transportation costs. While it is true that in the last two decades transportation costs have been greatly reduced - freight rates for overseas containers are, for many products, almost negligible - this trend may change with the increasing shortage of oil.

The value-to-weight ratio of the production output is a crucial variable for logistics costs. Bulky or large products, like bottled soft drinks or assembled furniture, are inexpensive to produce but weigh a lot. In contrast, mobile phones and luxury watches are light products with high value. With high value-to-weight ratios, transportation costs are not a major issue.

But logistics costs are more than just transportation costs. Longer supply chains often mean more damage in transit. Furthermore, longer distances and later delivery times usually create substantial inventory costs. If supply comes from Asia and takes four to six weeks to arrive in Europe, and if that supply is crucial to ensure just-in-time production, then a company will have to create larger safety stocks. **Inset 9.2** presents an analysis of total costs carried out by Electrolux.

Inset 9.2: Electrolux compares the cost of different sourcing locations (text based on Morschett/Schramm-Klein/Zentes, 2010, p. 339 f.)

At the beginning of the twenty-first century, Electrolux was confronted with a number of different challenges. One was to manage increasing production costs, mainly due to rising prices for materials and components.

A comparison of production costs showed that the total production costs of washing machines intended to be sold in the EU are highest when they are produced directly within the EU. For machines produced within the EU, the costs for materials and components alone are almost as high as the total production costs of machines produced in Eastern Europe or China. But although costs for materials and labor are lower in China than in Eastern Europe, high logistic costs from China to the EU outweigh the lower costs for materials and labour. Conversely, transport costs from Eastern Europe to the EU market are very low.

For the production of chest-freezers manufactured either in China or in Mexico and intended to be sold in the US market, the result was almost the same. Total production costs are even lower for Mexico than for China, again due to lower transport costs from Mexico to the USA than from China to the USA.

Figure 9.2 summarizes the two analyses. As Electrolux's product portfolio mainly consists of large and heavy products such as refrigerators, chest-freezers and washing machines, transport cost often plays a decisive role.

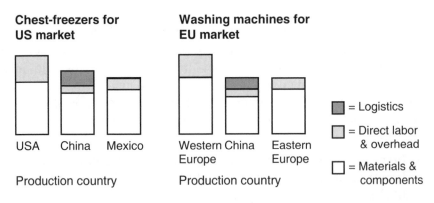

Figure 9.2: Total costs of Electrolux for products sourced in different regions (Electrolux, 2005, p. 4)

This is a strong argument for the trend towards what is called nearshoring, that is offshoring to a geographically close foreign country. Examples are Eastern Europe for German and Swiss companies, and Mexico for US companies. These are favorite destinations for nearshoring, which results in short delivery times, greater supply security and lower transportation and inventory costs. As a result, European car manufacturers, for example, source their parts and components from locations which are seldom in China and much more often in Eastern Europe.

Trade barriers between the production country and the home market, in particular customs tariffs, are an important consideration. If a company is mainly going international for production or sourcing, importing into the home country becomes necessary. Trade barriers are severe because there is no operation mode that allows the company to circumvent them. To avoid trade barriers, production countries within the same free trade region (like EFTA or the EU) may be chosen or countries with which the home country has a free trade agreement. For example, Switzerland is currently negotiating a free trade agreement with China. With regard to processing trade, companies should consider the benefits of free-trade zones within foreign countries. These are closed regions monitored by customs services where input goods can be imported without the usual customs requirements.

Additional cost factors include the cost of land in the foreign country (in cases where the company wants to build a factory), costs of raw materials and other input goods, tax rates, and costs for quality inspections. On the positive side, host countries may offer subsidies for the establishment of production sites.

Figure 9.3 shows the main cost elements that have to be considered when deciding upon foreign sourcing.

Purchasing cost or production costs abroad
+ **Logistics**
   - Inland freight in the production country
   - International freight
   - Inland freight in the home country
   - Transfer charges
   - Additional safety stock
+ **Customs duties and fees**
   - Duties
   - Customs fees
   - Harbour fees
+ **Taxes**
   - VAT and/or import tax
   - ./. Tax incentives in the production country
+ **Other costs**
   - Cost of quality monitoring
   - Cost of damage
   - Supplier development and certification
   - Cost due to exchange rate volatility
= **Total cost of procurement**

Figure 9.3: Components of procurement cost (adapted from Deloitte, 2007, p. 3)

9.2.3 Strategic factors

Cost factors may be complex, but at least they can be quantified to a considerable extent. However, there are also a number of strategic factors which are important for the location decision.

The predominant criterion for production in a foreign location is the **availability of skilled workers**. For companies from Western Europe, in particular, which often position themselves with their product quality, in a relocation project it is important to avoid quality problems arising from low-skilled workers.

Furthermore, the **infrastructure in the country** is crucial for a smooth supply chain. Relevant infrastructure may include roads, airports, railroads, ports, the ITC infrastructure and utilities like water and energy supply, as **Inset 9.3** illustrates.

Inset 9.3: Infrastructure as a necessary requirement
(text based on Appel/Hein, 2010)

Due to rising labor costs in China, fashion firms have started to analyze production locations that were formerly considered third class: Bangladesh, Cambodia and Laos. But the poor infrastructure in these countries makes it almost impossible to meet the delivery times that are so crucial in the fashion industry. In Bangladesh, power shortages have forced companies to shift their production from weekdays to the weekend when the power network is less heavily utilized. Furthermore, in these countries no sub-suppliers exist and parts like buttons or zips have to be imported.

Another determining factor may be the existence of **regional clusters** related to the industry concerned. The term cluster refers to a geographical agglomeration of interconnected companies with complementary activities in a particular field (Porter, 1990). The advantages of a cluster stem from the presence of a specialized infrastructure, industry sector specific factors of production, information and knowledge spillovers and access to necessary inputs (Morschett/Schramm-Klein/ Zentes, 2010, p. 120).

The overall **competitiveness of the country** is another factor to be considered. Competitiveness is a comprehensive term which has many different facets (see **Figure 9.7**). In the long term, strong competitiveness of the sourcing country is likely to lead to better and/or cheaper production. The World Economic Forum assesses the competitiveness of nations every year (e.g., World Economic Forum, 2010). By assessing competitiveness and its different sub-criteria it is also possible to evaluate the **quality of production** in a country.

It may be an advantage to have sourcing locations in **other currency areas**. This allows companies to carry out what is called natural hedging in relation to exchange rate changes which would otherwise be unfavorable to the company. Sourcing from different currency areas may reduce the overall risk exposure of companies to such exchange rate changes, as **Inset 9.4** explains.

Inset 9.4: StarragHeckert balances the weak euro (text based on Sollberger, 2010a; Sollberger, 2010b)

In 2010/2011, the depreciation of the euro against the Swiss franc is a major concern for many Swiss companies. Between 50% and 65 % of Swiss exports go into the Euro-zone and those Swiss companies that do not produce in the Euro-zone or source from there have either to increase their prices or to accept decreasing profit margins.

Walter Fust, chairman of the machine producer StarragHeckert, was not suffering from the weakness of the euro. A production location in Chemnitz in Germany made exports to the dollar area even more profitable in 2010 because at that time the euro was also weak relative to the US dollar. In addition, the company bought components like engines and digital controllers for its Swiss factories from the German supplier Siemens and these imports had become cheaper. The advantages and disadvantages of the euro depreciation balanced out for StarragHeckert. Geographical diversification of sales markets and of production and sourcing markets led to natural hedging which reduces the negative impact of exchange rate volatility.

From a strategic perspective, it is important to enable management to coordinate the foreign activities effectively and efficiently. This may require **physical proximity,** since visits to the production site or the suppliers' factories may greatly improve successful integration into one's own operations. Time zones may be relevant. When trying to communicate with organizational units in distant countries, sometimes only a short time window is available during which working times overlap. This may create communication barriers.

9.2.4   Political factors

There are a large number of political factors that should be considered when evaluating a foreign country (Shenkar/Luo, 2008, pp. 280 ff.).

The **political risk** of a country is a measure of potential problems in the future. As discussed in **Inset 6.1**, political risk has different facets. Which risk facets are relevant for the company will depend on the specific operation mode.

Governmental regulations, like the FDI policy of the prospective host country, affect the operation modes and the payoffs. The general policy towards foreign companies should also be examined. While WTO regulations largely demand non-discrimination against foreign companies, such equal treatment is not guaranteed in all countries.

More generally, the **economic freedom** that is granted to companies in the country influences the room for maneuver or autonomy of the company, that is, the extent to which it can take decisions and implement them. Here data can be found in an annual report of the Heritage Foundation (e.g., Heritage Foundation, 2011), a think tank from the USA.

Legal enforcement may be important if, for example, intellectual property rights of the company are not respected by other companies.

Corruption has to be considered, since it may lead to unfair preference for competitors or the blocking of permits, and so on, for the company. Transparency International is an organization which evaluates the situation around the globe and publishes an annual corruption index for each country (Transparency International, 2010).

9.2.5   Other factors

Beyond the factors listed above, there is a universe of other country attributes that could be considered. While this is certainly not necessary in the first step, it may become necessary when the filtering process has proceeded. In many cases the variables to be considered depend to a great extent on the particular company, the particular industry, and the particular production stage.

For example, **demand factors,** like the size of the market or the similarity of demand, may play a role, since demand provides the company with an option to sell some of its output in that market. This could create economies of scale.

Social and environmental standards are playing an ever greater role since corporate governance regulation and corporate social responsibility concepts have led to an enhanced responsibility for the activities that a company carries out in a foreign country – even if these activities are carried out by external suppliers. While in the past there might have been a search for so called "pollution havens" or "social havens" where companies could produce without the high standards of their home country, this trend has reversed and high social and environmental standards in the host countries are now often seen as favorable since they protect the reputation of the company.

Cultural distance between the home country and the host country influences the ability of a company to manage operations in the foreign country on its own. The larger the cultural distance, the less a company can rely on its experience in the home country being applicable in the host country (see also Section 6.3.4.).

Companies that intend to relocate could also learn from other companies that may have regretted their relocation decision and reversed it. **Inset 9.5** describes the result of a survey in Germany.

Inset 9.5: Making and regretting the relocation decision

The German Fraunhofer Institute asked companies that decided to relocate parts of their production abroad why they did so. As **Figure 9.4** shows, labor costs are by far the dominant motive. Other important reasons were sales-oriented (which we describe in Part III).

Lower taxes abroad were also mentioned together with access to skilled workers and to new technology.

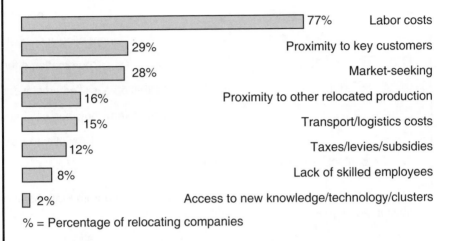

77%	Labor costs
29%	Proximity to key customers
28%	Market-seeking
16%	Proximity to other relocated production
15%	Transport/logistics costs
12%	Taxes/levies/subsidies
8%	Lack of skilled employees
2%	Access to new knowledge/technology/clusters

% = Percentage of relocating companies

Figure 9.4: Motives for relocating production abroad (adapted from Fraunhofer Institut, 2009, p. 7)

However, many studies have revealed that foreign divestment is quite common: companies often reverse their relocation decision within a few years (Morschett et al., 2009). The survey by Fraunhofer indicates that one fourth of all factories abroad are divested within 5 years of establishment. Such foreign divestment is often the result of earlier misjudgments. Looking into the most common reasons for divestment helps to highlight aspects that should be thoroughly analyzed before offshoring.

As **Figure 9.5** indicates, the most frequent reason for taking production back home reported by German companies is quality problems in their offshored production units. The main lesson from this is that the quality performance of the foreign country, the availability of skilled labor, etc. should be assessed very carefully before the selection is made.

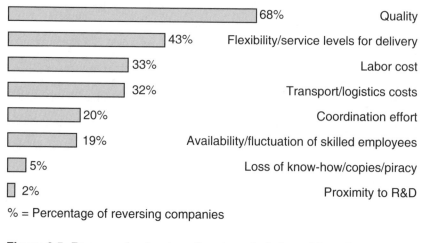

68%	Quality
43%	Flexibility/service levels for delivery
33%	Labor cost
32%	Transport/logistics costs
20%	Coordination effort
19%	Availability/fluctuation of skilled employees
5%	Loss of know-how/copies/piracy
2%	Proximity to R&D

% = Percentage of reversing companies

Figure 9.5: Reasons for foreign divestments (adapted from Fraunhofer Institut, 2009, p. 8)

Flexibility and service levels for delivery and transport costs are also aspects that lead to divestment. Companies have to evaluate the total cost of sourcing abroad, not only the purchasing costs.

It is noteworthy that labor cost abroad is given as a reason for divestment. In many emerging countries, wages may quickly rise. The country selection should not be based simply on current wage levels; wage development should be forecast over a longer planning period.

9.3   Process for evaluating new production and sourcing locations

9.3.1   Overview of the process

Figure 9.6 shows the proposed process for evaluating and selecting new production and sourcing locations.

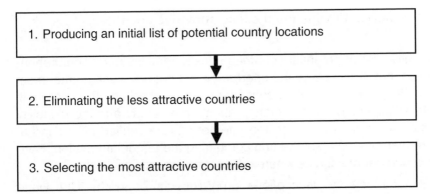

Figure 9.6: Process for evaluating new production and sourcing locations

9.3.2   Step 1: Producing an initial list of potential country locations

There may be a very large number of potential countries as production and sourcing locations. Clearly, a company cannot analyze all the countries of the world in a detailed manner. Instead, the company will start with an initial list of potential countries. This list usually results from information that the management already possesses: The management may have observed competitors relocating their production to Eastern Europe or there may be intensive public discussion of the attractive new sourcing opportunities in China or indeed a new free trade agreement between Switzerland and Japan.

However, it would be a mistake to narrow the analysis too quickly, based on prejudgments and lack of knowledge about other interesting locations. In this first step at least, systematic investigation of additional alternatives does not create substantial information costs. Including more locations in the selection process may result in a better final decision.

9.3.3   Step 2: Eliminating the less attractive countries

The initial list of potential countries usually remains fairly comprehensive so that at this stage the effort to collect data on each market must be limited. The collection of secondary data available on the Internet is quite sufficient. There are many data sources today and the reliability of the data that is found on the Internet can be verified by looking at more than one data source and comparing the target information. Here are a number of sources where information is readily available:

- General country descriptions on Wikipedia or in the CIA world factbook are sufficiently detailed for an initial analysis.
- Specific economic country data can be retrieved from the websites of OECD, the International Labor Organization ILO, and other international organizations.
- The official statistical offices of a country, or of the EU, provide a wealth of information.
- Country information from the Global Competitiveness Report (World Economic Forum, 2010) gives an excellent overview of different location factors (including, costs, innovation potential and infrastructure) and this is updated annually. The report even has an overview for each country on "The most problematic factors for doing business". **Figure 9.7** shows the country information in the Global Competitiveness Report for Romania.

To eliminate less attractive counties, sophisticated complex methods are not required. The most important criteria are defined on the basis of the dominant motives for the intended relocation of parts of the production process to another country. Threshold values for these criteria are set and these are then used to eliminate from the initial list those countries that do not exceed the threshold. The cost of the required production factors, usually labor, in the prospective sourcing country is the overriding consideration. The availability of potential suppliers and/or of a skilled labor force must also be examined. Political risk is usually also considered. Trade barriers are important in the first round as is the geographical distance between the home country and the prospective production or sourcing country as this is a major determinant of logistics costs and delivery times.

Key indicators

Population (millions)	21.3
GDP (billions USD)	161.5
GDP per capita (USD)	7,542

Global Competitiveness Index and its components 2010-2011

Criterion	Rank (out of 139)	Score (1-7)
Institutions	81	3.7
Infrastructure	92	3.4
Macroeconomic environment	78	4.5
Health and primary education	63	5.8
Higher education and training	54	4.5
Goods market efficiency	76	4.1
Labor market efficiency	76	4.3
Financial market development	81	4.0
Technological readiness	58	3.8
Market size	43	4.4
Business sophistication	93	3.5
Innovation	87	2.9
Global Competitiveness Index	**67**	**4.2**

The most problematic factors for doing business (% of responses)

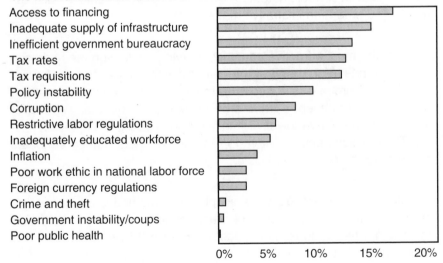

Figure 9.7: Evaluation of Romania in the World Competitiveness Report
(adapted from World Economic Forum, 2010, p. 284)

9.3.4   Step 3: Selecting the most attractive country locations

For the selection of the most attractive locations, more detailed and industry-specific data on the foreign countries is needed. This can be gathered from official government institutions in most home countries. In Germany, for example, the Bundesamt für Aussenhandelsinformationen (bfai) provides country reports. In Switzerland, the OSEC offers this service; for SMEs the OSEC usually provides an initial country analysis free of charge.

For more detailed data, investment promotion agencies in the foreign countries can be contacted. These are very willing to provide data on their country and on specific regions. While this information is likely to be biased - it will present usually the most attractive side of a country - it will be detailed and offer very useful insights. Official institutions, whether domestic (like the OSEC), or foreign (like investment agencies), or both (like joint chambers of commerce), can also help to organize visits to attractive countries: as soon as there is a short list of countries, the analysis for each country must be more detailed, so that visits are essential. These institutions can also help to establish contacts with potential business partners (suppliers, joint venture partners or even take-over candidates) or with local governments to discuss permits and other administrative matters.

To select the most attractive countries, varying evaluation methods can be applied, based on many of the criteria given above. The evaluation and selection process is based on a multi-attribute model. Generally, a company has to accept a trade-off. For example, countries with lower labor costs often have lower skill levels and/or are geographically distant. Thus, a company will have to rank and/or weight these attributes according to the company's goals.

To make an overall evaluation, a simple initial method is to choose two important dimensions and consider them simultaneously by illustrating the data in a two-dimensional space. As **Figure 9.8** demonstrates, this simple method allows decision-makers to grasp the essential information more quickly and makes it easy to compare the relative advantages and disadvantages of the various countries with regard to the most relevant criteria. Most countries that qualify as a potential production location from the perspective of labor costs are also characterized by a rather low degree of economic freedom. However, some countries in Eastern Europe are already reaching levels of economic freedom that are comparable to those of the US or the UK while maintaining hourly wages (including social costs) that are less than half the rates in those countries.

This first analysis is mainly used to illustrate the data and to reduce the country list further. In the next step, a more fine-grained analysis will be necessary. One possibility is a detailed analysis of the specific industry including investigation of (potential) suppliers and sub-suppliers, a review of wages in the specific industry, assessment of competition for production factors and various other factors.

Based on this fine-grained analysis, the final evaluation should be carried out with the help of a scoring model which can structure the decision. We described how such a model is developed in **Figure 6.12** above. Many different criteria have to be considered simultaneously. For a structured and rational discussion, we recommend first listing the criteria, then discussing the relevance of each criterion for the company and allocating it a specific weight and finally determining together the score for each location on each of the criteria. This system will produce an aggregate weighted score for each country. But again, we would advise caution: rather than simply accepting the result and choosing the option with the highest score, companies should try to find the reasons why a given solution has been recommended by the scoring model. This is usually a good starting point for a fruitful discussion.

The result of this evaluation process is not yet the final decision but a short-list of countries where the prospective sourcing or production is generally thought to be both feasible and attractive. This list is an essential basis for the development of the internationalization strategy for production and sourcing, which is presented in Chapter 11 below.

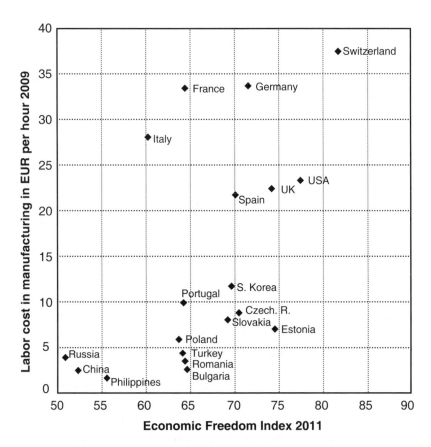

Figure 9.8: Labor costs and economic freedom in selected countries
(own illustration; labor cost data: Institut der Deutschen Wirtschaft, 2010; economic freedom: Heritage Foundation, 2011)

10 Evaluating foreign operation modes

10.1 Preliminary remarks and overview of the operation modes

When a company has decided that a product – a final product, a semi-finished product or a raw material – or a service should be sourced from a foreign country, it has to select a suitable operation mode. There is a wide range of options to choose from. In this chapter the different operation modes are described and then a number of tools are presented which can help companies to choose between them.

The available operation modes, illustrated in **Figure 10.1,** can be broadly categorized into four groups:

- A company can buy products from foreign manufacturers via trading companies. These can be located in the home country or in the host country.
- In the second group of operation modes the domestic company buys directly from an independent manufacturer abroad. In this case, the company is usually buying products from the standard product program of the foreign supplier. The product technology is owned by the foreign manufacturer.
- In the third category, a foreign manufacturer produces on behalf of the domestic company. The product specifications are determined by the domestic company which also owns the product technology. The manufacturer abroad is independent but bound by a manufacturing contract.
- The last group comprises production abroad. In this case, the domestic company uses foreign direct investment in the selected production market to own or co-own the production facilities. These modes are also referred to as internal sourcing, since the supplier is a foreign affiliate.

If the final product is sold in the home market of the company, all these options result in imports. While cases in which the foreign-sourced product is sold in a third country are possible and even common, in this chapter we focus on sourcing or production in foreign markets with the home market as the target market. The illustration of the modes in **Figure 10.1** refers to this situation.

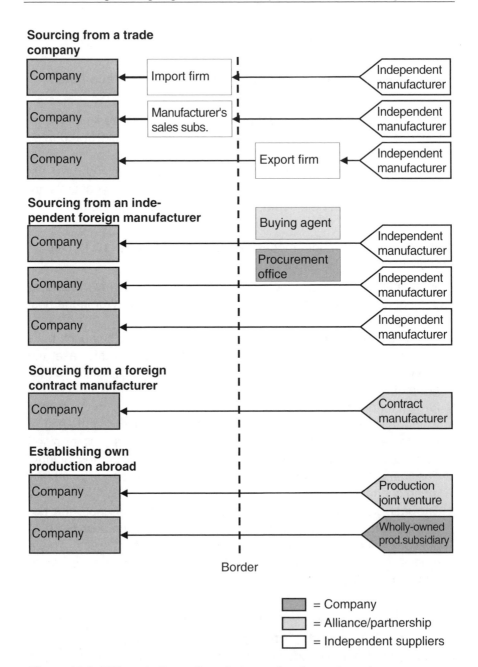

Figure 10.1: Different alternatives for sourcing from abroad

10.2   Sourcing from a trade company

Companies that intend to buy products of foreign origin do not necessarily have to internationalize themselves. In what is known as an **indirect import**, a company may buy products from an import organization and avoid the problems of international transactions. For example, small grocery stores can offer their customers bananas without sourcing directly in Latin America. Swiss industrial companies use tools in their factories that have been produced in China but bought from a wholesale company in Switzerland. And the PCs that are being used in companies in Western Europe are in most cases produced in Asia. Import firms in the procuring company's home market bring these products into the country.

In wholesale and retail channels throughout Western Europe, products are available that have been produced all across the world. In many cases, the buyer does not even know exactly where the products originate from:

- The main advantage of the indirect import operation mode is that the company can source from a wide array of foreign countries without the complexities and risks of international business. Contracts are domestic, negotiations take place in the mother language, payments are in the domestic currency and the company does not need to monitor international markets.

- However, the benefits of international sourcing can only be partially exploited via indirect sourcing. Low production costs in the foreign country are escalated by long supply chains between the original manufacturer and the company. Each actor in the chain adds its own profit margin on top of the profit margins of the other actors. In addition, a direct link to the original manufacturer abroad could help a company to gain a better control over quality. And buying in the foreign currency may help the company to hedge currency risks. Having an insight into a particular foreign market may also help the company to select a better manufacturer. This list of potential benefits could be extended further.

Sourcing from the sales subsidiary of a foreign manufacturer in the domestic market is a hybrid between sourcing from an independent import firm and sourcing directly from a manufacturer abroad. Formally, the sales subsidiary of the foreign manufacturer usually acts as the import firm. But this arrangement has some features of direct international sourcing since there is direct contact with the original manufacturer. It also has features of sourcing from an independent import firm, with the presence of an additional organization between the customer and the manufacturer. Furthermore, the contract may be concluded in a domestic setting, with the domestic legal basis and the domestic currency.

A first genuine step abroad is to **buy from an export firm** in the production country. Here, the company has an international business transaction, a contract that is often in the foreign currency. The company itself selects the sourcing country and then addresses itself to a trading firm in the selected country:

- The advantage is that the export company has very good knowledge of its own country and is usually able to identify a suitable manufacturer for the particular product. The export company handles all the necessary administrative processes, including customs clearing, and since the export company acts as the merchant, it is responsible for product quality, i.e. it will carry out quality monitoring. If a broader product range is sourced from this one country, the export company provides a single point of contact and can bundle the products. If a Swiss company, for example, wants to buy a number of different parts from China which are produced by different manufacturers, it may nevertheless interact with a single export company there which meets all its needs.
- The disadvantage is evident: there is no direct link to the manufacturers and as a result, the company cannot influence them directly. More seriously, the products that the export firm offers in its catalogue will be products that an average customer demands and which are chosen to maximize the export firms' sales and profit. These may not be the products that best fit the particular demands of the buyer.

10.3   Sourcing from an independent foreign manufacturer

Instead of sourcing from trading companies, a company can decide to **buy directly from an independent manufacturer** abroad. Foreign manufacturers that do not have a presence in the home country can be identified at international trade fairs where potential suppliers present their products. These fairs offer companies an efficient means to get an overview of the various suppliers in the different countries.

In the case of "arm's length" agreements, the domestic company buys with shorter term contracts, choosing from the existing product range of the foreign manufacturer. The product and production technology belong to the foreign manufacturer. The business relationship is a simple supply relationship between a supplier and its customer; and the supplier sells the same products to other customers too. Whether it is the supplier who arranges for the transport of the final products (or components or parts) to the customer's country, or the customer who buys "ex works" and then takes responsibility for the transport and associated costs always depends on the specific contract. Here, the company should consult the Incoterms of the International Chamber of Commerce. These are internationally recognized standards for international contracts for the sale and purchase of goods.

Given the geographical distance between the supplier and the domestic company, the company may **engage the help of a buying agent** in the source country. A buying agent acts as a facilitator, not as a merchant. The agent helps to identify a suitable manufacturer and supports the negotiation process with knowledge of the language and local customs. In addition the agent may help to organize the international logistics chain; however, the supply contract is directly between the domestic company and the foreign manufacturer, while the buying agent receives a commission. An agent can also support quality management and carry out inspections in the manufacturer's factory. One major advantage of quality control in the sourcing country is that quality problems can be detected before the products are shipped. This avoids supply interruptions and additional costs. Implementing quality monitoring as early in the supply chain as possible helps to avoid delays and unnecessary transport costs.

If the volume that a company buys from a specific foreign country is sufficiently high, it may make sense to **open a procurement office** in this country. For example, many retail companies have established procurement offices in Hong Kong to give them better access to Chinese suppliers. In 2007, BMW established a procurement office in Hungary in order to be closer to growing sourcing markets in Central and Eastern Europe and to be better able to identify suitable suppliers for the group. This move took place after the volume of procurement in this region had increased by 50% in two years (BMW, 2007).

The advantages of direct sourcing with the support of a procurement office are similar to those enjoyed when working with a buying agent. But in this mode the agent is owned by the company itself and is thus fully committed to company objectives. In most cases the procurement office does not act as a merchant but as an agent, that is, the supply contract remains between the foreign manufacturer and the domestic company.

10.4   Sourcing from a foreign contract manufacturer

10.4.1 General considerations about contract manufacturers

With contract manufacturing (international subcontracting), the domestic company asks a foreign company to manufacture parts of its product, or even the entire product, but it retains the marketing and sales of the product (Kotabe/Helsen, 2008, p. 296). The main difference between an entirely independent manufacturer abroad and a contract manufacturer is that the foreign contract manufacturer carries out production on behalf of the domestic company. The domestic company holds the proprietary rights over the product technology; indeed, often the production process is specified exactly by the domestic company and the company supplies the foreign manufacturer with raw materials, components or semi-final products. The foreign company manufactures this specific product for only one customer.

A manufacturing contract of this kind is similar to a **licensing agreement** since it grants the foreign manufacturer the possibility to use the intellectual property rights of the domestic company for a specific purpose and limited time. However, no royalties are paid by the licensee and the output is not sold to the external market but to the licensor for a price that is fixed ex ante.

The range of possible contract manufacturing relationships is wide. In most cases, the subcontractor carries out only individual production stages. But more far-reaching relationships are also possible. The sub-contractor may be involved in strategic R&D processes (this is often the case in the automotive industry). A **strategic alliance** with the sub-contractor can be established and the subcontractor may even be au-tonomous in the selection of its own suppliers or for the development of necessary components.

When a company starts sourcing final products or semi-finished prod-ucts from a foreign supplier which it formerly manufactured within its own domestic facilities, this is known as **offshore outsourcing**, and is based on a "make-or-buy" decision by the company.

Motives for offshore outsourcing can generally be grouped into the following five categories (Hollensen, 2011, pp. 407 ff.; Kotabe/Helsen, 2008, p. 297; Morschett/Schramm-Klein/Zentes, 2010, p. 262):

- **Cost advantages**: Cost savings is the dominant motivation for out-sourcing. The rationale is that an external firm can carry out a pro-duction step more efficiently than the outsourcing firm. Usually, the subcontractor is a specialist in its field; the activity belongs to its core competences. Furthermore, the subcontractor may also produce similar products (or at least products requiring similar machines, equipment and skills) for other customers, and this leads to econo-mies of scale.
- **Advantages in financing and low resource commitment**: Com-pared to owning its own factories, the domestic company's outsourc-ing of activities reduces the capital that the firm needs to commit to manufacturing activities. This immediately improves the financial ra-tios of the outsourcing company. Furthermore, it often transforms fixed costs into variable costs.
- **Risk reduction and strategic flexibility**: Subcontracting brings very little exposure to political risk for the international company. But the main advantage of buying from contract manufacturers is that the firm can maintain its flexibility and switch orders between suppliers, even between suppliers in different countries. After termination of the contract, the company can choose a new contract manufacturer in another part of the world if the circumstances and comparative ad-vantages have changed. This could include changes in wages, in trade barriers (e.g. sudden tariffs on products from China or India), in transport costs, and in foreign exchange rates. With own production

sites, a switch becomes much more costly. Price increases or quality problems with the supplier can also motivate a change. However, if a supplier invests in specific assets, it will usually demand long-term supply contracts with minimum levels of orders in order to compensate for this investment. In such cases switching orders from country to country on a short-term basis is no longer easy to do (Hill, 2009, p. 579 f.).

- **Concentration on core business**: From a strategic point of view, a move towards concentration on a core business is another important motive for outsourcing. By outsourcing peripheral or supporting activities, a firm can focus its resources on the core activities of the value chain. More and more, production processes themselves are not part of the competitive advantage of a company (take the iPhone, designed and developed by Apple, but produced entirely by other companies).

- **Improvement of performance and quality**: Using contract manufacturing services can lead to improvements in quality. Specialists have better know-how, better qualified personnel and are often more up-to-date with regard to technology than the outsourcing firm.

Large contract manufacturers even offer the flexibility to shift production to other world regions without changing the partner. They usually have production capacity in all relevant production regions, as **Inset 10.1** shows. These companies support their customer with advice and simulations to help ascertain which production region is optimal for their needs (Simflexgroup, 2011).

Inset 10.1: Contract manufacturing of the Microsoft Xbox by Flextronics (text based on Morschett/Donath, 2011)

Microsoft is basically a software company. When it introduced the game console Xbox in 2001, it did not want to invest in production facilities. Furthermore, production in the USA was considered too expensive. As a result, Microsoft signed a contract with Flextronics, the world's second largest "electronics manufacturing service provider" (EMS) to fully produce the Xbox following the specifications and the component list of Microsoft. At that time Flextronics already had production capacity established in more than 30 countries on four continents. Thus, Microsoft, together with Flextronics, could select the optimal production location.

However, it was not evident what the optimal location was. Geographical proximity to the main markets might have been important but that would bring higher production costs since those locations were not the lowest cost production sites. In this situation, cooperation with a contract manufacturer allowed Microsoft great flexibility:

- At first, demand for the Xbox was still uncertain. Long delivery times would have caused a problem since short-term orders were likely to come in, especially during the Christmas season. Thus, the production of the Xbox was initially started in the Flextronics industrial park in Guadalajara, in Mexico, close to the primary market of the USA, and also in an industrial park in Hungary, close to the Western European market. This made possible a quick response to the uncertain demand pattern.
- Once sales became steady and forecasts became easier, cost criteria came to the fore and proximity to the market was less relevant. After 2002, Microsoft shifted production from Hungary to a Flextronics industrial park in China, where the cost per unit was much lower.

In contrast to these advantages, the following **caveats of offshore outsourcing** have been identified (Hollensen, 2011, p. 408; Morschett/Schramm-Klein/Zentes, 2010, p. 262 f.):

- If transaction costs are taken into account, outsourcing may create **higher total costs** compared with the alternative "make". Production costs may be lower but the costs of identifying an adequate contract manufacturer, negotiating a manufacturing contract, monitoring the quality of the products, and so on, all cancel out part of the production cost advantages. Coordinating the activities of the foreign production company and linking them to the domestic company's activities may prove particularly costly, for example when the company decides to change its product, leading to changes in the specification. Moreover uncertainties about delivery times may bring additional inventory costs in the form of increased safety stock.
- There may be a risk of **opportunistic behavior** by the contract manufacturer. For example, a sudden surge in demand which leads

to extra orders may only be fulfilled for extraordinary high prices. The supplier may exploit the lock-in effect.

- **Quality problems** may arise if the contract manufacturer cannot fulfill the expected quality standards. Thus, it is necessary to ensure that the subcontractor uses total quality management and that it has gained international quality certifications like ISO 9001.
- If a firm outsources production to another party, then this partner gains insights into proprietary technology. There is the risk of **knowledge dissemination**. Over time the contract manufacturer may learn enough to develop into a competitor. Indeed, there are a number of examples of former contract manufacturers which have developed into main competitors. To maintain tight control over its technology, the firm should produce key components in-house (Hill, 2009, p. 579).
- In the case of contract manufacturing, a company transfers production activities that are not considered as **core competences** to other companies. But sometimes these activities have not been recognized as important for maintaining a competitive advantage. For example, production processes may bring important insights for product improvements. If outsourced to external suppliers, knowledge transfer between the production activities and the product development will be reduced. Over time, this may also erode the R&D competence of the company.
- Outsourcing reduces the company's level of control over the activities, yet the domestic company remains accountable, at least as far as public opinion is concerned. In the past, companies like Nike and IKEA have found that non-compliance by contract manufacturers with social or environmental standards has had a direct impact on their own **reputation**. In most cases today, outsourcing contracts include detailed descriptions of the required norms with regard to corporate social responsibility. Nevertheless, the monitoring of these standards is costly.

10.4.2 Processing trade as a particular form of contract manufacturing

In processing trade, a domestic company produces intermediate products in the home country which are then processed by a contract manufacturer in a foreign country and subsequently re-imported into the home country. For example, it is quite common to manufacture garments in North Africa from fabrics that have been woven in the EU. In such a fragmented international production process, it is usually the labor-intensive processing activities that are located abroad. This type of contract manufacturing is usually paid for with a processing fee. This avoids having to sell the products and then buy them back. Processing trade is also possible intra-firm.

There are a number of particularities of processing as compared to other forms of contract manufacturing. First, there are at least two trade flows: the export of intermediate goods to the contract manufacturer and the re-importing of the final goods. This makes logistics costs more relevant and as a result, job processing is usually carried out in proximity to the domestic market. From the perspective of Western European companies, processing is often located in Eastern Europe, North Africa or Turkey. For US companies, Mexico is a favorite location. Furthermore, processing is mostly done in free trade zones. This avoids custom duties being paid twice for the value of the intermediate goods. In addition, there is often preferential customs treatment of outward processing. For example, under certain conditions, quotas that limit the import of textiles into the EU do not apply to garments returning to the EU after processing in a third country.

Inset 10.2 describes Mexican "maquiladora" which serve as job processing companies for many US companies.

Inset 10.2: Global shift of production due to changing conditions (text based on Janetzke, 2008)

Processing companies, also known as maquiladora, have to be registered in Mexico in a special list and have strict reporting rules, so that Mexico can ensure that the output is re-exported. For the company to be included in the maquiladora list, 100 % of the output has to be re-exported. If the company is registered and acknowledged, it can import the intermediate goods duty-free.

After a drop in processing activities in preceding years, in 2008 this activity rose strongly again. The shift towards Asia was halted and traditional locations in Mexico on the US border became more prominent once more. There were two main reasons for this, both of which reflect the short-term flexibility of contracting:

- The drastically increased oil price had led to high transportation costs which favored geographically close locations for the US market. In 2008, about 30 % of the cost could be saved by having production in Mexico instead of Asia. Shorter delivery times were an additional advantage.
- Currency influences were also important. The Chinese currency gained value relative to the US dollar and the euro was strong which stimulated US companies and European companies to re-locate back to Mexico.

In the first four months of 2008, maquiladora contributed 80 % of the increase in Mexican exports. One example of the renaissance of processing in Mexico is Nike. Between 2007 and 2010, the final production of sport shoes in Mexico rose from only 250'000 to 1 million shoes per annum.

10.4.3 Business process outsourcing as an extension of process manufacturing

In recent years, offshore outsourcing of processes has gone beyond the production of physical goods. Increasingly, company-internal processes, e.g. IT, accounting, HRM, or call centers, have been outsourced, often to service providers in low-cost countries like India. India has become the leading location worldwide for such remote business functions, due to its mix of low costs, good technical and language skills and the availability of capable outsourcing providers. In the field of IT offshore outsourcing, Indian companies like Wipro, Tata Consultancy Services and Infosys all have well over 100,000 employees available to take over processes from other companies. These companies have developed into global players in their own right and have greatly benefited from the outsourcing of business processes by Western companies (see Morschett/Schramm-Klein/Zentes, 2010, pp. 272 ff.).

10.5   Establishing own production abroad

10.5.1 Preliminary remarks and overview

The fourth alternative to sourcing products from abroad is to establish own production facilities in the sourcing country. This leads to foreign direct investment, either through the establishment of an international production joint venture or by setting up a wholly-owned production subsidiary.

- The main advantage of direct investment is that it allows a high level of control over the activities in the foreign country. It is usually easier to ensure a certain quality level in an own factory abroad (or a co-owned factory) than with an independent manufacturing partner. In a (co-)owned factory there is full transparency of costs. The own production site can specialize in very specific products and components, something which independent companies may not be able or willing to. The production is fully devoted to and developed for the requirements of the domestic company. Supply is secure because the factory is (co-)owned. Environmental uncertainties, like strikes, cannot be eliminated. But direct investment avoids any uncertainty about the behavior of an independent foreign partner, who might decide to ask for a higher price for the following year, or who might decide not to deliver at all if there is a supply shortage.
- The major disadvantage of this alternative is that it requires considerably higher resources to be committed than the previously discussed alternatives. For many SMEs, establishing production abroad, even when sharing the investment with a joint venture partner, is simply too resource-intensive.

Production may be established in one of two ways: either a new factory is built in a greenfield operation (alone or together with a joint venture partner) or an existing production facility is acquired. This can be done alone, to establish a wholly-owned production subsidiary, or in cooperation with a joint venture partner. In joint ventures, the production facility has often previously been fully owned by the partner.

The advantages of an **acquisition** are the following:

- Acquisition allows a quick production start while a greenfield operation may take years from planning to the production start. And even after production starts, it takes quite a long time to acquire sufficient experience and to achieve acceptable cost and quality levels.
- With an acquisition, complementary resources may be acquired. When internationalizing for cost reduction, access to local sub-suppliers, local banks and to the local labor market are beneficial. Furthermore, the company usually also acquires the human capital of the factory, trained workers. How far their skills are compatible with future requirements is something that can be examined beforehand.
- The risks with an acquisition may be even smaller than with a greenfield investment. (Unlike cases where an acquisition is made with a view to market entry.) While it is certainly true that the valuation of the acquisition object is not easy, nevertheless it is mainly the tangible assets like the factory, the machines and equipment that are in focus, so it is not too difficult either. And since the factory is already operating, there is less uncertainty with regard to permits, etc. than when establishing a new factory.

A **greenfield investment** may have advantages too:

- Acquisitions are only an option if there is a suitable take-over object. If a company intends to enter a foreign country mainly for production purposes, the factory that is to be bought must be suitable for restructuring for the new product lines.
- The available object may not have the optimal size. When establishing a new factory, the company can choose how much production capacity to build. With an acquisition, the company may acquire a production site which is too large, leading to under-utilization of capacity.
- Acquisitions may produce negative reactions from employees who might fear foreign domination or restructuring.
- Acquisitions have to be integrated into the company's own production system (machines may have to be exchanged, the IT system adapted, etc.) which brings integration costs. In contrast, the establishment of a new factory means that the factory and all the systems can be constructed according to the company's standards.

10.5.2 Establishing a wholly-owned foreign production facility

Establishing a wholly-owned subsidiary abroad for production is the option that provides the greatest control over the foreign activities. In sole ventures like this, the own company strategy can be fully enforced. The foreign factory can be integrated into the company strategy and its production network so that coordination between the foreign subsidiary and the headquarters or peer subsidiaries is straightforward. This means that it is easy and quick to create product flows between the factory abroad, which delivers parts, components or final products, and domestic organizational units, either the sales organization or factories that use the intermediate goods to produce final goods. Furthermore, this operation mode allows much better links to the rest of the company. For example, knowledge generated abroad can easily be used by the company in the home country or in third countries. Benchmarking and the transfer of best practices are possible. The companies can all use the same IT system. Changes can be carried out flexibly, without negotiating with a partner. Cost reductions from experience curve effects fully benefit the company, whereas with other operation modes, part of the savings will be retained by a partner.

If the production process itself is part of the core competence of a company and gives it a competitive advantage, this knowledge should not be transferred to a partner. A wholly-owned facility can optimally combine firm-specific advantages, such as in-depth knowledge about optimal production processes, with country-specific advantages in the foreign location, such as low labor cost or availability of specific suppliers (Rugman/Verbeke, 2001).

This operation mode is, however, also the most resource-intensive option. And while a wholly-owned production subsidiary allows flexibility, since the domestic headquarters can decide autonomously whether or not the production program should be changed, or whether the production capacity should be expanded or reduced, or whether suppliers should be changed, the basic decision is not easily reversible, because establishing an own factory ties the company to the specific country for a long time. Divesting an own production site is usually costly, so this creates an exit barrier. It is also true that some countries which are attractive for production do not allow the establishment of fully foreign-owned companies or have legal restrictions. On the other hand, if the main purpose of the new production facility is to produce goods for export, host country governments are usually in favor and frequently even offer subsidies for such activity.

In **Inset 10.3**, a case is described in which a company established own production facilities in a foreign country which proved successful in the mid-term but problematic in the long-term.

Inset 10.3: Production shifting from Norway to Lithuania and Belarus by Devold (text based on European Foundation for the Improvement of Living and Working Conditions, 2008)

Devold of Norway AS produces high quality wool textile products, including sports underwear, and wool sweaters for outdoor and sports activities. In 1996, the company began looking for opportunities to reduce costs by internationalization. The basic reason for deciding to relocate production from Norway was the high labor cost. The company had been losing money and looking at ways of increasing profitability through the rationalisation of production. Because the production processes for the type of wool garments that the company sold were very labor-intensive, the opportunities for increasing productivity by substituting machinery for labor were limited – hence the focus on wage costs. The original intention was not to relocate the company's own production, but to purchase products from other manufacturers. However, having failed to find suppliers with suitable equipment, Devold decided to set up a new company in Lithuania.

The Lithuanian production company was set up in 1998. The location in central Lithunia was chosen for two reasons: the labor force was cheap at that time and skilled employees were available. From then on, a progressive relocation began for steps of the production, with the knitting, dying and sewing of underwear being relocated in 2002. According to a Devold executive, 95 % of overall textile production was relocated from Norway to Lithuania. At the beginning the company in Lithuania employed 15 people, but there are now 180 employees.

Profitability and competitiveness improved considerably as a result of the relocation. Costs were reduced, allowing the company to increase the volume of production. However, the company also reports that it took some time before it benefited from improved results – the period following the relocation being marked by concerns about quality. Overall, however, the company was initially satisfied both with Lithuanian labor costs and with the skills and qualifications of available employees.

However, due to the rapid rise in wages in Lithuania and increased emigration towards high-wage countries, the company began to have difficulty finding enough adequately skilled workers at reasonable wages. At this point the company started looking for opportunities to relocate production away from Lithuania. At the end of 2007, Belarus was chosen and it was decided to relocate some 10% of production there.

10.5.3 Establishing an international production joint venture

Establishing a production joint venture with a local company in the foreign country is a hybrid solution. It has some elements of working together with an independent manufacturer and it has some elements of establishing a wholly-owned subsidiary. Compared to a wholly-owned subsidiary, a production joint venture

- allows the company to share investments and risks,
- gives the company access to the resources of the joint venture partner (e.g. country-specific knowledge), including its relationships with suppliers, the local government, etc.,
- may help to overcome legal barriers, in cases where wholly-owned subsidiaries are not allowed,
- may increase economies of scale, if the joint venture partner also outsources some production to the new factory, and
- may help the company to learn from a local partner.

Because of this last point joint ventures are often seen as temporary solutions. Joint ventures may help a company to enter an unfamiliar country and to learn from a partner. Over time, however, the company gets to know the local conditions and may terminate the joint venture. Frequently, this termination is done by acquiring the partner's stake and the joint venture is then transformed into a wholly-owned subsidiary. A joint venture is therefore often characterized as a "real option" (Brouthers/Brouthers/Werner, 2008). It allows a company to invest limited resources in a foreign country and still have the option to expand later on, when the uncertainty around the venture is reduced.

But SMEs are often reluctant to enter into a joint venture abroad. The incompatibility of company cultures is the first problem. Further disadvantages of a joint venture stem mainly from the fact that the company is not independent in its decisions but control is shared with a partner which has its own objectives (Morschett/Schramm-Klein/Zentes, 2010, p. 288):

- Joint ventures make independent decisions impossible. Decisions cannot be fully tailored to the needs of one of the parent companies but always have to create win-win-situations. This makes joint ventures relatively slow in their response to external changes.
- As a consequence, joint ventures in the foreign country are difficult to integrate into a uniform global strategy. A company cannot decide alone whether the foreign venture should, for example, produce different components than previously or increase or decrease its level of vertical integration. Thus, the link between the joint venture activities and all the other company activities is not easy to manage.
- Since each partner intends to optimize the profits of his own company, conflicts in joint ventures are common.
- Profits from a joint venture need to be shared. This has a number of consequences. First, a cost reduction in the foreign production process does not entirely benefit the domestic company. Second, tax-optimizing transfer prices are usually not possible. Usually, the foreign joint venture partner will not accept a reduction of the transfer price since that would reduce his own profit.
- In a joint venture, a foreign company gains deep knowledge about the conduct of the company and its strategic competitive advantages. The domestic joint venture partner will contribute its firm-specific knowledge, e.g. by improving the production process abroad. The joint venture partner will learn from this. During the joint

venture, it may be possible to limit the negative consequences with contracts covering the intellectual property rights. But after joint venture termination, it is likely that the foreign partner will become a stronger competitor.

- Finally, joint ventures have rather low survival rates. As a consequence, since the partners both understand the risk of joint venture termination, the two partners may not fully commit to the joint venture.

10.6   Recommendations for evaluating foreign operation modes

10.6.1   Evaluation criteria

Whether the company produces necessary inputs by itself, or sources them from external suppliers, is a question of vertical integration. The reasons why a company may decide to buy, rather than to make, have to some extent already been discussed in the above presentation of the benefits and caveats of the different operation modes. On a general level, the evaluation criteria for the different operation modes are the same as for the different market entry modes:

- **Control**
- **Resource commitment**
- **Costs**
- **Flexibility**
- **Access to partner resources**
- **Risk of knowledge dissemination**

These are discussed in section 7.6.1.

With regard to production and sourcing, three more aspects should be considered in more detail:

- First, an important decision criterion is whether it is necessary to **invest in specific assets** in order to produce the required products abroad efficiently (e.g. Geyskens/Steenkamp/Kumar, 2006).
- Second, some operation modes are able to reduce the **supply uncertainty** that is associated with the dependence on certain input goods (e.g. Pfeffer/Salancik, 1978).

- Third, the **effectiveness of the knowledge-transfer** must be reviewed. How can the proprietary technology and know-how of the domestic company be transferred effectively to a business partner abroad (e.g. Kogut/Zander, 1993)?

10.6.2 Conditions influencing the evaluation

There are advantages and disadvantages of each operation mode, so there is no single optimal mode for each situation. Instead, the choice of operation mode depends on a number of contingency factors. For example, a SME may just not have the necessary financial assets to build or acquire a production plant in a foreign country. Or the foreign country may not allow wholly-owned foreign subsidiaries.

To choose the appropriate operation mode, the following aspects need to be considered:

- company-specific attributes (e.g. the financial restrictions of the company)
- product-specific attributes (e.g. confidentiality of the proprietary technology, relevance of the product supply for the company, sensitivity to quality problems)
- production process-specific attributes (e.g. necessary know-how for the production, specificity of the necessary production equipment, integration of this production stage with other production stages)
- host-country attributes (e.g. availability of adequate contract manufacturers, independent suppliers, potential joint venture partners, political risk in the country, legal restrictions, development of production costs, etc.).

Furthermore, a number of attributes have to be evaluated concerning the relationship between the host country and home country. First there is cultural distance which may make a mode without a foreign partner more difficult to implement. Next, the currency may play a role. In areas with the same currency, less flexible operation modes may be acceptable, while in foreign-currency areas, volatility in the exchange rate may have a strong impact on the cost of the product in the final sales market. This may require quick and flexible responses and operation modes have to be chosen accordingly.

10.6.3 Evaluation process

Operation modes are multi-dimensional concepts. And the specific situation of a company that wants to sell a specific product in a specific market is unique. However, there are methods available to support a company in evaluating operation modes. These can be combined in a heuristic process, shown in **Figure 10.2** below.

1 Eliminate the less suitable operation modes based on external and internal conditions

$$\downarrow$$

2. Select the most suitable operation modes based on a detailed evaluation

Figure 10.2: Process for evaluating foreign operation modes

In **Step 1** companies should identify the most important external and internal determinants of the operation mode in the particular situation and apply these criteria to filter out the less suitable operation modes in a coarse analysis. For example, for all modes that involve partners, the availability of these partners has to be evaluated. Furthermore, the financial constraints of the company can easily make the establishment of own production impossible. As a simple rule of thumb, **Figure 10.3** illustrates the fit of operation modes to a combination of country and asset characteristics. For example, in a country that has low country risk and in a situation where highly specific assets are necessary for production, a company may establish a production subsidiary. If the specificity of the assets required is medium, sourcing from independent manufacturers will not be possible. In this case, in a low-risk country a company may establish a production subsidiary but if the risk is medium or high, contract manufacturing is likely to be the optimal mode.

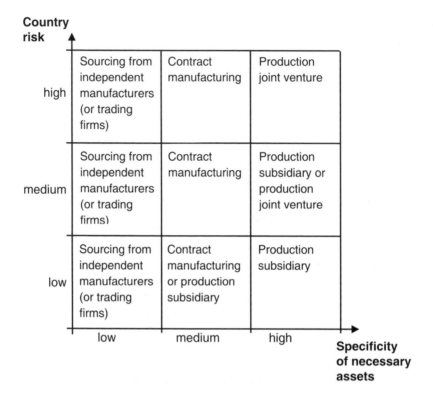

Figure 10.3: Fit between country attributes, production asset attributes and operation modes

Inset 10.4 compares sourcing from an independent manufacturer, sourcing from a contract manufacturer and own production with regard to basic criteria. The inset demonstrates how operation modes which are not feasible can be eliminated in Step 1.

Inset 10.4: Comparing sourcing from an independent manufacturer, sourcing from a contract manufacturer and own production ·

If we compare sourcing from independent suppliers with sourcing from contract manufacturers, contract manufacturing has two key advantages:

- First, it allows the sourcing of customized products. Contract manufacturing is usually employed if the necessary goods are specific to a particular company and therefore not available on the market. If proprietary technology is needed to manufacture products or components, the domestic company needs to provide knowledge and property rights to the foreign manufacturing company, establishing a manufacturing contract instead of a pure supply contract.

- Second, contract manufacturing reduces the supply risk. With contract manufacturing, a company basically buys production capacity for a longer period of time and it fixes the price for this capacity (or, depending on the type of contract, the price for the output of this production).

However, although contract manufacturers allow customized products, a certain level of standardization is necessary. Their institutional benefit comes from specialization advantages and economies of scale across a number of different customers. Obviously, economies of scale can only be achieved if the production requires the same or similar inputs, if more or less the same machines and factories can be used, and if the production processes are at least similar. This becomes evident when looking at the success of large electronics manufacturing service providers like Foxconn or Flextronics. They produce mobile phones or printers for different customers. In fact, the production and the hardware of these products are not highly specific and assembly lines can easily be used for the products of different customers. Only in this way can contract manufacturers offer great cost benefits.

Comparing own production abroad with contract manufacturing, we note the following advantages:

- Independent companies like contract manufacturers may not be willing to undertake substantial specific investment. A specific investment creates an asset whose value depends on a particular business relationship, i.e. it is only valuable as long as this customer buys from the company. An example would be a special machine designed to produce a specific component. Specificity creates negative effects for transactions between independent partners. The solution may be for the supplying factory to be owned by the customer. Thus, own production abroad is necessary if highly specific investment is needed.

- Furthermore, own production abroad greatly reduces the supply risk. In the case of resource-dependency, when the parts or components that a company sources from abroad are crucial for the operations of the company and the company uses a strategy of single-sourcing, which means that this part or component is only produced in one factory abroad, then ownership of the factory minimizes the risk that a supplier might at some time in the future stop the supply and decide to deliver scarce products to competitors.
- Finally, own production facilities abroad can be provided with the necessary firm-specific know-how much more effectively than can contract manufacturers. If, for example, the company has a lot of experience with production operations at home, has developed best practices and has experts for this activity, then these experts can serve as expatriates in the own factory abroad.

Once more, these benefits of vertical integration cannot be secured without a cost. The higher investment for own production abroad and the greatly reduced strategic flexibility with regard to the location of production are two major drawbacks. In addition, contract manufacturing usually allows a quicker start of production than does setting up own production. The manufacturing partner usually has capacity directly available.

In **Step 2**, the remaining feasible operation modes are analyzed in a more detailed manner, using a fine-grained analysis with more criteria. A scoring model can be applied to structure the decision. Since many different criteria have to be considered simultaneously, listing the criteria, discussing the relevance of each criterion for the company (which results in a specific weighting) and discussing the score of each operation mode with regard to each criterion produces an aggregated weighted score for each operation mode. More importantly, it helps to produce a structured and rational discussion. Analyzing why a certain solution is recommended by the scoring model is usually a good starting point for a fruitful discussion. **Figure 10.4** shows an example of a scoring model of this type.

Criteria	Importance of the criterion	Options		
		Independent manufacturer	Contract manufacturer	Wholly-owned production
Control over the production process and quality	3	1	3	4
Financial resources required	2	4	4	1
Cost per product unit	3	1	3	4
Flexibility to switch the sourcing location	2	4	2	1
Risk of knowledge dissemination to another company	1	3	2	4
Supply security	3	1	2	4
Effectiveness of knowledge-transfer to the foreign production site	1	1	2	4
Overall evaluation		**29**	**40**	**48**

Scores: 4 = very positive   3 = positive 2 = negative 1 = very negative
Importance of the criterion: 3 = high   2 = medium   1 = low

Figure 10.4: Scoring model for selecting the operation mode

11 Developing an internationalization strategy for production and sourcing

11.1 Overview of the process

In this chapter, a process is proposed for the development of the internationalization strategy for production and sourcing and its associated relocation programs. This proposal is based on the account of the evaluation and pre-selection of adequate locations in Chapter 9 and the evaluation of potential operation modes in Chapter 10.

Figure 11.1 illustrates the proposed process:

- In the preliminary step, the strategy project is planned. Here, the project organization is defined and the planning process itself is designed, including a time frame and a budget for the planning project.
- In two interdependent steps, potential sourcing countries are evaluated and, in close association with this, potential foreign operation modes are assessed.
- In Step 2 combinations of sourcing or production countries and matching operation modes are determined. This step also includes a more detailed analysis of different locations within one country together with the preliminary selection of partner(s).
- In the next step, feasibility studies are carried out for the suitable location - operation mode combinations. These then form the basis for the internationalization strategy that is crafted in Step 4.
- In Step 5, agreements with partners are signed.
- In the final step, building on the internationalization strategy, the feasibility studies and the final selection of partners, relocation programs for production and sourcing are produced.

The figure shows the usual sequence of steps in the process but it also indicates common loops. For example, if the negotiations with an intended partner fail, the company may have to modify the feasibility study for this country. It is clear that, in a heuristic process of this kind, other sequences or loops may also become necessary.

In the following sections, the steps in the process are described.

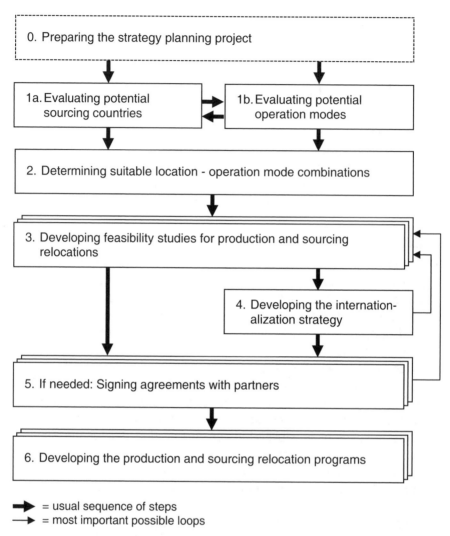

0. Preparing the strategy planning project

1a. Evaluating potential sourcing countries

1b. Evaluating potential operation modes

2. Determining suitable location - operation mode combinations

3. Developing feasibility studies for production and sourcing relocations

4. Developing the internationalization strategy

5. If needed: Signing agreements with partners

6. Developing the production and sourcing relocation programs

➡ = usual sequence of steps
→ = most important possible loops

Figure 11.1: Process for developing an internationalization strategy for production or sourcing

11.2   Step 0: Preparing the strategy planning project

Preparing the strategy planning project for an internationalization strategy for production and sourcing is the same as the preparation for an internationalization strategy for new markets. This is described in detail in Section 8.2.

For sourcing and production, there is an additional aspect to be considered: if a company is investigating the relocation of more than one production stage or the sourcing of a number of different parts from abroad, it is necessary to establish which of these different aspects can be handled separately and which aspects must be considered together. This discussion is crucial, as important links between the two processes must not be neglected. Suppose, for example, that two different production stages are closely connected to one another. If they are to be relocated abroad, then, it is sensible either to relocate both to the same location or, at the very least, to take the linkage between them into account when determining the two different foreign locations.

11.3   Steps 1a and 1b: Evaluating potential sourcing countries and operation modes

Step 1a involves identifying potentially attractive locations for sourcing. The criteria and the process are described in Chapter 9. The result of Step 1a is a short-list of attractive sourcing or production countries.

In Step 1b, potentially attractive operation modes for the company have to be identified. The criteria and the process have been described in Chapter 10. The result of Step 1b is a short-list of operation modes that seem generally feasible for the company.

These two steps, the evaluation of prospective sourcing or production countries and the evaluation of operation modes, are closely connected. Which of the two dimensions is determined first will depend on the specific case:

- A company with a large enough budget for all potential operation modes can first investigate all potential sourcing countries and determine the most attractive ones and then subsequently find the operation mode which may be optimal for that country.
- But often, the process has to begin with the selection of adequate and feasible operation modes. For example, a company may decide

to source from independent suppliers and not commit any of its own resources to the sourcing country. In this case the availability of good suppliers has to be the dominant criterion for the choice of country. A different example is a company which is determined to re-locate its production and establish a wholly-owned subsidiary abroad. The legal restrictions in certain countries may prohibit this operation mode and so these countries are eliminated from the be-ginning.

It is clear, then, that Steps 1a and 1b have to be resolved in an iterative process.

11.4   Step 2: Determining suitable location - operation mode combinations

11.4.1 Determining country - operation mode combinations

The starting points for Step 2 are the countries that have been consid-ered as attractive in Step 1a and the operation modes that have been considered as generally attractive and feasible in Step 1b. In Step 2, suitable combinations of attractive countries and suitable operation modes have to be determined. In practice, for an SME few countries will come under consideration at this stage of the process and few op-eration modes will be investigated for the countries selected.

However, in Step 2, two further aspects have to be considered:
- The **concrete location** within a potential country has to be fixed.
- If one is needed, the **partner** with whom a company wants to coop-erate has to be chosen.

These two aspects can be determined now, because at this stage of the process we already have at least a rough idea of the possible op-eration modes for each country still under consideration.

How the analysis now proceeds will depend on the operation mode:

- If the company has, for example, decided to procure parts in Vietnam from an independent manufacturer, then the selection of the supplier is the next step.
- If the company has decided to enter into a joint venture in Romania, then the determination of a potential joint venture-partner is the next step. Since this partner will often offer to use his own plant for the joint venture, the location of the plant is already fixed.
- If the company has decided on the establishment of own production in Poland, then it remains entirely free to pick a location. Consequently, a detailed analysis of production locations within the country becomes the most immediate task.

11.4.2 Identifying production and sourcing locations within the prospective countries

In the previous steps, the company has mainly focused on the selection of the potential sourcing or production country. Naturally, the question of potentially interesting locations within the country will already have been looked at, as this is a relevant criterion for the evaluation of countries. However, the various possible locations have not yet been systematically compared.

The evaluation criteria (cost factors, infrastructure etc.) must now be investigated for each specific location within a country: the heterogeneity of different regions is often extreme, as the example of China, in **Inset 11.1,** illustrates.

Inset 11.1: Locations within China are highly heterogeneous
(text based on Baizhu, 2011; Ramasamy, 2010; Rohde, 2011; Shirong, 2009)

When considering China as a production country, the specific location within the country has to be carefully chosen since differences within this huge country are enormous.

One consideration is labor costs. On average, rural workers earn only a third as much as workers in urban locations. In 2008, the average annual income for a worker in rural China was around USD 690, while those in the cities earned USD 2,290. Wages in the first tier cities like Shanghai or Beijing are even higher, substantially more than in the average city. Experts believe that this income disparity may widen even further in the coming years, despite official government policy to create more wage equality. The development of many second tier cities is so fast that rural development lags behind and this makes wage inequality unavoidable.

As regards the different regions, the coastal regions have seen strong growth in the first decade of the new millennium and wages have increased accordingly. In these regions, companies are now regularly confronted with labor shortages which creates even more pressure to increase wages. As a result, companies like Intel, Dell and Pfizer have moved inland and relocated their production sites to other regions within China. The Western and Central provinces still offer substantially lower labor costs. Foxconn, the electronic contract manufacturing giant, has built a facility in Henan province in Central China where it now employs about 200,000 people. It expects to save more than 2 billion US dollars annually in comparison to its other Chinese location in Guangdong.

In mid 2011, disparities in labor costs even increased. A new social security law has come into effect in China. How exactly it is implemented and the specific details are in the power of local governments and city administrations. This produces strongly divergent regulations. The well-developed first tier cities have the greatest additional labor costs, an increase of 44 % on top of basic salaries which are already higher than in other regions. In Zhongshang, for example, the additional social security costs amount to less than 20%.

However, most low-cost regions within China are still characterized by substantially less well developed infrastructure and much longer distances to the ports. Together these factors mean greater logistics costs and longer delivery times.

The evaluation criteria for locations for production and sourcing and the relevant information sources have been described in chapter 9 and this account is not repeated here.

11.4.3 Identifying potential partners and suppliers in the prospective countries

In the previous steps, the company evaluated various operation modes, some of which require a partner or a supplier. In this discussion, the company must have already considered whether there are potentially attractive suppliers or partners within the host country. But these possible partners have not yet been compared to each other.

This is now the task in Step 2, though the final decision is not yet required. For example, when considering sourcing from independent manufacturers, it is important to identify a number of different manufacturers which fulfill the relevant criteria. Final supplier selection can be carried out in a later step. Since the criteria for the selection of suitable business partners depend largely on the operation mode, they cannot be discussed in detail here. Nevertheless, some advice should be given.

When the intended operation mode is sourcing from an independent manufacturer, potential suppliers should be evaluated mainly in terms of their ability to deliver the required quality, their price level and their reliability. With this mode of operation, short-term contracts are usual. This allows companies to switch suppliers without major problems, so the initial evaluation of intended partners need not be too exhaustive.

But if the company intends either to produce in the foreign country together with a joint venture partner or to outsource production to a contract manufacturer, then the prospective partners should be analyzed in depth. The following information should be gathered:

- **General information**, e.g. size of the company, product portfolio, financial assets, economic business situation.

- Information about the **physical assets**, e.g. production locations, available production capacity, existing technical infrastructure, quality certifications like ISO.
- Information about **capabilities**, e.g. innovation capability, organizational capability, managerial competence.
- Information about the company's **network**, e.g. relations with the local government, with suppliers, etc.
- Information about the **organizational structure** and the decision makers.
- Information about previous alliances and the company's **reputation** as a cooperation partner.

Some of this information can be requested from the potential partner directly. In addition, neutral information sources in the host country should also be contacted, such as the economic section of the home country's embassy in the partner's country or a joint chamber of commerce.

It has to be emphasized that beyond the relevant hard facts about the prospective partner, **soft factors** are also important for the longevity of the partnership. Whether the company cultures are compatible and whether the relevant individuals in the partner companies get along, may crucially determine the success of the partnership.

11.4.4 Result of Step 2

Having specified suitable location - operation mode combinations and identified potential partners and suppliers, the company has determined the suitable options. This is the result of Step 2.

Figure 11.2 shows an example of a result from Step 2. Here it is assumed that the company wants to source a rather unspecific part from a foreign country, so that procurement from an independent manufacturer is an option.

Product	Most attractive locations		Operation modes		
	Country	Location within country	Sourcing from a domestic import firm	Sourcing from an independent manufacturer	Sourcing from a joint venture
P1	China	C1			a
		C2			b
	Vietnam	V1	c		
P2	Ukraine	U1		d	
		U2		e	
	Romania	R1	f		

▭ = selected operation mode at that location
a - f = suppliers/partners

Figure 11.2: Location - operation mode combinations as result of Step 2

As the result of Step 2, the company has determined the countries which remain under consideration and identified locations within those countries. It has also decided how the operation in each location would be realized. For each of these "location-operation mode" combinations, a feasibility study must be produced. This is the next step.

11.5   Step 3: Developing feasibility studies for production and sourcing relocations

In Step 3, a detailed feasibility study for each of the selected location-operation mode combinations needs to be produced. A final decision is not yet taken but the feasibility studies are written up in order to allow a well-informed and rational decision in Step 4. **Figure 11.3** shows the main elements required in a feasibility study for a production or sourcing relocation option:

- A description of the specific requirements of the product to be sourced or produced abroad and of the production steps concerned.
- A description of the selected country and the specific location within the country. The criteria that should be included in this description have been listed in chapter 9.
- An analysis of the characteristics of the intended operation mode, presenting the main advantages and disadvantages.
- A detailed description of the selected partner. In almost every case sourcing from abroad requires a business partner in the host country. Since this is crucial for the final decision in Step 4, negotiations with potential partners should be taken up in the course of the feasibility studies. If the company intends to acquire a factory abroad, these facilities must be described in detail in the feasibility study.
- A formulation of quantitative objectives with forecasts about relevant external conditions together with internal figures. These are essential components of a feasibility study. Sales planning in the home country should indicate likely demand. An estimation of the future development of costs is also required.
- An analysis of the legal situation. Since many operation modes involve the transfer of proprietary knowledge to the sourcing country, intellectual property rights protection must be reviewed, together with other crucial legal aspects of the business relationship.
- A statement of required resources. With indirect foreign sourcing, the company does not commit any human resources, assets or working capital to the new sourcing location. In contrast, joint ventures or wholly-owned subsidiaries require substantial resources both abroad and at home.
- A description of all relevant aspects of the cross-border supply chain. Sourcing or producing abroad for the home market implies a supply chain from the selected location which should be described in the feasibility study.
- A list of the practical measures to be undertaken and the time required for these actions. Depending on the type of relocation, the focus must also be on the existing operation mode. If, for example, a factory in the home country must be closed because production is to be relocated, then this divestment process must be carefully planned.

1. Product and production step characteristics

2. Country characteristics

3. Characteristics of the specific location within the country

4. Operation mode

5. Supplier, contract manufacturer, partner and/or acquisition object

6. Supply chain

    6.1   Transport and warehouses, including costs

    6.2   Delivery times

    6.3   Supply security

    6.4   Other decision-relevant aspects of the supply chain

7. Legal aspects

    7.1   Protection of intellectual property rights

    7.2   Other aspects of contracts with foreign partners

8. Resources required

    8.1   Human resources

    8.2   Assets

    8.3   Working capital

9. Quantitative objectives and forecasts with regard to labor costs, production volumes, etc.

10. Measures

    10.1 Steps and time needed to build up activities

    10.2 Steps and time needed to terminate current activities that will be relocated e.g. supplier contracts in home country

11. Responsibilities

12. Budget

    12.1 Initial investments

    12.2 Annual expenses

13. Economic evaluation

Figure 11.3: Table of contents of a feasibility study for a relocation option

- A statement of responsibilities in the company for the relocation project showing which department in the company will be responsible and identifying competent executives available in the company to lead the project. In addition, it should make clear where the project team is to be located during each stage of the project.
- An estimate of the necessary initial investment and a forecast of annual expenses. A major purpose of the feasibility study is to reveal the financial consequences of the relocation option. But revenues are not influenced by the project because the products are intended to be sold in the home market, exactly as before the relocation.
- An economic analysis. The final element in the feasibility study is the calculation of its profitability. Given that cost-reduction is the major motive for internationalization for production and sourcing and that revenues achieved from home country sales are relatively independent of the operation mode, it is sufficient to compare the costs of the feasible alternatives. **Inset 11.4** describes the Net Present Value method (NPV) which is frequently used for an analysis of this kind.

Figure 11.3 presents the content of a feasibility study for relocation as a logical sequence. However, as with market entry strategies, the determination of the content will be an iterative process.

Inset 11.2: The Net Present Value as an approach to assessing location - operation mode combinations

NPV (see **Inset 8.1** for a more detailed explanation) discounts the cash flows of different years to provide a present value. For this calculation, the discount rate which is used must include a risk premium.

Figure 11.4 gives an example of the application of the method to the evaluation of a specific location - operation mode combination. A proposed production joint venture in China in location C2 together with Partner a is evaluated in comparison to the continuation of existing production in the home country.

Elements of the NPV	Initial in-vestment	Cash flows year 1-15	NPV
Maintaining production in the home country		-1,000	
Production joint venture in China with a partner in location C2	-2,900	-300	
Cost of closing down the production in the home country	-600		
Difference	-3,500	700	**593.2**

All figures in thousands of Swiss francs

Figure 11.4: The Net Present Value of a relocation option

To establish production in China, the company would need to invest 2.9 million Swiss francs. The rest of the investment is carried by the joint venture partner. To this must be added the cost of closing down production in the home country.

Annual cash outflow for production in China, including the logistics of returning the products to the home country and a profit for the joint venture partner, would be only 300,000 Swiss francs. A planning horizon of 15 years is assumed, after which the production site in China would have depreciated to a value of zero. Annual production costs in the home country are higher, due to higher labor cost, higher cost for land, etc. Taking all these costs together, annual cash outflows of 1 million Swiss francs are estimated. A comparison between the two alternatives points to an annual saving of 700,000 francs.

The high risk of the investment, including currency risk, political risk, etc., is taken into account by a discount rate of 15 %.

Despite this, the result of the calculation is clearly favorable: this relocation option has an NPV of 593,200 francs.

The main problem in this type of analysis is the reliable estimation of future costs. Wages change and exchange rates fluctuate. The NPV calculation should be made for a number of different future scenarios. In particular, a sensitivity analysis should be used to evaluate how robust the results are if certain expectations are not fulfilled.

11.6   Step 4: Developing the internationalization strategy

The feasibility studies for each location-operation mode combination are the main element in the internationalization strategy. The internationalization strategy for production and sourcing must now determine which of these relocation options will be realized and in what order and what time frame. This decision will be based on a number of criteria:

- An important basis is the financial assessment of each location-operation mode combination, carried out in the context of the feasibility studies in Step 3 (see **Inset 11.2**).
- Other important criteria are the investments required and the possibilities for financing. Financial restrictions usually do not allow the (immediate) realization of all feasible and attractive relocations.
- It is possible to choose the best operation mode and location for each product. Alternatively, a multi-sourcing approach can be used. Since supply security is a major criterion for the internationalization strategy, a company often decides to use several sourcing possibilities simultaneously. In this approach the company may sacrifice the economies of scale which it might gain by sourcing all of its parts from one location, but this option increases the security of the supply. For example, companies that had relocated all their processing work to Northern Africa had supply shortages in the first few months of 2011 due to the political conflicts in this region. In the same year, car companies that sourced critical parts from Japan had production interrupted after the Japanese earthquake and tsunami. In addition to flexibility, a second advantage of the simultaneous use of more than one operation mode and sourcing location is that benchmarking can be used to transfer best practices between locations and to negotiate lower prices.

In order to achieve an overview of the numerous consequences of each location-operation mode combination, and to determine and compare the overall consequences of these combinations, it is best to use a scoring model (see **Figure 10.4**).

Once the best location-entry mode combinations have been identified and selected, the internationalization strategy for sourcing and production has to be formulated. The strategy document summarizes the decisions and gives an overview of their financial and organizational consequences. Usually, a few pages suffice. The details are all included in the relocation programs, which are produced in the next step.

Figure 11.5 shows a proposed structure for an internationalization strategy for new sourcing and production locations:

- First, the products and production steps concerned are listed.
- Second, the decisions in favor of the specific countries and locations are formally stated.
- After this, the operation modes for each product and location are itemized and the business partners named, in cooperation with which the operation modes will be realized.
- Next, the most important quantitative objectives are summarized, mainly with regard to sourcing or production volumes.
- Then, the schedule is detailed for the different relocation projects.
- The allocation of responsibilities for the various projects is specified.
- Finally, the expected investment budgets and financial targets for the different sourcing countries are listed.

1. Products and production steps
2. Countries and locations
3. Operation modes and partners
4. Quantitative objectives
5. Timetable
6. Responsibilities
7. Investment budgets and free cash flow targets

Figure 11.5: Table of contents of an internationalization strategy for sourcing and production

11.7   Step 5: Signing agreements with partners

After the internationalization strategy has been developed and formally accepted, final negotiations are begun with the selected business partner, who may be a supplier, a contract manufacturer or even a joint venture partner.

These negotiations are based on the talks with the partners that were held earlier in the course of the feasibility studies. If detailed discussions have already taken place, the signing of the contracts can be achieved in a short time. But often there are relevant aspects which remain to be tackled and will need to be negotiated before the final agreement is made. Sometimes these negotiations with the partner lead a company to a reassessment of the relocation. If there is a severe deterioration in this assessment, then another partner may be chosen. Sometimes it may even become evident that a partner strategy is simply not viable. In this case, a new feasibility study may become necessary.

11.8   Step 6: Developing the production and sourcing relocation programs

In Step 6, the detailed relocation programs for production or sourcing have to be developed. There are three main bases for these programs:
- The feasibility studies detail the main aspects, such as quantities, expected costs per unit, necessary production technology, general aspects of the supply chain, etc.
- The internationalization strategy specifies quantitative objectives, the timetable and the budget.
- The partner selected in Step 5 now integrates its own knowledge, ideas and insights for a more detailed program. Thus, in most cases the relocation programs have to be developed in cooperation with the local business partner.

In the case of a joint venture or own production, the establishment of a factory must be planned or perhaps the restructuring of an existing facility, in the case of an acquisition. In any event, production planning, the integration of production or sourcing abroad with other production processes of the company, IT systems, quality monitoring, and other factors will be finally determined in this step.

Part V

Strategies for being international

Part V deals with the strategic planning in an international company.

Chapter 12 first explains how to determine the appropriate level of integration and responsiveness:

- After brief preliminary remarks Section 12.2 presents the three strategic orientations which are possible within the integration-responsiveness framework. Three insets present examples of each: an example of global strategy, one of multinational strategy and a transnational strategy.
- Section 12.3 sets out recommendations for fixing the level of integration and responsiveness. First the forces for global integration and for local responsiveness are outlined. These are important terms of reference which must be respected. Next a process is described which allows companies to select the level of integration and responsiveness for an industry market. An inset reveals how IKEA has successfully realised a global strategy in the multinationally oriented furniture industry.

Next Chapter 13 shows how to define the strategic businesses in an international company:

- Section 13.1 explains why it is crucial to define strategic businesses.
- Section 13.2 defines what a strategic business is, and distinguishes between two different kinds of strategic business.
- The next section looks at the process required for the definition of strategic businesses. An inset gives the strategic businesses in an internationally active medium-sized company.
- Finally in Section 13.4 business patterns in international companies are presented.

Chapter 14 then deals with the definition of strategic objectives in international companies:

- After brief preliminary remarks, Section 14.2 distinguishes five dimensions of strategic objectives.

- Section 14.3 then introduces a process for defining the strategic objectives in an international company. An inset shows the strategic objectives of a producer of consumer goods.

The standardization or differentiation of the market offers is discussed in Chapter 15:

- After brief preliminary remarks, in Section 15.2 the difference between domestic and international marketing is explained.
- Next, in Section 15.3 the basic options for international marketing are presented and then Section 15.4 reviews the advantages and disadvantages of standardization and differentiation.
- From a practical point of view, in most cases neither complete standardization nor total differentiation are sensible. Hybrid strategies are preferable, and these are discussed in detail in Section 15.5. Hybrid strategies attempt to combine the benefits of standardization and differentiation. Examples of these strategies are given in three insets, while a fourth inset explains how an international company can set up its product and brand portfolio for the various different markets in which it operates.
- Finally, in Section 15.6 recommendations are given for determining the level of standardization and differentiation of market offers. The discussion begins by examining influencing conditions and concludes by recommending a procedure.

Chapter 16 explains the configuration of the value creation process and the determination of the operation modes:

- After preliminary remarks, Section 16.2 shows the basic types of configuring the value creation process. Three insets give examples of the world market factory, parallel production and cross-border production. The end of this section discusses current trends in the value creation system. An inset outlines the hub-and-spoke network used for the production of the Dacia Logan.
- Next, Section 16.3 examines operation modes. First, the basic options are listed. An inset gives the operation modes used in parallel by Dacia. After this, three special aspects of operation modes are discussed: we show how the choice of operation mode may change as the company gathers international experience; then, we look at combinations of operation modes; finally, we raise the question of the standardization or local adaptation of the operation mode.

- Section 16.4 offers recommendations for developing an operations strategy. We begin by showing why the configuration of the value creation process and the determination of the operation modes, described in the preceding sections, form the core elements of an operations strategy. Next, influencing conditions are outlined and the section closes by proposing a process for developing an operations strategy.

Chapter 17 introduces a process for strategic planning in an international company:

- After preliminary remarks in Section 17.1, an overview of the process is given in Section 17.2. The process consists of one preliminary step and seven main steps. The following sections describe the content of each of these steps.
- The preparation of the strategy planning project is described in Section 17.3. In an inset, examples of questions for initiating the project are given.
- Next, Section 17.4 shows how to carry out strategic analysis and Section 17.5 describes how to revise or produce the mission statement.
- In Section 17.6 the development of the corporate strategy in an international company is explained. An inset mentions how Nestlé uses different levels of integration and responsiveness in its various divisions.
- Sections 17.7 and Section 17.8 describe how business strategies and functional strategies are produced.
- The next sections offer information about how to draw up implementation programs and how to make the final assessment of strategies and implementation. The concluding section deals with the formulation and formal approval of the strategic documents.

12 Determining the level of integration and responsiveness

12.1 Preliminary remarks

Companies that are active internationally must avoid to look for good solutions for each foreign engagement separately. Instead, their main competitive advantage results from an integrated review of all their worldwide activities (Holtbrügge/Welge, 2010, p. 132). In this context, the present chapter focuses on a basic decision for the company to make in terms of the levels of global integration and local responsiveness.

For medium-sized companies, the level of global integration and local responsiveness – a basic orientation to international business – is mostly determined at the corporate level. For very large companies, different divisions may follow different orientations.

The strategic orientation of the company or of a business is a basic attitude of management or a "state of mind" (Perlmutter, 1969). Obviously, a company should consider the external environment, especially the situation in the industry. But companies can differ in their strategic response to the external environment (Morschett/Schramm-Klein/ Zentes, 2010, pp. 36 ff.) and determine their position in the integration-responsiveness framework themselves.

12.2 Three strategic orientations in the integration - responsiveness framework

All companies that are active in different countries are confronted with two, often conflicting, sets of demands, namely the requirement to adapt to the local environment in the different host countries ("local responsiveness") and the potential benefits of a standardized approach ("global integration"). More specifically, the two dimensions can be described as follows (Doz, 1980; Prahalad/Doz, 1987; Bartlett/Ghoshal/ Beamish, 2008, pp. 88 ff.):

- An international company operates under heterogeneous conditions in many different host countries. In each country the local unit is confronted with different local customers and host governments, different market and distribution structures, different competitors and substitution products. The attempt to exploit the opportunities that arise from heterogeneity pressures the company towards **local responsiveness**. This pressure varies by industry.
- **Global integration** means interconnecting the international activities of the firm across all countries, leveraging the strengths of a large company, and trying to achieve synergy effects. For instance, strong economies of scale can push a company towards internationally standardized products. Or the comparative cost advantages of one country may be an incentive for the company to specialize the activities of certain foreign subsidiaries, leading to interdependencies between the activities worldwide.

In the mid 1980s, a number of well-known authors proposed that these two requirements are not the extreme points of one dimension but that companies could, instead, see each as an independent dimension. Based on this view, basic types of international strategies have been developed that describe the different responses of companies to the two requirements (see **Figure 12.1**). Some authors describe these types as "**archetypes of international companies**" (Kutschker, 1999, p. 110). Each type is a bundle of strategy elements expressing the fundamental strategic orientation of an organization.

Although a two-dimensional framework implies four strategy types, often only three types are conceptualized. Many authors cannot identify a strategy with low global integration and simultaneously low local responsiveness (see the overview in Morschett, 2007, p. 58). A strategy like this would consider foreign activities only as remote outposts whose main role is to support the parent company by contributing additional sales. The focus would be on exploiting the knowledge, products or processes of the parent company by transferring them to foreign markets. Accordingly, the company would not adapt to the specific host country and the foreign activities would also not be systematically integrated in the company. While this situation may be the emerged approach in the first stage of internationalization, the authors do not recommend this strategy type for companies developing a strategy for being international.

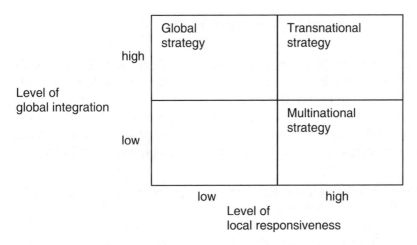

Figure 12.1: Integration - responsiveness framework (adapted from Bartlett/Ghoshal/Beamish, 2008)

In the following part of the text, the three viable strategic orientations are described in detail (Bartlett/Ghoshal/Beamish, 2008, pp. 203 ff.; Harzing, 2000; Morschett/Schramm-Klein/Zentes, 2010, pp. 32 ff.).

Companies with a **global strategy** focus their organization on achieving economies of scale and a worldwide uniform image. Such companies are usually found in industries where forces for global integration are strong and forces for local responsiveness rather low. Often, price competition in global industries is high, thus, the dominant strategic need is efficiency. The most relevant resources are directly controlled by the headquarters and decisions are highly centralized. The company attempts to rationalize by producing standardized products in focussed plants that meet a worldwide demand volume. In the past, these production plants were almost always located in the home country. Today, companies often choose to concentrate their production in one location in a low-cost country. The predominant task of the other foreign subsidiaries is to act as a pipeline for the parent company, selling products in its local market. R&D and innovation is usually concentrated in the home country. Information flows and product flows are unidirectional: the company headquarters is a centralized hub for the company. Apple, Porsche, IKEA, Nespresso, Cartier and Victorinox are examples of this strategy. **Inset 12.1** outlines the case of Victorinox.

Inset 12.1: The global strategy of Victorinox

Victorinox is a Swiss company that is still controlled by the family that founded it in 1884. It is the manufacturer of the famous Swiss army knife. After the acquisition of its former competitor Wenger in 2005, it became the sole supplier of pocket knives to the Swiss army. While the company also offers other products, e.g. watches and travel gear, this inset focuses on multi-purpose pocket knives.

Although the company has been a supplier to the Swiss Army for more than a hundred years, international success began with the distribution of the knives in US army shops after World War II. The term "Swiss army knife" originated at this time.

Today, the company produces almost 30 million pocket knives a year. The pocket knives are all manufactured in a factory in Ibach in Switzerland under the brand Victorinox and carry the well-known emblem of a white cross in a red shield.

In terms of industry forces, the industry supports a global strategy. Customer demand for pocket knives is global and there is no strong divergence of customer needs with regard to this product. While some cultural influences on pocket knives exist – for example, though the knife is often used as a gift, this use is inappropriate in Asia – they do not create a need for product adaptation to each foreign market.

The country-of-origin effect is of great importance for a Swiss army knife, and any decentralization of production to different host countries would negatively influence the image. Furthermore, economies of scale from central production are substantial. And given the relatively high value-to-weight ratio, transporting the final products to the sales countries does not produce major costs. For this specific product, competition around the world is rare, in particular since the major competitor (who also followed a global strategy) has been acquired. There are no strong influences of governments on the international trade in pocket knives.

Victorinox sells a broad range of standardised products around the world and the brand positioning is uniform around the world. The Swiss army knife is a symbol of the ultimate ingeniously designed, super-functional product. The global brand strategy is managed centrally by the Victorinox corporate headquarters and its agency partners from Switzerland.

A globally successful TV series, MacGyver, demonstrated to the world how the hero frequently used his Swiss army knife to save him or others in dangerous situations. NASA equips astronauts with this army knife. It seems that a uniform image has been successfully transported around the globe.

To ensure that the global strategy is enforced at the point of sale and to have even better control of the worldwide image, in 1992 the company started to open its own stores. In recent years, a number of flagship stores have been opened that represent all the different products of the brand, including stores in New York, London, Tokyo and Geneva.

In contrast, a **multinational strategy** accentuates national differences to achieve its strategic objectives. In many aspects, it seems the reverse of the global strategy. It follows a polycentric approach. Products, processes, strategies, even management systems, are modified in each country to adapt to local needs and sometimes to local government regulations. This adaptation to the host country is accompanied by local production and local R&D. The main task of subsidiaries is to identify and fulfill local needs and the foreign subsidiary is provided with the necessary resources to respond to these local needs. The subsidiaries enjoy a degree of independence from the headquarters and they are also not linked to peer subsidiaries in other countries. The organization takes the form of a decentralized federation. An example of this strategy is given in **Inset 12.2**.

Inset 12.2: The multinational strategy of Carlsberg (text based on Carlsberg, 2011)

Carlsberg is the world's fourth largest brewery group. It employs 41,000 people. It has a strong position in Northern & Western Europe, Eastern Europe and Asia, the three regions in which it is based.

While the company has a small number of global brands, mainly Carlsberg, it has the number one position in 13 European markets and 4 Asian markets with strong local beer brands and locally targeted activities. For example, the company is no. 1 throughout Scandinavia, in Russia, in Kazakhstan, in Germany, in France and also in China.

In the beer industry, the market-leading brands are not the same across countries. The main competitors are often large multinationals like Anheuser-Bush InBev, but these offer many local brands, often traditional brands in each country which have been acquired in recent decades. Thus, competition is a mix between global and local. Consumer demand is rather fragmented: national beer markets are characterized by different tastes in beer, different types of beer and loyalty to national brands (like Feldschlösschen in Switzerland).

Since beer is a heavy product which usually cannot be transported over long distances profitably, production is often decentralized to the countries of consumption. The Carlsberg Group operates at least one brewery in each of the countries in which it has the number one position, usually to produce local beer brands for that market.

In Germany, Carlsberg offers Holsten, Astra and Lübzer. In Switzerland, it owns Feldschlösschen, the no. 1 brand, and Cardinal. In France, Kronenbourg and Kanterbräu, both originating from and produced in the Alsace but owned by Carlsberg, are among the market's leading brands. In Russia, the Carlsberg Group has a market share of almost 40%, with a variety of brands. Among them is Baltika, Russia's most popular domestic premium brand. Uralsky, Nevskoe and DV are other local beer brands in Russia. In China the Carlsberg Group sells some of its international brands which are exported there, but it reports that the major part of its sales growth stems from relaunches of local beer brands in key provinces in China. For example, the company now offers Dragon 8 Beer, Wind Flower Snow & Moon, Wusu and Dali Beer, which it produces in its breweries in different regions of China.

Altogether, the Carlsberg Group's brand portfolio includes more than 500 brands which vary greatly in volume, price, target audience and geographic penetration. Many of them target a specific country or even a specific region. This enables the sales teams to offer to regional retailers and other customers like restaurants and hotels a product range that is adapted to the local tastes and a supply chain which is usually fully embedded in the host country. The variety of brands allows Carlsberg to make arrangements with important customers in the different markets.

While global strategies and multinational strategies emphasize either global efficiency and integration on the one hand, or multinational flexibility and local responsiveness on the other, the **transnational strategy** attempts to respond to both these strategic needs. Transnational organizations aim to achieve the benefits of both, emulating both global and multinational companies. This means that a transnational strategy is one in which a company becomes strongly responsive to local needs while still achieving the benefits of global integration. In such cases the company can be described as an integrated network, where key activities and resources are neither centralized in the headquarters nor fully decentralized into each country. Instead, resources and activities are geographically dispersed but specialized, leading to economies of scale and flexibility. A certain level of product adaptation to local needs is combined with cross-border production processes that can still concentrate production in single locations, for example for specific common components. This leads to horizontal product flows, that is, the reciprocal flow of different finished products between different foreign subsidiaries. Innovation can occur in different locations and is subsequently diffused to all countries; and foreign subsidiaries can serve in strategic roles, either for producing specific products, or as centers of excellence. An example of this strategy is given in **Inset 12.3**.

Inset 12.3: The transnational strategy of Electrolux (text based on Zentes/Swoboda/Morschett, 2011)

Electrolux is the one of the world's largest manufacturers of home appliances, with sales of about 12 billion euro in 2010. It sells its products in more than 150 countries and many of the elements of its strategy suggest that it can be categorized as transnational.

While the company has a mix of local brands, regional brands and one global brand, it is clearly committed to increasing the share of products sold under the Electrolux brand to leverage its global reach. Given that there are still very strong local and regional brands in the Electrolux portfolio, this is often achieved by dual-branding, with the (global) Electrolux brand name added to the original (regional) brand name (e.g. AEG-Electrolux). This is intended to combine the advantages of a global brand with a regional one. Since the year 2000, sales of Electrolux branded products, including those that are dual-branded, have risen from 18 % to almost 50 % of sales.

The different country markets mostly do not have their own production because production is optimized on a global scale. However, the same product type may be manufactured in different local variants in different locations, depending on the target market. In a restructuring program which started in 2004, Electrolux greatly reduced the number of plants and increased the proportion of production in low-cost countries. In a mix between a global and a local strategy, it looked for optimal production locations to serve its markets while reducing costs. With large domestic appliances, logistics costs are a crucial factor in location decisions. This aspect of Electrolux was discussed in **Inset 9.2**. One result of the company's analysis was the opening of new plants in Poland and Hungary (close to the Western European markets) and in Mexico (close to the US market) while many plants in Western Europe and North America were closed.

Local tastes and requirements for domestic appliances remain heterogeneous around the world, calling for a certain degree of local adaptation in the market offer. But the severe reduction in the number of plants was possible because it was accompanied by a reduction in the number of product platforms that the company used. Reducing the number of product platforms generated benefits that included enabling greater standardization of components, fewer product variants and simpler production in fewer locations. This is a frequent element of transnational strategies because it allows companies to adapt the final product to the specific tastes of the customer in a specific country while still achieving global economies of scale from the standardized platforms.

While the transnational strategy type is often seen as an ideal in the literature, it is highly complex, costly and difficult to implement. Bartlett and Ghoshal recommended the complex transnational strategy only for companies that are confronted with an environment with simultaneously strong forces for integration and responsiveness. "Organizational complexity is costly and difficult to manage, and simplicity, wherever possible, is a virtue" (Ghoshal/Nohria, 1993, p. 24). To realize a transnational strategy successfully requires many years of experience in managing international operations.

12.3 Recommendations for determining the level of integration and responsiveness

12.3.1 Conditions influencing the decision

To determine the optimal level of global integration and local responsiveness, a company must consider the external demands that are specific to the industry or industries. These can be described as forces for global integration and forces for local responsiveness (Morschett/ Schramm-Klein/Zentes, 2010, pp. 30 ff.).

In a global industry, a firm's competitive position in one country is strongly affected by its position in other countries. The **forces for global integration**, also called industry globalization drivers, stem from four different sources (Bartlett/Ghoshal/Beamish, 2008, pp. 88 ff.):

- First of all, homogeneous **customer needs** in the different markets may create opportunities to sell standardized products. With common customer needs, marketing becomes transferable across countries. Almost 30 years ago, Levitt (1983) wrote about the "Globalization of Markets" and in his culture convergence thesis he suggested that different cultures are becoming more similar, and lifestyles and tastes are converging worldwide. While this thesis is still disputed, it can certainly be observed in many industries (e.g., smart phones, TVs, home appliances), where globally similar demand has emerged with the Internet enforcing this trend. In B2B markets, companies meet global customers. Consider, for example, automotive suppliers which deliver to global car manufacturers. Similarly, large international retailers like Carrefour, Tesco or Media-Saturn, and global e-commerce channels like Amazon are emerging as customers for suppliers in different countries. All these aspects enhance the need for globalization in an industry.

- From a **cost perspective**, different industries have different incentives to standardize. For example, economies of scale at a particular production plant can be increased with standardized products that are exported to different country markets. But economies of scale and scope and experience curve effects differ from industry to industry. This can be caused by different production technologies. The greater the potential economies of scale and the steeper the experience curve, the more likely an industry is to turn global. Furthermore, in those industries where product development is expensive, and at the same time product lifecycles are short, companies usually try to exploit global scale effects. Comparative differences in labor costs will often make concentration of production in one optimal location useful.

- **Governmental drivers** also have an influence on the need and potential for globalization in an industry. For example, compatible technical standards are necessary for product standardization. Liberal trading regulations with low trade barriers and common market regulations are important drivers for globalization, making cross-border trade easier. Conversely, high trade barriers reduce the forces towards globalization, protecting local particularities. Deregulation of formerly protected industries (like energy, telecommunications, and transport) also pushes industries towards globalization.

- The presence of **global competitors** enhances the need for globalization. Only companies that manage their international operations interdependently can implement a coordinated strategy and use a competitive strategy that is sometimes called "global chess" (Bartlett/Ghoshal/Beamish, 2008, p. 90). This means responding to threats in one market by reactions in other markets. In addition, large multinational companies offering the same products and brands around the world also promote the convergence of tastes and customer demand.

On the other hand, in certain industries companies are facing different factors, which push them towards **local responsiveness:**

- The dominant reason for local responsiveness is profound difference in **customer demand**. This may be caused by strong cultural differences in tastes, by different environmental conditions (climate, topography, etc.), or by different income levels and income distribution.
- Differences in the **industry structure** might make adaptations necessary. A different competitive situation in different markets might force a company to change its strategy and to adapt it to the local market conditions.
- Furthermore, **protectionism** by governments often creates a need to produce locally and/or to adapt products to specific markets.
- Local responsiveness can also become necessary or beneficial due to different **labor conditions**, e.g. labor costs or skill levels that require adaptation of production processes. Furthermore, cultural influences might make different leadership styles more or less effective in different countries.
- Similarly, the availability or non-availability of good **suppliers** has an influence. A low number of potential suppliers might make a higher level of vertical integration necessary.

These forces describe the external influences on a specific industry. Strategic management usually assumes that a degree of match between the external situation and the company strategy is more efficient than a mismatch. Yip (1991) pointed out that to achieve balanced global and national competitive advantages, the globalization of the strategy has to be aligned with the globalization of the industry. Nevertheless, companies have a certain level of freedom in the development of a strategy (Child, 1972). So, although industry forces are strong influences, "managers can and do change the rules of the game" (Prahalad/Doz, 1987, p. 30; Devinney/Midgley/Venaik, 2000, p. 674). Terms such as "state of mind" or "strategic orientation" clearly indicate that the industry characteristics are important, but companies can choose alternative strategies based on their resources, strategic objectives and other considerations (see **Inset 12.4**). Big companies even have the possibility to pursue a **shaping strategy** and to redefine the industry forces.

12.3.2 Process for determining the level of integration and responsiveness

In **Figure 12.2**, a process for determining the level of global integration and local responsiveness for a business field is proposed.

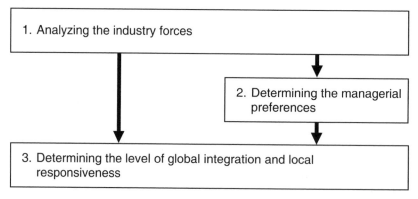

Figure 12.2: Process for determining the level of integration and responsiveness

In **Step 1**, a thorough analysis of the industry forces has to be undertaken to identify the position of the industry in the integration-responsiveness framework. The relevant industry forces were explained in Section 12.3.1.

In **Step 2**, the company should determine its managerial preferences. Obviously, the industry forces will have an influence on the managerial preferences but they will not fully determine them. The company must analyze the available resources for the business field, and managerial beliefs about the current and future situation of the industry (Devinney/Midgley/Venaik, 2000), the corporate strategy and the strategic objectives of the business, including the intended market position. Often, the chosen level of integration or responsiveness for other strategic businesses of the company influences the basic orientation of corporate management.

In **Step 3**, the company can determine the level of global integration and local responsiveness for the business field in question. This decision must consider the industry forces and the managerial preferences in an integrated manner. If both point to the same decision, there is a fit which does not need further justification. If, however, the chosen level of integration-responsiveness goes against the industry forces, the company must vigorously assess whether it genuinely has the power to change the rules of the game. This could produce a sustainable strategic advantage since it would give the company a true USP. But to be successful in opposition to the industry forces takes much more effort.

Inset 12.4 highlights the case of IKEA where the industry forces clearly imply a multinational strategy but the company has become world market leader with a global strategy.

Inset 12.4: The global strategy of IKEA in a multinational industry (text based on Morschett/Schramm-Klein/Zentes, 2010, pp. 42 ff.)

Furniture is an industry that can be categorized as multinational. Tastes with regard to home furnishing are still very different around the world. For example, the typical home in Asia looks different from the typical European home. Given the high transportation cost, furniture is often produced in proximity to the final markets (e.g. in Eastern Europe for Western European markets). The number of globally active furniture manufacturers is small and the retail industry in this field is still very fragmented, even at a national level. It is difficult to identify any worldwide retailers. Thus, the forces for global integration are rather low and the forces for local responsiveness can be seen as strong.

Despite this, the largest furniture retailer worldwide, IKEA, clearly follows a global strategy. Of the range of around 9'000 products that

IKEA offers in its stores around the world, 95 % are the same in each country. The company operates big box speciality stores for home furnishing that have a very similar exterior and interior design around the world. IKEA uses the same advertising message around the world and the catalogue, one of its main communication tools, is to a great extent identical around the world.

13 Defining the strategic businesses

13.1 The importance of defining the strategic businesses

Companies are complex multi-layered systems. For this reason, it is difficult to achieve an adequately comprehensive overview of a company: both company staff and outsiders will typically look first of all at sales statistics and/or at the organizational chart. These two approaches offer an overview from different perspectives. The sales statistics link current sales to products, markets and customer groups, while the organigram shows how tasks are distributed between organizational units.

Both of these views focus on daily business and can therefore be described as operational. They are of very limited use as the basis for strategic decisions. The sales figures do not show the links between markets served, products offered and resources required. The organigram neither shows how the company produces its offers nor explains the interfaces between the organizational units in the value creation process.

For good quality decisions in strategic planning, a strategic view of the company is required. This is achieved by defining the strategic businesses. Defining these businesses divides the company into strategically important subsystems. The strategic businesses which have been identified then form the basis for generating strategic options and assessing them at the corporate level. The strategic businesses are also the basis for the formulation of individual business strategies. Thus the definition of strategic businesses is a central task. It defines the entire structure for the ensuing work of strategy development.

13.2 Understanding strategic businesses

Management literature uses the word "business" in both strategic and organizational contexts (Thahabi, 2010, p. 63). However, the use of the term in organizational theory is not of relevance in the context of the present book, which has an exclusively strategic perspective. So from here on we use the term "business" in its meaning within strategic management: the terms "business" and "strategic business" will be used interchangeably.

A (strategic) business is (Grünig/Kühn, 2011, p. 128 f.):

- a market offer
- which can be distinguished from the other market offers of the company
- and which contributes critically to the success of the company.

The three elements are understood as follows:

- **Market offer** includes not only the central products and services, but complementary services, communication, price conditions and so on. The offer includes all the various measures within a marketing mix. It is important to understand that when identifying strategic businesses, it is not only differences in the basic products or services that must be taken into account, but also differentiated use of other elements of the marketing mix (Grünig/Kühn, 2011, p. 123).
- The identification of a particular market offer as **distinct from the company's other market offers** can be based on a number of different criteria. The most important ones are different industry markets, different industry segments within an industry market and different country markets (see section 12.3).
- As Chapter 3 shows, strategic planning must focus on essentials and not get bogged down in detail. For this reason, a strategic business has to make an **important contribution to the success** of the company or at least must have the potential to do so in the future (Grünig/Kühn, 2011, p. 124 f.). Typically, this condition is set in terms of a fixed percentage of turnover or contribution margin. Activities contributing less than this value, for example less than 5%, can be dismissed as strategically irrelevant, unless of course they have the potential to contribute significantly in the future. Obviously the figure which is set will depend on the specific context; it is not possible to give a standard figure.

Two different types of strategic businesses can be distinguished (Grünig/Kühn, 2011, p. 127 ff.):

- **Strategic business units** share the market and/or important resources with other such business units. For this reason, their autonomy of action is somewhat constrained.
- **Strategic business fields** do not to any significant extent share
  markets and resources with other businesses in the corporation.
  This makes the business fields autonomous; they are like companies
  within the company.

Even with business fields, there are nearly always relationships which
link them. But these links will be weak ones. For example, one business field may be able to exploit distribution channels built up by another. And all business fields may have recourse to the corporate legal
department. Business fields will also be mutually dependent in financial
terms. What is necessary is that the business fields are sufficiently
independent at the market level and at the resource level in order that
they can be strategically planned and managed as separate entities.
As a practical rule of thumb, one should only speak of a business field
if the activities concerned could be sold off without endangering the
survival and success of the remaining businesses in the corporation.

Figure 13.1 summarises this account of businesses, business units
and business fields. As can be seen, there are three requirements for a
business and two further requirements for a business field. If the latter
are not met, then the business is a business unit. The business unit is
outlined on the diagram with a dotted line, reflecting the fact that there
are no extra requirements, as compared with business fields.

This distinction between business units and business fields is of great
importance in practical terms:

- A strategy can be developed for a business field quite independently, that is without taking into account what the strategies might be for
  other businesses. This makes it possible to consider radical options,
  such as disinvestment, spin-off and merger. For example, in 1997,
  one year after the merger of Ciba-Geigy and Sandoz to form Novartis, Ciba was set up as a spin-off, separating specialty chemicals. In
  2000, the Novartis agribusiness was merged with the agribusiness
  activity of Astra Zeneca to form Syngenta. These two strategic
  moves were only possible because the businesses involved were
  strategic business fields.

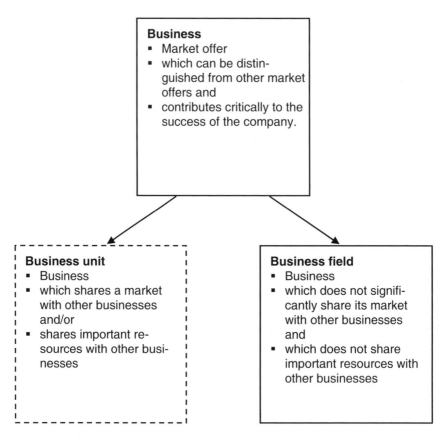

Figure 13.1: Business, business units and business fields

- For a business unit, the strategic planning situation is quite different. Because they are linked in terms of the markets they serve and/or the resources they require, business units need strategies which take account of the requirements of other business units. If different business units operate in the same market, then their products have to be differently positioned, otherwise they may cannibalize each other's sales. If a watch producer has a number of different labels, it is necessary for these brands to be positioned differently in terms of design, quality and target customer segment. Where business units require similar resources, their strategies should be designed to promote cost synergies. For example, a small manufacturer of injection moulding items may produce parts for the auto industry, for toy manufacturers and for mobile telephones. It is obviously preferable if the parts supplied to all three sectors could be produced with the same type of machines. The larger the parts are, the greater the holding pressure specifications of the injection moulding machine required. This means that it is a good idea to offer all the various customers parts of a similar size. In this way the company may limit its production machinery to a smaller number of machines whose capacity will be used more fully.

As **Figure 13.2** shows, medium and large enterprises often have a hierarchy of business fields and business units: Several interdependent business units together form a strongly independent business field.

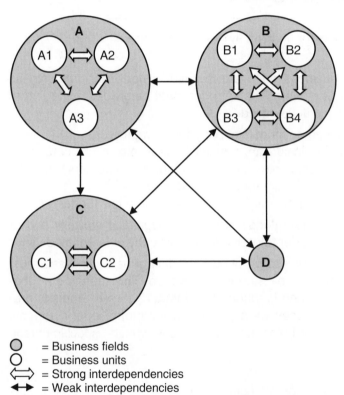

○   = Business fields
○   = Business units
⟺   = Strong interdependencies
◆▶   = Weak interdependencies

Figure 13.2: Business units as parts of business fields

13.3   Process for defining the strategic businesses

Figure 13.3 shows the proposed process for defining the strategic businesses (Grünig/Kühn, 2011, p. 132).

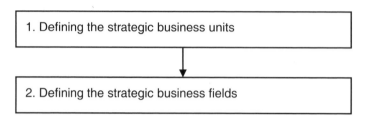

Figure 13.3: Process for defining the strategic businesses

In **Step 1**, the business units are defined. When defining business units, the company's overall market offer must be divided according to clear criteria. Such criteria include:

- industry markets, e.g. chocolate, baby food, water etc.
- industry segments inside an industry market, e.g. micro cars, sub-compacts, compacts etc. or price-oriented customers, quality-oriented customers, design-oriented customers etc.
- country markets, e.g. products for Germany, products for Italy etc.

In simple contexts one criterion may be enough, but typically two or three are required in order to generate a sufficiently differentiated view.

The choice of the criteria to be used for defining the businesses must be made according to their strategic relevance. This means that specialist industry knowledge is required. In **Inset 13.1** an example is presented of how businesses were defined in an international company. This concrete example helps the reader to see why the specific criteria were chosen.

Step 2 is the identification of business fields. There are two possibilities here:

- Different business units may be grouped together in a business field if they share markets and/or resources.
- Individual businesses which do not share markets or resources with any other company businesses are upgraded to business fields.

There are no exact criteria for assessing interdependencies at the market and resource levels. Different individuals or working groups may therefore come to different conclusions on these points. But we should only speak of a business field if it is possible for it to develop in the long term largely independently of the rest of the company. This has nothing to do with size. There are very large businesses which do not meet this criterion and for this reason cannot be classified as business fields. To take a striking example, Schindler refers to the "elevator and escalator business" and the company is right to group these two together (Schindler, 2011). Although elevators and escalators bring an annual turnover of more than 8 billion Swiss francs and the division employs a staff of more than 40'000, this activity represents a single business field. All the various products address the need to transport people and goods vertically within buildings. Moreover, they are often marketed as a total package for which after-sale maintenance is carried out by a regional subsidiary or dealership.

The result of the process is that a business structure is produced which is closely adapted to the specific features of the company concerned. **Inset 13.1**now offers an example of a customized business structure of this kind.

> **Inset 13.1: The strategic business structure of Ricola** (text based on Thahabi, 2010, pp. 195 ff.)
>
> Ricola is a Swiss producer of herb drops, tea and chewing gum. The herb drops include both hard and soft herb drops. The tea is either packaged in teabags or sold as an instant tea powder.
>
> All of these three product types are manufactured within Switzerland, using separate facilities for each type. To distribute the products abroad, the company has set up wholly owned subsidiaries in its most important export countries.
>
> **Figure 13.4** presents the strategic business structure for Ricola.

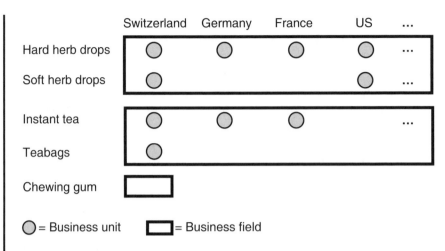

Figure 13.4: Business structure of Ricola

The product groups address different customer needs (herb drops, tea, gum) and different preferences (hard and soft herb drops, instant tea and teabag). The different geographical markets confront the company with varying customer habits, competitive situations and distribution structures. A strategic business structure in two dimensions is able to represent all these differences.

The three business fields serve different industry markets: Indeed, in retail chains the products fall into different categories. And production is also quite separate for each type of product. While it is true that the distribution companies are responsible for marketing all Ricola's products, nevertheless within those companies the different business fields are handled separately.

Beginning the strategy planning project of an international company by determining the strategic businesses creates a basis for further planning. At the same time, these further steps in planning can lead to changes in the strategic businesses. In particular, the strategic structure may change as a result of the decision either to have a standard offer or to differentiate the offer (see Chapter 15) or may change as a result of decisions concerning the value creation process (see Chapter 16). For this reason, loops in the process must be anticipated.

13.4   Patterns of businesses in international companies

Comparison of a sufficient number of individual cases shows a limited number of patterns occurring in practice (Thahabi, 2010, p. 260 ff.). These can be divided into two: first, patterns of businesses for industries in which the country markets form separate competitive arenas and second, patterns where the world market is the competitive arena. The world market is the rarer case. For most consumer goods, in retail and in many services too, competition takes place within a country or a country group. There are markets, however, where the competitive arena is the world. Examples are trade in raw materials or production of investment goods like avionics. As the world continues to grow closer (see Chapter 1) more global markets will appear.

Figure 13.5 gives the patterns for cases where the competitive arenas are individual countries:

- In this case the business units are formed according to the different countries and industry segments (see **Inset 6.2**). These industry segments can be product groups, customer groups or product-customer combinations.
- The question of whether business units can be grouped together in business fields, and how this would be done, depends on resources: can resources be allocated to individual country groups, or to different individual industries, or even to combinations of industry and country groups? As the figure shows, there are four possible patterns and all four occur in practice.

Figure 13.6 displays the pattern where a world market is the competitive arena:

- In this case the business units are industry segments (product groups, customer groups or product-customer combinations).
- For a worldwide competitive arena too, the formation of strategic business fields is a question of resources. If key resources and processes can be allocated to the industries, then they form business fields. If not, there are no business fields.

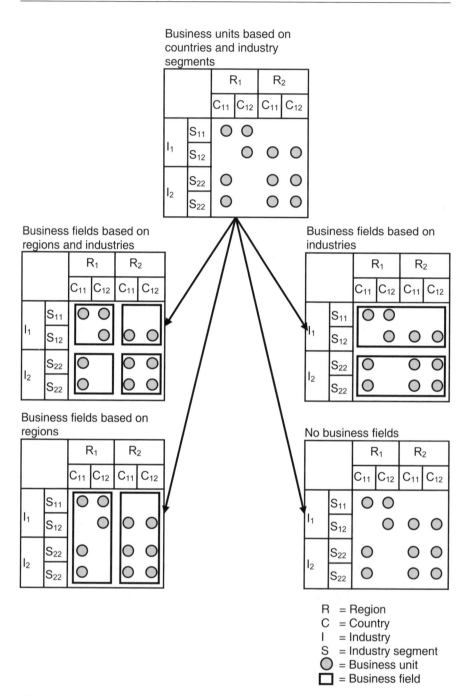

Figure 13.5: Patterns of strategic businesses where countries are the competitive arenas

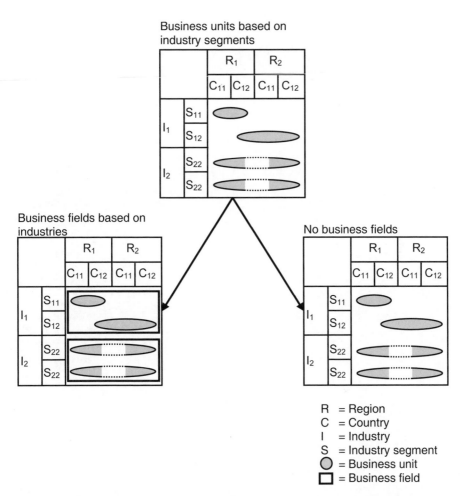

Figure 13.6: Patterns of strategic businesses where the world market is the competitive arena

14 Defining the strategic objectives

14.1 Preliminary remarks

The central task of a corporate strategy is to determine the strategic goals of the company, in particular target market positions for its different businesses, for a fixed planning period, such as five years. By setting out the planned development of the company in this way, a framework of reference is created which the company's leaders can orientate themselves to.

But determining the strategic goals of an international company is a very demanding task. There are two reasons for this:

- First, as Section 14.2 will show, determining goals is a multidimensional task. Because of this multidimensionality, it is not easy to set up a system of goals which are internally consistent with one another.
- Secondly, the goals must be both ambitious and achievable. To take an example, it is extraordinarily difficult to set realistic market share targets for a foreign industry market. This is all the more true when the company has not been operating in that market for very long and cannot use past performance as a basis.

14.2 Dimensions of strategic objectives

When fixing strategic goals for an international company there are numerous dimensions to consider. The most important ones are listed in **Figure 14.1** and explained in what follows.

Diversified companies which are active in a number of industries need to specify **goals for each industry market**. This is because the competitive arena is the industry market, and targets, whether in revenue or market share, only make sense in relation to these markets. For Nestlé, for example, target market positions would be specified separately for the various markets in chocolate, baby food, dairy products and so on.

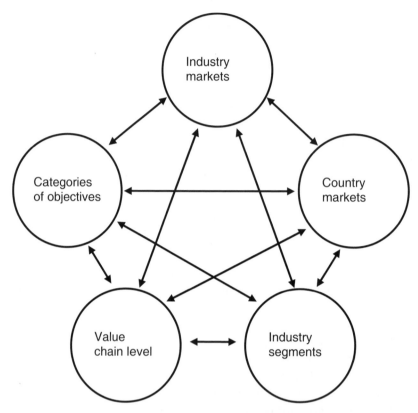

Figure 14.1: Dimensions of the strategic objectives in an international company

In most industries competition takes place at the level of countries (or groups of countries) rather than worldwide. The competitive situation as regards dairy products differs between, say, Thailand and Vietnam. There are strong nationally-based competitors in each country and the distribution channels are different too. As a result, a dairy producer like Nestlé would specify target market share **objectives separately for each country** or region. However in global markets, such as the market for airplane production, it would be pointless to devise different goals for each country or country group.

Most industry markets are not homogenous but can be divided into a number of product groups/submarkets and/or customer groups/segments. For chocolate in Switzerland, the market differentiates between chocolate bars, chocolate blocks, pralines and children's products. The market can also be divided into price/quality segments: premium products, medium-price and low-price.

The market for clothing offers even more possibilities for subdividing:

- Customer segments would include children, young males, young females, adult males and adult females.
- A second approach would divide the market according to the type of clothing, such as outer wear, underwear, sports wear, plus sizes.
- As with chocolate, the clothing market can also be divided according to different categories of price and quality.

A good approach to subdividing markets is industry segment analysis, which was outlined in **Inset 6.2**. To get specific targets, we **need objectives related to the relevant industry segments** and not for the whole market.

An internationally active company needs more than just general objectives. Of practical importance are **objectives on three different value chain levels**:

- First objectives for each of the strategic businesses are required. As we saw in Chapter 13, businesses are product and/or customer groups which belong to an industry market and also often to a geographical market.
- Long-term planning of operations is done by setting specific objectives for each production unit. For practical reasons, it is better to set these objectives for larger units, such as factories. The objectives can be expressed in terms of capacities or in unit production costs for the various products. The operation objectives may also include the closure of existing facilities or the opening of new ones.
- Finally sourcing is also of great strategic importance and requires strategic targets too.

The fifth dimension concerns the content of the objectives. There is a wide range of possible goals. **Figure 14.2** lists what we consider to be the primary **categories of objectives** for the company as a whole, for the businesses, for the operation units and for sourcing:

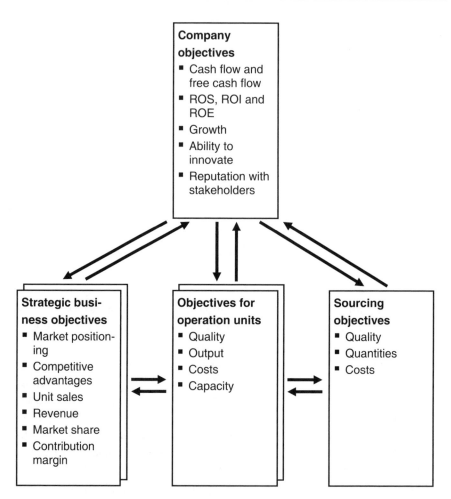

Figure 14.2: Possible strategic objectives

- As the chart shows, these suggestions include qualitative objectives like the company's reputation or ability to innovate, alongside quantifiable objectives, such as growth. The financial objectives form an important subcategory within the quantitative goals. Such quantitatively expressed objectives, especially the financial ones, are absolutely essential at the strategic level. The strategy cannot have a binding effect without them. But we recognize that it is difficult to set quantitative targets for several years into the future.
- The arrows on the chart indicate that these are not separate goals but form part of a system of objectives. If positive synergies are to be

created between the different parts of the firm, then the various goals must be carefully adjusted in order to create an internally consistent system of objectives.

14.3   Process of defining the strategic objectives

Figure 14.3 gives our recommended process for the definition of strategic objectives.

In **Step 1** a list is made of the various areas for which strategic objectives need to be formulated, including objectives for the company as a whole:

- Normally objectives are required for each strategic business. Most medium-sized or large international businesses will have business fields as well as business units. Here the objectives should be ordered hierarchically: the business field objectives are divided into business unit objectives.
- Production in most international companies involves a large number of different value activities. For the purpose of defining goals, these need to be combined into bundles. Strategic goals can only be formulated for such bundles, for example for specific factories.
- As **Figure 14.2** shows, an overall statement of sourcing objectives should be included. Although a company may be active in several industries and countries, an overall view can lead to significant synergies.

Step 2 is the definition of categories of objectives. Here what is necessary is a list of categories for each of the following: the company as a whole, the businesses, the operation units and sourcing. Sometimes it is useful to make separate lists of objectives for the business fields, which enjoy significant autonomy, and for the business units, which are more closely linked together.

It is our recommendation that the numbers of objectives should be kept quite small. There are two reasons for this:

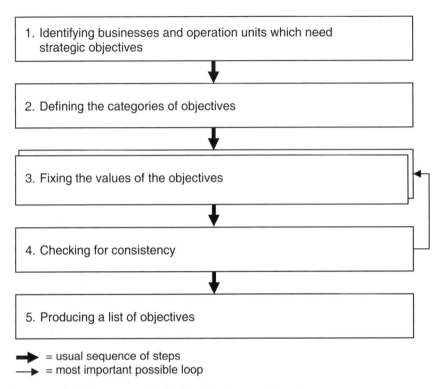

1. Identifying businesses and operation units which need strategic objectives

2. Defining the categories of objectives

3. Fixing the values of the objectives

4. Checking for consistency

5. Producing a list of objectives

➡ = usual sequence of steps
→ = most important possible loop

Figure 14.3: Process of defining strategic objectives

- The strategic objectives are not only required for further planning, but also form the basis for fixing the personal objectives with the managers. For this to succeed, what is required is a small number of key objectives. Only in this way can the right motivation be obtained.
- The system of objectives must be internally consistent. This is vital for the further planning and for the creation of synergies. And it is much easier to achieve this consistency if the lists of objectives for the company as a whole, for the businesses, for the operation units and for sourcing are kept to a small number. For example, for business units, the objectives might be no more than a specification of target sales and contribution margin. In **Figure 14.2** we provided quite a full list of possible strategic objectives, but this should not be understood to suggest that in a concrete case all of these objectives should be specified.

Step 3 is the determination of target values. While Steps 1 and 2 defined the areas for which objectives are needed and specified the types of objective, now in Step 3 values must be introduced. However, these will be provisional ones, as further stages in the planning will check them and correct them if necessary.

The target values are typically given in a sequence with a value for each year in the planning period, beginning with the expected value for the current year, the year in which the planning is carried out. This first value acts as a reference point.

These targets are normally set top-down. But as the targets for the businesses, for the operation units and for the sourcing department may turn out to be unrealistic, the values may be revised bottom-up. Sometimes this process has to be repeated a number of times.

In **Step 4** the whole system of objectives is checked for internal consistency. First the consistency of the buying, production and sales quantities must be assessed. This is a relatively easy matter. Much more difficult is assessing the consistency of the financial values. In order to arrive at a fully consistent system of financial targets, the values for each year need to be based on a forecast profit and loss statement, a forecast balance sheet and a forecast cash flow statement. This takes a great deal of time and effort.

Step 5 finally brings this work together in the form of a document giving an overview of the objectives. For an example of what this might look like, and the rationale behind it, see **Inset 14.1**.

Inset 14.1: Strategic objectives of FFA

FFA, an Austrian producer of consumer goods, produces four prod-uct groups in four different factories: product groups A1 and C are produced in two factories in Austria. Product B is produced in the Czech Republic and product group A2, a cheaper version of A1, is produced in China.

The company's principal markets are Austria and Germany. The company has also been able to enter the Chinese market with product group A2. In the coming years the company intends to launch A2 in Indonesia too. Indonesia also seems a promising mar-ket for product C. **Figure 14.4** summarizes this situation, showing both the existing businesses and the planned new ones.

	Austria	Germany	China	Indonesia
Product group A1	●			
Product group A2	●		●	○
Product group B	●	●		
Product group C	●			○

● = Existing business unit   ○ = Planned business unit   ▭ = Business field

Figure 14.4: Businesses of FFA

The system of strategic goals has been based on the following con-siderations:

- The strategic businesses are governed by contribution targets and cash flow targets. **Figure 14.5** shows the system of contribu-tion margins and cash flow values underlying the objectives.
- The four factories and the sourcing department are purely cost centres. The cost objectives are formulated so that they can be tied to the contribution margin targets of the businesses.

```
         Revenue
./.      Cost of raw materials and components
=        Contribution margin 1
./.      Direct production cost
./.      Sales cost
=        Contribution margin 2
./.      Fixed cost of the factory/factories *
./.      Overhead cost of the business field *
=        Contribution margin 3
./.      Overhead cost of the company *
=        Cash flow
./.      Investments
=        Free cash flow

*  = without amortisations and depreciations
```

Figure 14.5: Contribution margin and cash flow definition for FFA

- Based on the strategic objectives for the businesses, for the operations units and for sourcing, cash flow and free cash flow objectives can be formulated for the company as a whole.

Figure 14.6 sets out the strategic objectives of the company. The entry into the Indonesian market planned for 20xx+2 will have a number of consequences.

- In 20xx+1 some 2.2 million EUR will be invested in Indonesia which will lead to a corresponding reduction in free cash flow to 0.8 million EUR.
- For the years 20xx+2 and 20xx+3 this market entry will also cause a temporary drop in the percentage contribution margin 2 in business field C.
- Nevertheless the market entry is justified. Existing production capacity can be used, so that fixed costs will not rise significantly. According to the plan, the additional contribution margin 2 from Indonesia will increase the profitability of the company.

Business objectives

Businesses	Years	Turnover	Contribution margin 2	Contribution margin 3
A1 Austria	20xx	6	3	—
	20xx + 1	6	3	—
	20xx + 2	6	3	—
	20xx + 3	6	3	—
	20xx + 4	6	3	—
A2 Austria	20xx	10	3	—
	20xx + 1	10	3	—
	20xx + 2	10	3	—
	20xx + 3	10	3	—
	20xx + 4	10	3	—
A2 China	20xx	15	3.8	—
	20xx + 1	16	4	—
	20xx + 2	17	4.3	—
	20xx + 3	18	4.5	—
	20xx + 4	19	4.8	—
A2 Indonesia	20xx	0	0	—
	20xx + 1	0	0	—
	20xx + 2	2	0.4	—
	20xx + 3	2.5	0.6	—
	20xx + 4	3	0.8	—
A Total	20xx	31	9.8	5.2
	20xx + 1	32	10	5.4
	20xx + 2	35	10.7	5.9
	20xx + 3	36.5	11.1	6.3
	20xx + 4	38	11.6	6.8
B Austria	...	...	...	—
B Germany	...	...	...	—
B Total	20xx	20.5	6.8	2.5
	20xx + 1	21	7	2.5
	20xx + 2	21.5	7.2	2.6
	20xx + 3	22	7.4	2.6
	20xx + 4	22.5	7.6	2.7
C Austria	...	...	...	—
C Indonesia	...	...	...	—
C total	20xx	8.5	2.8	1.9
	20xx + 1	9	3	2.1
	20xx + 2	11.5	3.3	2.3
	20xx + 3	12.5	3.8	2.8
	20xx + 4	13.5	4.5	3.5

Figure 14.6: Strategic objectives of FFA

Factory objectives

Factories	Products	Years	Output	Direct cost per unit	Fixed cost
A1 Austria	A11	...	...	...	...
	A12	...	...	...	
A2 China	A21	...	...	...	...
	A22	...	...	...	
B Czech Republic	B1	...	...	...	...
	B2	...	...	...	
C Austria	C1	...	...	...	...
	C2	...	...	...	

Sourcing objectives

Products	Raw materials and components	Years	Quantities	Cost per unit
A11	A111	...	...	...
	A112	...	...	...
A12	A121	...	...	...
	A122	...	...	...
A21	A211	...	...	...
	A212	...	...	...
A22	A221	...	...	...
	A222	...	...	...
B1	B11	...	...	...
	B12	...	...	...
B2	B21	...	...	...
	B22	...	...	...
C1	C11	...	...	...
	C12	...	...	...
C2	C21	...	...	...
	C22	...	...	...

Company objectives

Years	Turnover	Contribution margin 3	Cash Flow	Free cash flow
20xx	60	9.6	3.6	2.6
20xx + 1	62	10	4	0.8
20xx + 2	68	10.8	4.6	3.4
20xx + 3	71	11.7	5.5	4.3
20xx + 4	74	13	6.8	5.6

Figures in millions of EUR

— = not possible to calculate at this level

... = not displayed to shorten the figure

Figure 14.6: Strategic objectives of FFA (continued)

15 Determining the level of standardization and differentiation of market offers

15.1 Preliminary remarks

In this chapter, the focus is on the market offer, the most visible part of a company's international strategy. The market offer is shaped by the marketing of the company. Marketing can be defined as an organizational function made up of a set of processes for creating value, and for communicating and delivering this value to customers together with processes for managing customer relationships (Keegan/Green, 2008, p. 4). Marketing is implemented via the marketing mix which is often referred to as the 4 P's: product, pricing, promotion and place. Within marketing, the main topics of this chapter are the product offer and the company's brands. While the other elements are also of relevance, product and brand are usually the core of the marketing mix.

15.2 Particularities of international marketing

International marketing refers to marketing in at least two different countries. It has a number of characteristics which distinguish it from domestic marketing. The information requirements, for example, are more complex and gathering information is far more challenging. Reliable market research data is not available for every country and secondary data which can be found easily for Western European countries often simply does not exist for emerging countries, making primary market research necessary. The complexity of international marketing is higher, due to geographic distance, different languages, different cultures, different consumption patterns, etc. Furthermore, the risks are usually higher in international marketing. Resource commitment and the costs of entering a foreign market are usually high while the management's intuition and market knowledge is less well developed for foreign markets (Zentes/Swoboda/Schramm-Klein, 2010, pp. 5 ff.).

The basic question which companies need to answer with regard to marketing for foreign markets is this: Can the company successfully use the same, or very similar, marketing in the foreign markets or does the marketing need to be adapted to the specific local conditions?

However, there is a more profound challenge in international marketing. International marketing implies more than just a multiplication of the domestic marketing efforts in a number of foreign markets and approaching the customers in those markets with the best possible marketing. Beyond this, international marketing is characterized by interdependencies, both between each foreign market and the home country and between the different foreign markets (Backhaus/Büschken/ Voeth, 2003, p. 56 f.). This is illustrated in **Figure 15.1**.

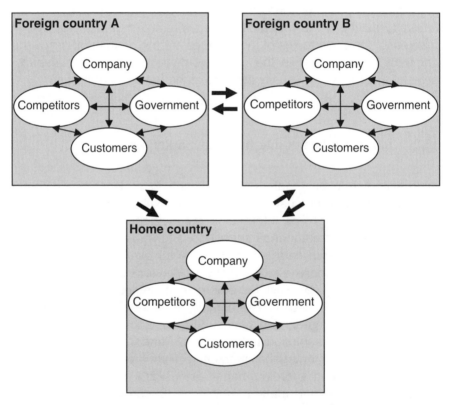

Figure 15.1: Interdependencies between marketing in different countries

Different country markets can be coupled in many ways:

- **Coupling with regard to customers:** Customers will often be aware of the company's marketing in another market, through media and travel. Lower-quality products abroad may damage the image at home. Lower prices abroad for identical products may irritate the customer and lead to arbitrage, i.e. cross-border buying. For example, European customers increasingly import their cars from other European countries. The same positioning in different countries can help to reinforce the company image, while a different positioning will water it down. With the rise of the Internet, the coupling of markets has drastically increased and customers now regularly search for information on the foreign websites of companies and in this way are exposed to the marketing in those countries. In B2B markets, coupling may mean that a specific home country customer also buys from the company in a foreign country and expects the same products, the same price and the same level of service there. In some industries, there may be global lead markets. If a company is successful in the USA, that gives it an image advantage in all other markets. In this case, committing resources to the US market may have spillover effects into other markets.

- **Coupling with regard to the company** itself refers, e.g., to economies of scale that can be achieved through standardized marketing. If a company enters a foreign country with a standardized market offer, it may be able to reduce its prices in the home market. Alternatively, a company may serve a new market demand in a foreign country with a product which can also be offered in the home market at a later stage. Operations in different markets can be cross-financed, at least in the short run. Thus, cash-flow in one foreign market may be used to enter a second foreign market. And losses in a foreign market may be offset, for a while, by profits in another market.

- **Coupling with regard to competition:** Companies may face the same competitor in different markets. This may influence the company's conduct in those markets. If the competitor uses globally standardized marketing, the accompanying economies of scale may force a company to do the same, simply in order to remain competitive. An alternative response would be to to avoid the price competition by offering a locally adapted product. In every case, being confronted with the same competitors abroad requires coordination between the different markets. Companies can observe the competitors' behavior and strategy in one market and become better able to respond in a second market. Or companies can attack a competitor in one market, e.g. by lowering prices, in order to reduce its contribution margins with the ultimate objective of weakening the competitor's strategic positions in other markets.

- **Coupling through governments** and other institutions: Country markets are influenced by governments in many ways. For example, the freedom of trade cannot be restricted within the EU and this makes locally adapted pricing difficult. Governments of different countries may also decide jointly upon technical standards. In another scenario, the introduction of a product in one market may lead to governmental pressure to introduce it in other markets as well, as the pharmaceutical industry illustrates. In price-regulated industries governments may use the price in a foreign market as the reference price for the home country. Companies may be met with anti-dumping measures if they try to sell products more cheaply in a foreign market than at home.

15.3   Basic options for international marketing

Companies have a number of different options when designing their international marketing (Hollensen, 2011, pp. 455 ff.). These can be shown along a continuum from full standardization to full differentiation (full local adaptation), as **Figure 15.2** illustrates.

At one extreme, a company may adapt its marketing fully to each host market. **Locally adapted marketing** identifies the differences in the customer demand in the various countries and tries to provide a market offer that is fully aligned with local conditions. At the far end of the scale, products are developed specifically for each foreign market. This exploits the market opportunities in each market optimally, since the product characteristics, the price level, the advertising campaign, the distribution channels, etc. are all chosen with regard to this country market. A strategy of this kind often follows the acquisition of a successful brand in a foreign country. In Chapter 13, **Inset 13.2** on Carlsberg showed the use of locally adapted marketing through local brands.

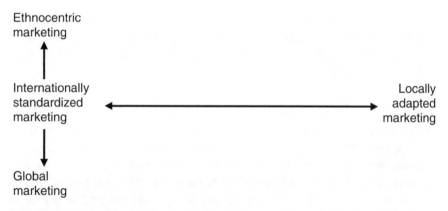

Figure 15.2: Standardization, differentiation and types of international marketing

At the other extreme, a company often tries to sell the same product worldwide, with the same (or least very similar) pricing, the same positioning, and the same advertising campaign via the same distribution channels. This **internationally standardized marketing** is based on the idea that customer demand is converging internationally and that customers are willing to buy the same product worldwide. An additional argument that is made in favor of this strategy is that an internationally standardized product offer will greatly bring down costs and, as a result lower product prices too. Although customers might still have different preferences, they will be willing to sacrifice them for lower prices (Levitt, 1983). In company practice, internationally standardized marketing emerges in two different ways:

- Often, companies just extend the market offer which has been developed for their home country to the foreign market. This is called **ethnocentric marketing:** the domestic marketing mix is used in the foreign markets as well. This may seem naive but some of the most successful companies in the world have used ethnocentric marketing and just imposed their products in other countries where they were welcomed as innovations and symbols of a new lifestyle. US companies like Coca-Cola, Levi's and McDonald's did this in the decades after the Second World War.
- A more modern approach by companies that are already active in many different countries applies standardization in another way. In **global marketing**, all countries in which the company is active are seen as one market. The market offer is developed with this overall

market in mind and with the objective of achieving global efficiency and economies of scale while appealing to the (uniform) tastes of customers in different countries. Victorinox provides an example (see **Inset 13.1**).

There is an interesting trend to note with regard to these basic options: In the past, companies assumed that customer needs in different countries were very varied, and at that time marketing was the company function that was most closely adapted to the local conditions. However, in recent years the convergence of customer demand that was predicted by marketing guru Levitt 30 years ago has become a reality in many industries. Sony Playstations, Apple iPhones, Red Bull Energy Drinks, Dyson vacuum cleaners, Rolex watches, Cartier jewelry, and Zara clothing are all sold in a standardized way around the world. More and more often, companies centralize, or at least tightly coordinate the marketing in different countries, to achieve a coherent market offer in globally interlinked markets.

There is another important remark to make with regard to global marketing: If the company wishes to sell standardized products in all its markets, then this needs to be recognized as a dominant criterion when new foreign markets are being selected. For this means that only markets with a rather similar customer demand may be selected, i.e. countries where demand for the standardized market offer of the company is expected to be sufficiently high. In contrast, locally adapted marketing is more flexible: if a company is willing to develop specific market offers, then it can select any market which is generally attractive.

15.4   Benefits of standardization and differentiation

Standardizing the market offer in all foreign markets has a number of **benefits** for a company (Ghauri/Cateora, 2006, p. 246 f.):

- The predominant benefit is **cost advantages**. With standardized products, companies can achieve global economies of scale. A supply chain aspect adds to these savings: standardized products greatly reduce logistics costs because they can easily be stocked centrally, safety buffers can be lower, handling is much easier, etc. Together, these cost advantages reduce the price per unit. This enables the company to sell for a lower price which leads to higher market shares. This, in turn, leads to even larger production volumes and on this basis the company can become the cost and price leader in an industry.

- While cost is the reason most often cited in literature, the argument is one-sided. In fact, standardization is not applied only to products that are facing strong price competition. At the other end of the product range, luxury brands like Cartier, Rolex or Porsche are frequently marketed in a standardized manner around the world. Here, the value of the products stems to a large extent from a brand that creates aspirations in any part of the world. This adds to the luxury appeal of the brand. These examples show that a global brand can create a **uniform international image** which enhances customer demand.

- Standardized products can maintain or increase the **loyalty of customers** that travel or move around the world. If customers can visit the familiar McDonald's restaurant in another country or buy the same cosmetics brands, this enhances their commitment to the brand. However, if this effect is to be created, the product offered under the brand should be the same or at least similar.

- Another advantage of standardized market offers is **easier international coordination** of marketing processes. Experience, know-how and best practices can be transferred from one market to another. Good advertising campaigns that are successful in one country can be used in another country, etc.

On the other hand, there are **good reasons to adapt** the market offer to each country market:

- The most important reason for adaptation is to optimize the appeal to **heterogeneous customer demand** in different countries. Standardized products are the equivalent to a mass market approach in domestic marketing. Targeting the "average" customer may not optimally appeal to any local customer and, thus, not fully exploit the sales potential in the host country. This may be the consequence of cultural influences and different consumption patterns, and is very common in many industries. For example, the consumption of beef and pork around the world reveals extreme differences, influenced by tradition and religion. Taste with regard to alcoholic beverages like beer, wine and spirits also differs strongly. Clothing styles, too, are influenced by culture. The demand for winter tires or air conditioning is influenced by the climatic situation. Furthermore, the spending power of the average consumer in different countries remains extremely divergent, which leads to different price-demand functions. And if prices for standardized products diverge too far in different countries, arbitrage will occur. To avoid this, different income levels often imply an adaptation of the product offer to the local market and the spending power of its consumers.

- It is also beneficial for sales if the market offer is adapted to the **competitive situation**. Competitive advantages only exist relative to other companies in the market. It may be that the market offer in the home market would not allow the company to achieve the same position in a foreign market. For example, although Walmart is the price leader in US grocery retailing, when the company entered Germany, it faced stiff competition from the discounters. And the market offer that was sufficient to make it superior to its US competitors was not cheap enough to make it superior to Aldi and Lidl in Germany.

- Sometimes a company has to comply with **legal requirements** (e.g. technical standards) which may make it necessary to adapt the market offer. This is, for instance, the case for switchboards.

Standardization and local adaptation represent extremes of a continuum. In company practice, such extremes are rather rare. No company really sells exactly the same product for exactly the same price through the same distribution channels with the same advertising slogan (not translated into the foreign language) placed in exactly the same media worldwide. And hardly any company creates a totally different set of products for each country market. There is a wide range of positions along the continuum; hybrid strategies try to combine the advantages of standardization and of local adaptation. These are described in the next section.

15.5   Hybrid strategies to combine the advantages of different basic options

15.5.1 Considering different product features

Products are complex entities, combinations of tangible and intangible elements. Beyond the core product there are additional elements such as packaging, branding and other augmented features, like support services (Czinkota/Ronkainen, 2008).

With regard to the core products, it is possible to offer completely standardized products or to develop specific products for each country market. But it is also possible to modify products sold in the home market (to a greater or lesser degree) to meet the specific needs of the host countries. In such cases the basic product remains standardized but certain product features are adapted. An example of this is given in **Inset 15.1**.

Inset 15.1: Volkswagen adapts its cars to the US consumer

In 2007, Volkswagen realized that its cars were too expensive in the USA. The VW models Jetta and Passat were substantially more expensive than the comparable models Toyota Camry and Toyota Corolla. Unsurprisingly, the Toyota models were selling much better.

Volkswagen realized that it had built in too many technical features that the consumers were not willing to pay for. The company started to offer "lighter" models, with fewer features and accessories. This enabled it to offer the models for a few thousand dollars less and to reduce its prices to the level of the Toyota models.

The USA is far from Europe and as a result, coupling between the markets is weak. Despite this, in 2011, with a weak US dollar, the unwelcome side effects of VW's strategy became evident. With the US Jetta much cheaper than the same model in Germany, German customers increasingly started to import Jettas from the USA. Even after all the additional costs for logistics, and for minor modifications

└ to the cars so that they would comply to legal standards in
  Germany, German customers still saved thousands of euros.

To minimize the cost of modification for a foreign market, companies
can use product design policies that allow them to modify their products to meet local requirements at little additional expense. For example, modular design approaches allow the firm to assemble individual
products for each country market by selecting from a range of standardized product components that can be used worldwide. Such common platform approaches start with the design of a uniform core product or platform to which customized attachments can be added for
each local market (Kotabe/Helsen, 2008, p. 355 f.; Morschett/Schramm-
Klein/Zentes, 2010, p. 370).

One strategy that allows a company to sell a standardized product in
each country market despite specific local requirements is a strategy
referred to as "built-in-flexibility". This is common in electronic products.
The products incorporate all possible local differences and adapt flexibly to the local requirements. For example, mobile phones adapt to differences in voltage, different network frequencies and multiple menu
languages (Morschett/Schramm-Klein/Zentes, 2010, p. 71).

15.5.2 Considering different marketing mix elements

The advantages of standardization and of adaptation are not the same
for all the elements of the marketing mix. For this reason, companies
may standardize their various marketing mix elements to a different
degree. The benefits of economies of scale are most strongly influenced by a standardization of the product. This is, therefore, the element that is most often highly standardized.

But even for exactly the same product, prices in different countries may
be differentiated to a greater or lesser extent. There are two main factors which influence the decision on how far product prices should differ between countries:

- **Price elasticity of demand**: for many reasons, the price-demand
  function can differ between countries. Different income levels, differ-

ent consumer taste and different competing offers often lead to different demand functions. This means that companies should attempt to charge different prices in different countries in order to optimally exploit the customers' willingness to pay.

- **Degree of separation of markets**: Price differentiation is only possible to the degree that markets are separated. Otherwise, arbitrage will occur, together with other negative overspills between the markets, as explained above in section 15.2. Large distances between countries, tariff barriers and information barriers are examples of separating factors which lead to higher transaction costs and this increases the range within which a company can differentiate its prices.

A company can also actively exploit the marketing mix to increase the separation between markets. Ways to do this include offering different products (or products with slightly different features) in different markets and using different brand names. In such cases the price differentiation is supported by differences in other elements of the marketing mix.

15.5.3 Considering the product and brand portfolio

As most companies offer a range of products, rather than a single product, companies may adapt the selection of products that they offer in each market. With wide product ranges, it is often possible to adapt the product offer to the specific needs of the customers: for example, to adapt to a lower income level in the foreign market by offering mainly products at the lower end of the price range. Linked to this option is the question of the **product lifecycle**. While older products have already been eliminated from the market offer in more sophisticated markets, they may still be part of the range in other countries. As an example of different products and different lifecycles, **Inset 15.2** outlines Volkswagen's offer in selected countries.

Inset 15.2: Volkswagen adapts its product range to countries

Volkswagen does not offer the same selection of models in all country markets. Instead, it adapts the product range to the specific customer demand. For example, in India for a long period it offered only the Passat, the Jetta and the Touareg. In **Figure 15.3**, the availability of selected car models in different countries is listed.

Model	Country				
	Germany	USA	India	Brazil	Japan
Gol				X	
Golf	X	X		X	X
Touran	X				X
Fox	X			X	
Scirocco	X				X
Sharan	X				X
Polo	X		X	X	X
Vento			X		
Eos	X	X			
Jetta	X	X	X	(x)	
Voyage				X	
Passat / CC	X	X	X	X	X
Routan		X			
Tiguan	X	X		X	X
Touareg	X	X	X	X	X
New Beetle	X		X	X	
Phaeton	X		X		

Figure 15.3: Availability of selected car models of Volkswagen in different countries

For example, the Gol is a model that was specifically developed for the Latin American market and has for many years been the best-selling model there. It is produced mainly in Brazil. The old Volkswagen beetle was produced and sold in Mexico until 2003 but had been withdrawn from Europe as early as 1985. Different generations of the Golf have been sold around the world. Since 2008, the Golf VI has been the model sold in Europe and most other advanced markets. But in Latin America the company still builds the Golf IV, which is also sold in Canada. The Golf V is still produced and sold in South Africa. The VW Routan is sold only in North America (USA, Canada, Mexico). The Routan is a minivan, a rebadged variant of a former Chrysler model. In Brazil, the Jetta is not sold as a limousine but only as a wagon. The Touareg is sold in all countries. The Phaeton is offered in Germany and in India, but not in Brazil or the USA. This demonstrates that the decision to offer a luxury car model is not necessarily a question of the average income in the country.

With regard to branding, which is strategically closely linked to the product policy, very different strategies can be observed. **Global brands** can be used to create a uniform image but the opposite strategy, using **local brands** to apply brand differentiation, can also be used to separate markets or to appeal better to the local customer. Sometimes brand differentiation is the result of the acquisition of local brands that have substantial brand equity and are therefore retained. For example, Unilever sells a similar range of ice cream products under the brand Lusso in Switzerland, Langnese in Germany, Frigo in Spain, Good Humor in the USA, Walls in the UK, Algida in Italy and many other brand names. Some companies have a complex architecture of different brand layers, as **Inset 15.3** demonstrates.

Inset 15.3: Different types of brands at Anheuser-Busch InBev
(text based on Anheuser-Busch InBev, 2011)

Anheuser-Busch InBev is the world's leading brewery company. It was created after the acquisition of the American brewery giant Anheuser-Busch by the Belgian InBev company. The company owns about 200 brands worldwide, of which 14 achieve sales of over 1 billion USD annually.

The brand architecture is composed of three different layers of brands: global brands which are sold in virtually every country in

Brand type	Brands
Global brands	Budweiser, Stella Artois, Beck's
Multi-country brands	Hoegaarden, Leffe
Examples of local brands	USA: Michelob, Bud Light; Argentina: Quilmes Belgium: Jupiler Brazil: Skol, Antarctica China: Sedrin, Harbin Germany: Diebels, Franziskaner Russia: Bagbier UK: Bass, Whitbread

Figure 15.4: Brand structure of Anheuer-Busch InBev

which Anheuser-Busch InBev operates, multi-country brands which are sold in dozens of countries, and local brands which are usually only sold in a single country market.

The three **global brands** are all very strong in their home markets and from there have been internationalized. Budweiser is one of the most valuable beer brands around the world and is offered in markets from the USA to Russia or China. Stella Artois is the best selling Belgian beer worldwide and is sold in about 80 countries. Beck's is the world's best selling German beer, sold in more than 80 countries.

Two traditional Belgian brands (of the former InBev group) have become **multi-country brands**. Leffe Blonde and Leffe Brown are Belgian Abbey ales dating back to the 13th century. Hoegaarden, currently one of the company's fastest growing brands, is a Belgian wheat beer which dates back to 1445. Hoegaarden is successfully marketed in countries as diverse as Russia, France, USA, Ukraine, Spain and Austria.

The **local brands** often have a strong heritage and position in their national markets. For example, Antarctica is the third best selling beer in Brazil and has been produced since 1885. Skol is the leading beer in the Brazilian market. Quilmes is the market leader in Argentina and Bud Light is a strongly selling beer in the USA.

With this brand architecture the company tries to reap the advantages of global brands while simultaneously adapting sufficiently to local markets to exploit the full market potential.

To determine which products should be introduced in which country, the company needs to analyze the demand in the different markets it serves, including preferences for certain product features, price levels, etc. But it also needs to consider the cost of adaptation or of creating new products for a specific market, a cost which usually reduces economies of scale. **Inset 15.4** proposes a process for determining the international product and brand portfolio.

Inset 15.4: Determining the product and brand portfolio

In **Figure 15.5**, a process is proposed for determining the product range for a specific foreign market and for modifying the product and brand portfolio in the home market. This presents the simplified case of one foreign market. However, the process can also be applied if the foreign market is a country cluster or if the company is already active in a larger number of foreign markets.

In **Step 1**, the company has to evaluate the demand in the foreign market concerned and to compare it with the existing product portfolio of the company. In the illustration, this is limited to the home country product portfolio but a company that is already international can use the entire product portfolio in all established country markets as the starting point.

In **Step 2**, the company selects from its existing portfolio the products that best fit the demand in the foreign market and introduces them to the market. In this step, the market entry mode for the products needs to be decided as well. This decision has been discussed in detail in Chapter 7.

Figure 15.5: Process for determining the product and brand portfolio

In **Step 3**, for each of the products the company must determine whether it should be offered on the foreign market in a standardized way or whether it should be modified to adapt to the specific needs of the foreign market:

- For this analysis, the **cost of modification** has to be calculated. This cost will depend on the extent of necessary changes, and vary according to the extent that the product has a modular design, and also the production technology used. There must be an assessment of the impact on the entire company of reduced economies of scale together with the increased complexity of production and logistics.
- The principal **benefits of modification** are increased sales. Obviously, the size of the foreign market plays a major role in the calculation. The larger the market, the more likely that adaptation to this market will more than offset the modification cost. If the company is active in many different markets, it should evaluate whether the modified product can also be offered in the home market or in third markets.

As **Step 4**, the company should conduct a benefit/cost analysis for the development of new products for the foreign market under consideration. Again, it is not only the cost of developing a new product that needs to be considered, but also the increased complexity for the company.

In **Step 5**, the company may decide to introduce the newly developed products from the foreign market to the home market or other third markets.

Figure 15.6 illustrates the product and brand portfolio in the home country and the foreign market during the process.

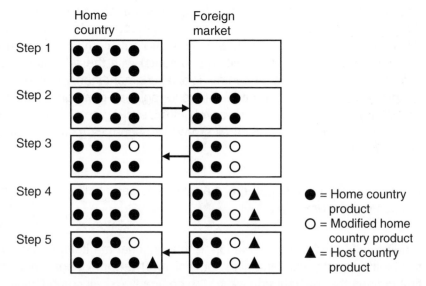

Figure 15.6: Product and brand portfolio in the foreign market and the home country during the process

Sometimes the product portfolio produced in this way for the home market and all foreign markets becomes the starting point for further analysis. Given that complexity in the international product portfolio is a major cost driver, the company should constantly review whether it can reduce the number of product variants and models. Eliminating variants and attempting to sell the same or similar products in many markets often proves beneficial.

15.5.4 Considering different market segments

Markets consist of many different customers and even in the domestic market these customers are not homogeneous but differ in their needs, income levels, buying attitudes, etc. This heterogeneity is usually drastically increased in international marketing contexts. With customers from different countries, it is difficult or impossible to find a marketing approach that wil appeal to all. On the other hand, it is very expensive to target the marketing to individual customer needs.

One solution to this problem is to divide the entire, heterogeneous market in which a company is active into a number of smaller, distinct segments which are characterized by homogeneous demand. Market segmentation allows the company to approach each segment in a rather standardized way while the different segments are targeted with a different market offer. This is a hybrid strategy combining the advantages of standardization (within segments) with the advantages of differentiation (between segments). Typical segmentation variables are geographic criteria (e.g. countries or world regions), demographic criteria (like age, family size, income or religion), psychographic criteria (like lifestyle) and behavioral criteria (like product usage) (Armstrong/Kotler, 2007, p. 166).

In international marketing, there are two basic segmentation methods, illustrated in **Figure 15.7**.

Traditionally, market segmentation in international marketing has tried to identify country clusters. This form of **international segmentation** first defines the relevant criteria for the company (e.g. income levels or product usage or lifestyle) and then on this basis groups countries together. Local adaptation to each country market can be seen as an extreme form of international segmentation, since it considers each country as a segment on its own.

For practical reasons, companies often group countries within one region together and treat them in a similar way. Western Europe, Eastern Europe, Latin America, North America, etc. are regions that are often

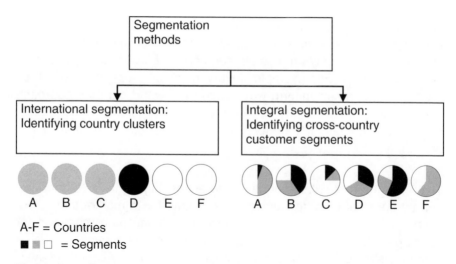

A-F = Countries
■ ▪ □ = Segments

Figure 15.7: Basic methods of market segmentation in international marketing

combined into country clusters. But segmentation criteria must be company-specific. Pharmaceutical companies may distinguish between liberal and regulated markets, while food companies may use religion (which influences the consumption of some food types) as a criterion.

After this, the company develops a specific marketing strategy for each fairly homogeneous country cluster. In this approach too, a company should always consider coupling between market segments and seek to exploit synergy effects among the clusters, only adapting the market offer when necessary.

Nowadays multinational companies often use another approach. Having observed that differences within a country may be larger than between countries, they use **integral segmentation** to identify cross-country customer segments that have similar needs. With regard to consumer electronics, for example, the difference between a twenty-year old Swiss, a twenty-year old American and a twenty-year old Japanese may be much less than between two different generations within Switzerland. The same is likely to be true for clothing styles, music, and entertainment. The idea here is that, no matter where they are located, each of these segments may be approached in a similar way (e.g. MP3 players for the younger group and CD players with expensive loudspeakers for the older group). Another option for a company is to identify a single target segment in different countries and to use a niche strategy, to focus only on a single segment worldwide (Keegan/Green, 2008, p. 245 f.). For example, luxury manufacturers often sell their products in a rather uniform way around the world but they approach only a single cross-country segment or a small number of segments. Integral segmentation, therefore, is basically a global marketing approach.

The existence of within-country differences highlights a further important consideration: few companies, if any, try to market their products to all the customers in a country. It is much more common for companies to target specific segments. What this means, is that a company should not evaluate a potential target country based on average country values but on the characteristics of its target segments. For example, the average income in India or China may be very low but the average income of the target segment for luxury goods is often higher than in developed countries. And the size of this segment is substantial in both markets.

15.6   Recommendations for determining the level of standardization and differentiation of market offers

15.6.1 Conditions influencing the decision

As the previous sections have illustrated, the determination of the appropriate level of standardization and local adaptation is influenced by many different factors (Hollensen, 2011, pp. 456 ff.).

As a first factor, the **intended strategy** with regard to local responsiveness and global integration must be considered. It is important to note that there are almost always factual differences between countries. But some companies prefer to emphasize the differences while others prefer to emphasize the commonalities.

Second, the homogeneity or heterogeneity of **customer demand** in the different countries must be examined. This includes factors such as consumer socio-demographics, tastes, consumption patterns, purchasing power, etc. The convergence of customer demand is different for different product groups. In **Figure 15.8**, the culture-boundedness of different product groups is shown. The less culture-bound the product category, the more feasible is product standardization.

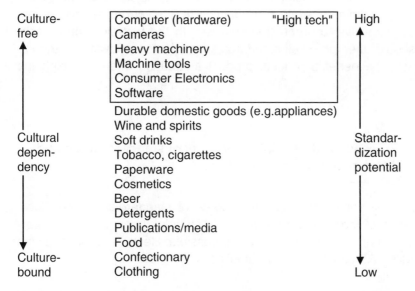

Figure 15.8: Culture-boundedness of different product categories
(Müller/Gelbrich, 2004, p. 555)

The **relevance and size of the market segment** is another influence factor. The more important the segment, due to its size, perhaps, or strategic relevance in the industry, the more likely a company is to adapt to its specific needs.

The **competitive situation** is another factor. The presence of many national or global competitors influences a company's own market offer and its competitive situation.

The relevance of **governmental influences** has already been mentioned. Heterogeneous legal requirements usually lead to differentiated products. Trade barriers have a more indirect effect. These usually lead to local production in the host country which often makes the local adaptation of products less expensive.

Finally, the **product and the production technology features** must be considered. Modification costs differ greatly between products. Product adaptations may only require changes in minor features that are not costly to modify. Some production processes are more flexible than others with regard to different production batches. Importantly, some production technologies may make it possible to achieve substantial economies of scale in production (e.g. electronics) while others are less sensitive to production volumes. In the first situation companies should attempt to sell standardized products worldwide; in the latter case, the benefits of local product adaptation often outweigh the costs.

15.6.2 Process for determining the level of standardization and differentiation of market offers

The process for determining the degree of standardization and local adaptation of the market offer is highly complex because many different options and hybrid strategies are possible. Here, the process given in **Figure 15.9** can serve as a guideline.

There are two starting points. First, the markets in which the company is currently active, and those in which it intends to be active in the near future, need to be researched with regard to customer demand, etc. (**Step 1a**). Second, the strategic position in the integration-responsiveness framework has to be considered (**Step 1b**).

In **Step 2,** a basic decision must be made as to whether the company considers the differences found to exist between the country markets to be relatively unimportant, and therefore intends to target them with one offer or, in contrast, whether the company is willing to adapt the offer to heterogeneous country markets. This decision is based on the homogeneity or heterogeneity of the markets and on the strategic international orientation.

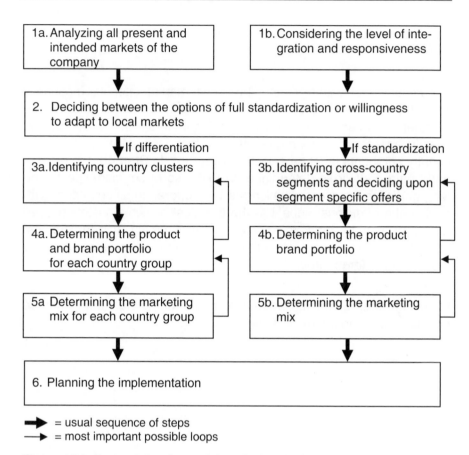

Figure 15.9: **Process for determining the level of standardization and differentiation of market offers**

If the company wants to adapt to local market conditions, it needs to segment the total market, following relevant segmentation criteria (**Step 3a**). The result of this step is a set of country groups with fairly homogeneous demand. In the extreme case of fully locally adapted marketing, each country is a separate segment. In **Step 4a**, the company must develop the product and brand portfolio for each country cluster. The process for this step has been explained in detail in **Inset 15.4**. In **Step 5a**, the other elements of the marketing mix are determined for each country group. Couplings between the different country groups have to be considered in this step. Since the product policy is usually dominant, the other elements of the marketing mix are often a direct consequence of Step 4a. But the different mix elements can be adapted to local markets to some extent, even if the product is the same.

A company that wants to use the same market offer internationally should first identify cross-country customer segments and decide whether the heterogeneity between the segments requires a segment-specific adaptation of the market offer. In that case, the targeted cross-country segments must be selected (**Step 3b**). In **Step 4b**, the product and brand portfolio is determined. In the case of segment-specific offers, portfolios are created which are then offered in all countries. Otherwise, the offer must appeal to the broadest possible customer base across all country markets served by the company. In **Step 5b**, the marketing mix is determined, either in a uniform way or adapted to the cross-country target groups.

In the final **Step 6**, the implementation of the marketing strategy can be planned, including the market offer.

16 Configuring the value creation process and determining the operation modes

16.1 Preliminary remarks

The **configuration of the value creation process** refers to how the different value-adding activities of the company are set up in different geographical locations. The company has to determine the number of locations for each activity and fix the specific locations. In this chapter, we will mainly focus on operations: the sourcing, production and logistic processes. R&D processes are not considered (for R&D processes see Morschett/Schramm-Klein/Zentes, 2010, p. 347 ff.).

In Part III, we discussed the selection of new markets and the various market entry modes. The selections made will lead to a configuration of sales activities in different countries with related production activities for each sales market. In Part IV, the perspective was that of a SME intending to sell in its home market and searching for a production and sourcing location abroad. These selections lead to a configuration of production activities with the home market as the target. These two steps are both crucial when going international, but a company that has reached the next stage and is becoming a truly international company has to solve more complex configuration questions:

- Production locations abroad can serve two purposes simultaneously: they can produce for the home market and for the host country market at the same time.
- Furthermore, a foreign production location can (in addition or exclusively) serve as an export platform (Monteiro, 2010). In this case, the affiliate's output is sold to a large extent in third markets.

Taking all this together, a company has to select production and sourcing locations for all the markets that it serves and this decision must not be approached on a country-by-country basis but in terms of the overall optimization of the sales and production network.

The location decision is closely linked to the **determination of the operation mode**. A company not only has to decide where it wants to locate its different activities but it also has to decide who will carry out those activities, since either outsourcing to independent companies or joint activities with partners may be appropriate options.

In this chapter, options for the configuration of the value creation process and for the operation modes will be presented, followed by recommendations for determining an operations strategy.

16.2   Configuring the value creation process

16.2.1   Configuring the value creation process as a two-dimensional problem

A company has on one hand **to decide whether to produce a product group for all the various country markets concentrated in one single factory or whether to produce decentralized**. For example, Swiss manufacturers of luxury watches, like IWC, often locate all their production activities in Switzerland and serve the world market from there. In contrast, Japanese car manufacturers started to relocate their production facilities to target regions in the USA and Europe in the 1980s and nowadays often serve regional markets from regional production sites.

The **advantages of decentralizing production** activities to different countries include the following (see Morschett/Schramm-Klein/Zentes, 2010, p. 326f.):

- **Circumvention of trade barriers**: Companies can save customs duties and overcome non-tariff barriers by locating production in the target markets.
- **Acceptance by local governments**: Host country governments prefer local production, which has benefits for their labor market, trade balance, etc. Often, they are willing to give incentives to companies locating production in their countries.
- **Easier adaptation of the market offer to local markets**: Locating production facilities in the target markets leads to increased sensitivity to local market needs.
- **Advantages in distribution logistics**: By locating production closer to the markets, companies reduce delivery costs and delivery time to their foreign customers. This shortens their time-to-market (which can be very important, for example, for clothing companies like Zara or consumer electronics like the Sony Playstation). Local production also facilitates just-in-time delivery to commercial customers.

- **Increased flexibility and reduced supply risk**: By having production capacity in different countries rather than in one single location, companies can reduce their risk exposure and can shift production to secure supply, for example, in the case of strikes. Furthermore, using different factories makes it possible to reduce costs if there are changes in the cost structure or in the currency exchange rates. In addition, the company becomes less dependent on currency volatility since more of the production costs are incurred in the currencies of the various sales markets.
- **Increased innovation power**: Companies with a decentralized production system benefit from exposure to influences in different countries and this may help them to innovate faster, transfer knowledge better across borders, etc.
- **Better access to local inputs and better relations with local suppliers**: Local production not only facilitates access to customers but also to local inputs. These can be natural resources (oil or ores), agricultural products (coffee or rubber), or other input goods. Relations with suppliers in a foreign market are also improved by locating facilities close by.

In contrast to this, **concentrating production in one location,** often the home country of the company, also has major benefits (Morschett/ Schramm-Klein/Zentes, 2010, p. 327 f.):

- **Economies of scale**: Having one large production plant instead of several smaller ones increases the output volume of the factory, which results in economies of scale.
- **Ease of coordination**: While the dispersion of production processes might reduce production costs, it usually grossly increases coordination costs for the various factories in different countries working in the same production chain. Concentrating production activities in one location reduces the challenge of coordinating dispersed production processes.
- **Better bundling of procurement volume**: Concentrated production usually leads to better bundling of the inputs required. If prices for input goods are centrally negotiated for a large volume delivered to one location, they will often be substantially lower. The coordination effort required to bundle the procurement needs of factories in different countries is high (despite the common use of IT systems for enterprise resource planning) and even if coordination is perfect, suppliers still demand higher prices for decentralized deliveries.

- **Better availability of capabilities in some home countries**: From the perspective of companies from industrialized countries like Germany, the availability of skilled labor at home offers quality advantages that are often not available in other countries.
- **Country-of-origin effect**: For many companies, the home country is still a major source of its image advantage. Producing Swiss watches in Switzerland or a Porsche in Germany provides the companies with a competitive advantage.

There is a second dimension to be considered. In many industries, **the production process can be split into different stages**, which means that the different stages have to be linked to form production chains. The automobile industry is a typical example of multi-stage production. Often, engines and car bodies are produced in specialized factories, usually by the car company itself. Many other parts and components, like the braking system, the seats and the lighting, are produced in other factories, often by independent suppliers such as Bosch or Johnson Controls. In the last stage of production, all these components are transported to an assembly plant where they are combined into the final product.

The different stages in a split production process may all be located in the same location or at least in the same country. Large automobile manufacturers often situate the final assembly plant and the production of the main components in a single location in order to integrate the different production stages optimally. On the other hand, there are products for which the production stages can easily be moved to different locations. If the locations are in different countries, this leads to **cross-border production processes**.

16.2.2   Basic production configurations

The combination of the two dimensions lead to four basic production configurations. In **Figure 16.1**, a three-stage production process is used to illustrate them:

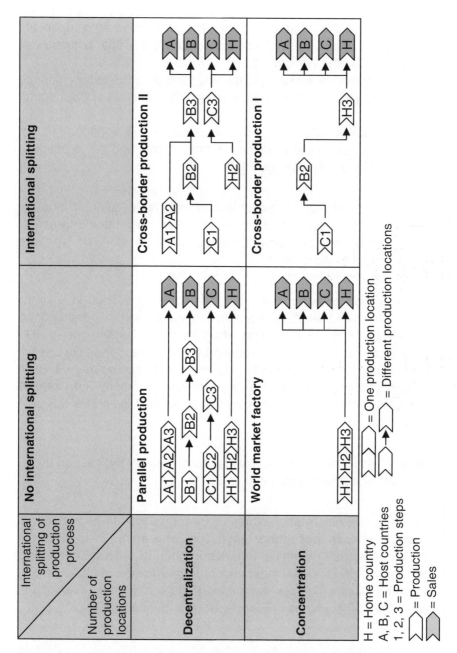

Figure 16.1: Basic types of production configurations (adapted and extended from Knüppel, 1997, p. 139ff.; Kutschker/Schmid, 2011, p. 1001; Morschett/Schramm-Klein/Zentes, 2010, pp. 330f.)

- The three stages are the manufacturing of parts from input goods and raw materials in stage 1, then the production of components with these parts in stage 2 and subsequently the final assembly of the finished product in stage 3.
- In the illustration, it is assumed that the finished product is sold in different countries and that the sales activities are always decentralized.
- The four basic configurations of production are the world market factory, parallel production and two forms of cross-border production (see also Holtbrügge/Welge, 2010).

The four types will now be explained and examples given. It must be noted though, that these ideal types are hardly ever found in practice. Varying hybrid configurations combining features of each type are much more common.

In a **world market factory**, a product is wholly produced in a single factory throughout the different production stages and then transported from there to the international markets. This choice is often the result of a global strategic orientation. It represents the highest possible level of concentration and all the benefits of concentration can be reaped. But it also suffers from all the disadvantages of concentration. The example of Ricola's production of confectionery in **Inset 16.1** illustrates this configuration.

Inset 16.1: Ricola using a world market factory (text based on FAZ, 2010; Lebensmittel Zeitung, 2011)

Ricola, the Swiss manufacturer of herbal cough drops and throat drops, produces these drops entirely in Switzerland, in its factory in Laufen. The raw materials, in particular the 13 different herbs, are grown in Switzerland by independent farmers who are closely monitored by Ricola. The company exports 90% of its output, selling in more than 50 countries in Europe, North America and Asia.

The company uses its Swissness in its advertising, with the Alps as part of its image. It is known world-wide and one of the top 20 Swiss brands. Concentrating production in the home country is crucial to support this positioning.

However, the negative side of this strategy is currently becoming evident. As the company pointed out in 2010, an exchange rate of less than 1.30 CHF to the EUR is having a strongly negative impact: Sales volumes in euro are now worth much less in CHF. In 2010, although the company sold more in foreign currency than in previous years, its turnover in CHF was lower.

Raising prices abroad to offset the exchange rate developments would be almost impossible, since Ricola drops are already a high-price product. Yet the fact that all the production costs are in Swiss francs has put pressure on company profits. To counter this development, the company is using two strategies. First, more purchasing is being done abroad. For example, the sweetener for the sugar-less variants is now bought in Germany and more of the marketing expenses have been shifted to the different target countries and thus paid for in the target country currencies. Second, a modest move into cross-border production has been made. While the products are still produced in Switzerland, the packaging – which can be seen as the last step in the production process – is more and more often being done abroad. Ricola now maintains two foreign facilities, one in France and one in the USA, for packaging the drops. The costs for this production stage are now in euro or dollars.

With **parallel production**, full production chains are replicated in different country markets and each factory serves its local market. This is a manifestation of a multinational strategic orientation. Frequently, high trade barriers are the motivation for this production strategy, which is also used in cases where different or locally adapted products are produced for the different markets. Daimler's production of certain car models can serve as an example (**Inset 16.2**).

Inset 16.2: Daimler relocating parts of its production to the USA
(text based on FAZ, 2009)

The locations for the production of Daimler's main volume model, the C-class, have traditionally been Sindelfingen and Bremen in Germany. However, a number of developments in recent years have led Daimler to reconsider this configuration. The dollar has steadily decreased in value, making imports from Germany into the USA much more expensive. Furthermore, sales of the C-class in the USA have been rising and the competition in this car segment has intensified.

So Daimler decided to relocate its production, a decision which brought intense protests from the workers in Sindelfingen. Starting from 2014, the C-class will not be produced in Sindelfingen any longer. While 60% of the world production of the C-class will be manufactured in Bremen, 20% will be produced in the USA, 10% in China and 10% in South Africa. With this move to parallel production, Daimler intends to reduce production costs (by moving more of its production to lower-cost countries), to achieve more independence from exchange rates (by moving some of its production to the currency areas of its sales) and to lower logistics and transport costs.

One factor that contributed to this decision was the fact that Mercedes has had a positive experience in the USA. The production of the Mercedes M- and R-class in the USA did not hurt the brand's image.

Multi-stage production processes are frequently designed as **cross-border production** processes. These are characterized by geographically dispersed production stages that are linked by the international flow of goods between different production units. Given the interrelatedness of production and sourcing, some of the production units might not even belong to the company, but to suppliers. Production processes of this kind are manifestations of a transnational strategy in which companies try to meet local requirements and achieve global synergy effects at the same time. With cross-border production I, each production stage is concentrated in a single country but no two consecutive stages are located in the same country. In the case of cross-border production II, each production stage is partly decentralized, that is, realized in more than one location. In addition, the different production stages are located in different countries. Cross-border production is almost always realized in a hybrid combination of these ideal types.

Cross-border production has major advantages. In cases where the production chain is not split, all the production stages are exposed to the same country conditions. However, as different production stages have different requirements (e.g. different labor intensity), it is clear that if there is only one location, then there will be suboptimal locations for some stages. This disadvantage can be overcome by splitting production and selecting optimal locations for each specific production stage. In this way the specialization advantages of different country locations can be optimally exploited. For instance, labor intensive manufacturing steps can take place in low-wage countries while knowledge- and capital-intensive stages can be located in countries where skilled labor and the necessary infrastructure are available. However, the interrelatedness of the production stages must also be considered and the coordination efforts and logistics costs that result from fragmentation must be taken into account. **Inset 16.3** describes the example of PrecIn GmbH. This is a real company but the facts and data have been modified to preserve the company's anonymity.

Inset 16.3: PrecIn optimizes the configuration of a split production process

PrecIn is an SME located in Southern Germany. It produces complex precision instruments in a two-stage process: in the first stage complex sophisticated components are produced and in stage two these are assembled into final products. There are basically two types of products: most markets require sophisticated and complicated high-end final products but two developing countries, China and Mexico, have a large demand for fairly simple, standard-level precision instruments.

The products are sold in more than 80 countries around the world. In most countries, this is done by independent distributors. In the most important foreign markets, PrecIn has bought a stake in its former independent distributors or created joint ventures with them.

And in a few recently entered foreign markets, the company has established wholly-owned sales subsidiaries.

The production configuration is illustrated in **Figure 16.2**. All the factories are wholly-owned by the company. Components are produced in the factory in Southern Germany. Even though wages are high in Southern Germany, these components require highly skilled workers and they also contain the core of the company's competitive advantage: its engineering superiority. Keeping this under tight control is important to the company. The procurement of parts and raw materials is carried out centrally at headquarters, also in Southern Germany. The final production of the complex, high-end preci-

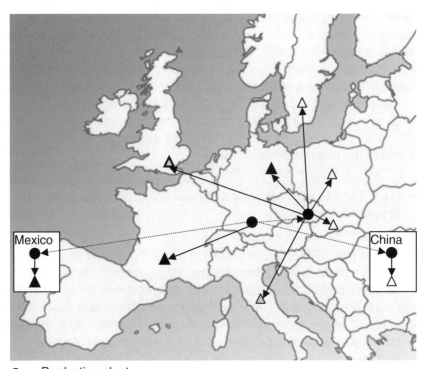

● = Production plant
▲ = Wholly-owned sales unit
△ = Sales joint venture or partially owned sales unit
△ = Independent distributor
→ = Flow of finished products
⋯▶ = Flow of components

Figure 16.2: Configuration of PrecIn GmbH

sion instruments is completed in a factory in Slovakia. From here the products are transported to all the sales units around the world.

However, for the simple standard products that China and Mexico need, this process would be too expensive. For these two markets, PrecIn uses dedicated factories in those two countries. The factory in Germany still supplies the components; only the assembly stage is located in Mexico and in China, exploiting the very low wage levels in these two countries. What makes own production for these countries worthwhile is the combination of a low wage level and the very large and specific demand in these two markets, the demand being different from the demand in most other countries.

16.2.3   Trends

In a general trend in recent decades, **production processes** are becoming **increasingly fragmented,** split into different production stages located in different countries.

At the same time, each stage in the production process is becoming relatively more concentrated, to avoid inefficient duplication. Lower logistics costs and reduced trade barriers have caused this trend. For instance, in areas of regional integration like the European Union, many companies no longer retain dedicated factories for each country but have centralized production to a small number of factories that deliver throughout the region. This trend can be observed clearly in the fast-moving consumer goods industry: whereas in earlier decades national factories were created, now these have been concentrated into **regional factories**. Examples are companies like Nestlé, Unilever and Procter & Gamble.

A further, very common hybrid configuration type is the **hub-and-spoke system**. In this process, many production stages are carried out in a central location but the final assembly is decentralized. The use of this system results from the varying advantages of concentration or decentralization for different production stages. While components can still be transported around the world rather cheaply and tariff barriers are often not very high, the situation is quite different for many finished products. Finished cars and computers are bulky and fall into a different customs tariff category. Leaving them disassembled until they reach the sales country and assembling them there brings many benefits, especially as final assembly is often a fairly simple process which does not require skilled labor. **Inset 16.4** provides an example of a hub-and-spoke system from the automobile industry.

Inset 16.4: Hub-and-spoke network for the Dacia Logan (text based on Schmid/Grosche, 2008, pp. 77 ff.)

The decision of Renault to acquire Dacia was part of its strategy to introduce a low-cost car onto the world markets. With the rise of emerging countries and their need for cheap cars, this is of major importance for the future of a car manufacturer. Producing a car of this type in France would be almost impossible. So in 1999 Renault bought a majority stake of 51% in the Romanian car producer Dacia, a stake which it had increased to 99.3% within three years.

Renault bought the company for a little more than 50 million US dollars but then invested approx. 500 million EUR to restructure and rebuild the production plants as modern facilities. It is noteworthy that the company decided on a low level of automation. For example, the welding is largely carried out manually, which is only usual in the production of high-end cars. Manual production can be used to enhance quality and Renault estimated that the low labor cost in Romania would allow the company to maintain a high level of labor-intensity, even over the longer term. Another advantage of their policy is that the necessary investment in the plants was much lower than it would have been for a highly automated facility.

In addition, the production of the Dacia Logan has a high degree of vertical integration. Almost all the production stages are carried out in two plants in Mioveni in Romania. In addition to the final assembly, also located in Mioveni are the press shop, the weld shop, the paint shop, the engine shop and other component productions. Thus Renault profits from the low labor cost in the country for large parts of the production process. Wages in Romania are more than

90% lower than in France, Renault's home country. Furthermore, 80% of the sourcing volume comes from Romania.

However, some of the sales markets for the Dacia Logan are far from Romania and are characterized by high tariff barriers. For example, Russia has an import tariff of 25% for completely assembled cars, which would destroy the low-cost advantage of the Logan. To counteract this, the Logan is assembled in different locations around the world. For sales in the European market, assembly is in the factory in Romania and the finished cars are transported to the other countries. For other countries, Romania produces completely knocked down kits (CKD) which are transported to the geographically dispersed plants where they are assembled. Thus the car factory and the engine factory in Romania act as central hubs in the production network but the last production stage, assembly, is carried out in plants in Morroco, Colombia, Brazil, South Africa, Russia, Iran and India. In some of these locations (Brazil and Iran), parts for engines are also manufactured locally.

16.3   Determining the operation modes

16.3.1 Basic options

A number of different arrangements are possible for organizing and conducting international business activities (Andersen, 1997, p. 29). These are export modes, contractual operation modes (like licensing, franchising, contract manufacturing) and investment modes (like joint ventures or wholly-owned subsidiaries). A detailed explanation of the available foreign operation modes is given by Welch, Benito and Petersen (2007).

A company that is active in a number of foreign countries and has a complex international configuration has to determine the operation mode for each foreign operation. In **Inset 16.5** the example of the Dacia Logan is used to illustrate the variety of operation modes that companies apply. The example is based on **Inset 16.4** which explained the hub-and-spoke network of Dacia.

Inset 16.5: The operation modes of Dacia
(text based on Schmid/Grosche, 2008, pp. 77 ff.)

As described in **Inset 16.3**, the Dacia Logan is produced in a hub-and-spoke network. Most of the production stages are carried out in Romania but the final assembly takes place in eight different sales regions. However, Renault has not established new production locations in all of these regions but uses a very flexible strategy to identify the best operation mode in each region.

In Russia, the Avtoframos plant was established in a joint venture between Renault and the city of Moscow.

In Morroco, the Logan is assembled by the contract manufacturer SOMACA (Société Marocaine de Construction Automobile) in Casablanca. Renault owns 54% of the company but competitors Fiat and Peugeot also hold stakes in SOMACA. SOMACA assembles the Logan for all Northern African countries. Renault also uses SOMACA for the assembly of the Renault Kangoo for this region.

In Colombia, Renault acquired 60% of the Columbian company Sofasa S.A. which assembles the Logan kits for several countries in Latin America. Three other Renault models are also produced by Sofasa. The company also assembles for Toyota, which holds a 28% stake in Sofasa.

In Iran, Renault has a joint venture with the Iranian authority for industrial development. The joint venture "Renault Pars" is responsible for the sales of the Logan (here, the model is called Tondar) and it produces engines for the model. The final cars are assembled from the CKD kits using engines made locally by the contract car manufacturers Iran Khodro and SAIPA.

In Brazil, Renault owns a factory in Curitiba which produces other Renault models as well as engines for the Logan. Here, the Renault factory is used for the assembly.

In India, Renault created a joint venture with the largest Indian car manufacturer, Mahindra & Mahindra. This assembles the Logan in a Mahindra plant in Nashik.

The production in South Africa will be carried out by Nissan, the strategic alliance partner of Renault in all world markets. Nissan has a factory in Rosslyn in South Africa where the Logan is produced. It will be sold under the Nissan brand in that country.

This example reveals that a company does not always use the same operation mode – even for the same type of operation – in all of its host countries. The choice of operation mode is influenced by many different factors. Among these factors are different host-country conditions (legal restrictions, availability of partners, availability of production capacity, etc.). But the choice of operation mode is also greatly influenced by emerging relationships and existing factories.

A general trend with regard to operation modes, which has continued for several decades, is a reduction in the amount of value added by the company as opposed to external suppliers. The car industry, with the Japanese manufacturers leading this trend, has demonstrated the benefits of this strategy. This reduction in own value-adding activity was combined with a movement from traditional sourcing to modular sourcing. In traditional sourcing, a one-tier model was used in which numerous suppliers delivered single parts or raw materials to a car manufacturer company. This company then carried out the complex assembly task. In modular sourcing, a number of module suppliers deliver complex pre-assembled modules to a company that only engages in the final assembly, completing few of its own production steps. Close relations are established with these few vertical cooperation partners, or first-tier suppliers, including joint development, open information and knowledge exchange. This leads to tight coordination with a small number of business partners and a reduction in coordination efforts required. Instead, the first-tier suppliers coordinate their own supplier networks in a pyramid-like structure of supplying companies (Morschett/Schramm-Klein/Zentes, 2010, p. 336).

16.3.2 The operation mode as a dynamic phenomenon

In Parts III and IV, strategies for going international were described, including the selection of an optimal initial operation mode. However, it is very common for the initially chosen operation mode to be changed after some time. In fact, the concept of internationalization stages highlights the fact that a company has to choose the initial operation mode based on its initial limited market knowledge. At this stage the company usually chooses an operation mode requiring a low specific investment in the country. Over time, however, and with experience in the country, the company increases its market knowledge. Frequently, this leads to operation modes with a higher commitment .

The best-known internationalization stages model, from the Uppsala-school, argues that with regard to any one foreign country, the internationalization process often takes place as follows (Johanson/Vahlne, 1977):

- At the outset companies do not have any regular exports to the specific foreign market.
- Then, regular exports are taken up via a foreign intermediary (e.g. a distributor).
- In the next step, once the company has more insight into the country, it often establishes a sales subsidiary.
- Eventually the company begins own production in the foreign country.

This so called "establishment chain" can often be observed in practice. A company's experience of a foreign country is an important determinant in the decision to commit the necessary resources to establish a wholly-owned company there.

But reality is more complex. Over time companies may also learn that they have committed too many resources to a particular country and so switch to operation modes with fewer own resource requirements (Swoboda et al., 2006). They may sell their production facilities in a country and from then on only serve the market via export.

To sum up, operation modes are not stable but often change over time. These mode switches can occur either as corrections of former managerial misjudgments or as adaptations to new circumstances (Welch/Benito/Petersen, 2007).

16.3.3 Bundles of operation modes to optimally adapt to the specific situation

While a company may replace one operation mode by another, as described in the previous section, it may also use a number of operation modes in parallel. This phenomenon is discussed in detail by Welch, Benito and Petersen (2007, pp. 393 ff).

This approach is often used for unrelated business fields, as the different industry conditions imply a different operation mode for each business. But it may also occur within the same business field. If, for example, a Japanese company sells printers in Germany to private consumers via retail channels and also sells them directly to commercial customers, it could create a sales subsidiary in the country to deal with the small number of German retail companies in this sector while at the same time using a local wholesale company as an independent distributor to sell the products to the many commercial customers. Frequently, the business field would then be divided into two different business units.

But even in the same business and with the same customers, a company may use a combination of operation modes. For example, in most countries the hotel group Accor uses franchising, management contracts and wholly-owned hotels in parallel (Morschett/Schramm-Klein/Zentes, 2010, pp. 253 ff.).

In production, a company may have a production joint venture in a foreign market which simultaneously acts as a licensee for the company's products. Thus, the company's profits stem partially from the licensing fees, and partly from the profit in the foreign joint venture of which it takes a share. Another example would be that production of crucial components may be carried out in a wholly-owned subsidiary of the company, while, in the same country, assembly into the final products is done by a contract manufacturer. This may be justified if the assembly activity is less of a core competence of the company. Thus, it may be optimal to choose different operation modes for different production stages.

Although different ownership and different operation modes may make coordination between the different activities more difficult, this effect may well be compensated for in cases where each operation mode for each value chain activity is optimally aligned.

16.3.4   Standardization versus local adaptation in the operation mode decision

A company that is active in more than one country must decide whether it wants to use the same operation mode in every country or whether it is willing to adapt and select the optimal entry mode for each country.

As has been pointed out in Section 10.6.2, a number of aspects need to be considered when choosing the appropriate operation mode:

- company factors, e.g. the financial restrictions on the company
- product factors, e.g. confidentiality of the proprietary technology, sensitivity to quality problems
- production-process factors, e.g. necessary know-how for the production, specificity of the necessary production equipment
- host-country factors, e.g. country risk, legal restrictions, availability of adequate partners.

While some of these factors will point towards standardization, others may seem to favor local adaptation of the operation mode.

Some **factors in favor of standardization** are:

- **International orientation**: A global strategic orientation implies tight control over foreign activities. It is much more difficult to implement a global strategy if the various partners in different countries have to be persuaded to adopt certain policies. Such partner modes are more likely to function well with a multinational strategic orientation. Note that the strategic preferences imply a certain set of operation modes, regardless of the specific host country.

- **Company resources**: The choice of an operation mode is partly determined by the available resources. The resources remain the same, no matter what country the company operates in.
- **Product strategy**: A company's product strategy is a major influence on its choice of operation mode. And regardless of the country, the underlying product strategy remains the same.
- **Learning effects**: A company amasses experience, not only with regard to particular foreign countries but also with particular operation modes. For example, a company may use licensing, make a mistake, correct this and learn from it for further licensing contracts. Similarly, some companies become experts in managing joint ventures and can use this competence internationally. In such cases, best practices can easily be transferred around the world.
- **Same partner in different countries:** Using the same partner in different countries (e.g. the same partner in several joint ventures) facilitates coordination and binds the partners closer together. Having the same partner in Germany and in China means that opportunistic behavior is much less likely since the consequences for a partner are more severe. For example, Renault and Nissan are strategic alliance partners who cooperate in many countries around the world.

Using the same operation mode internationally also facilitates the exploitation of global synergy effects. This is particularly true if the company decides to employ wholly-owned modes in every country (Malhotra/Agarwal/Ulgado, 2004). Very often, SMEs prefer such full-control modes which give them increased flexibility, in particular, the possibility to take decisions without negotiating with a partner and to integrate the different foreign activities into the international strategy of the company more easily. If, for example, a company sells the output of a production unit in one country to a sales unit in another country, then it can easily change the transfer prices for these transactions if it fully controls both activities. But if production takes place in China in a production joint venture with partner A and sales are carried out in Japan in a sales joint venture with a partner B, then shifting profits from China to Japan is usually not possible.

On the other hand, **local adaptation of operation mode** choice is mainly driven by the specific attributes of each host country (Morschett/Schramm-Klein/Swoboda, 2010) and by the different tasks that have to be fulfilled in a specific foreign activity:

- Even if companies have a preferred operation mode, **legal restrictions** in some countries often render this choice impossible. For example, retailing activities in India are usually only permitted in the form of a joint venture. And currently, China is discussing whether to require companies producing certain car parts to enter into joint ventures with Chinese partners.
- Furthermore, different countries represent different **political risks**. To protect a company's resources, operation modes with low own resource commitment are preferred in high risk countries. In riskless countries, companies may still prefer to establish wholly-owned subsidiaries.
- **Market size** greatly differs from market to market. While it may be worthwhile to build an own factory for the US market, small country markets can be exploited by exports from the home country or from third countries.
- Companies usually locate **different production stages** for different products in different countries. And the mode choice for each activity is influenced by other factors. For example, for the extraction of natural resources in a country (e.g. oil digging in Russia), it may be very beneficial to ally with a local company that often has a first-mover advantage in this field. For other activities, a partner may be much less valuable. Furthermore, in certain production stages, the risk of knowledge dissemination to a foreign partner is fairly small while in other production stages, core technologies are produced which should be protected by full-control operation modes.
- The operation mode selected for a certain activity in a specific country may differ because of the existence of **other activities** in this country. As the Renault case has shown, the company may already have a production platform in some countries while it would have to start from scratch in another country.
- A company may prefer cooperative arrangements, e.g. the use of a local contract manufacturer. However, the **availability of skilled and reliable partners** varies greatly from country to country.
- As has been shown above, access to partner resources is necessary for different reasons. Often, a company uses a local partner in a specific country because its **own knowledge of that country** is limited. Cultural distance may underlie the need to use local partners. But this will vary according to the country concerned and, of course, the company's familiarity with a country changes over time. Thus, the operation mode for a company in a country in which it has al-

ready been active for twenty years can differ from the operation mode in a newly entered country.

16.4   Recommendations for developing an operations strategy

16.4.1   The operations strategy as an approach to configuring the value creation process and determining the operation modes

As Chapter 5 shows, operation strategies are an important type of functional strategy for an international company. The operation strategies determine how each of the different industry-country markets will be supplied with the required products.

At the centre of any operations strategy are the two issues considered in detail in Sections 16.2 and 16.3:

- What is produced where and what form does the value creation process take?
- Will production take place in the company's own facilities, or in co-operation with a partner, or be carried out by a third party? Which operation modes will be used in the different countries for the different production activities?

Once these central questions have been answered, two further questions can be asked and answered:

- What will be procured where?
- How will the logistics tasks be fulfilled which arise from the configuration of the value creation process?

Whether the answers to these questions are provided in the operations strategy or whether they are addressed within the framework of short and medium term planning will depend on the degree of complexity involved. For an SME in most cases it should be sufficient to set out the value creation process and the operation modes within the operations strategy.

16.4.2   Conditions influencing the decision

16.4.2.1 Conditions influencing the configuration of the value creation process

Given the conflicting advantages of concentration and of decentralization, it is necessary to examine the particular influence factors for this decision (Hill, 2009, p. 567 ff.; Zentes/Swoboda/Morschett, 2004, p. 390 ff.). These influence factors help executives to determine the optimal production configuration for the company. At the same time, they explain why the configuration decision is highly specific to each company.

The first set of influence factors consists of **product- and production technology-related factors**. These include:

- **Product-specific trade barriers**: While some products are not confronted with major trade barriers anymore, which encourages centralization, others are are still exposed to high customs tariffs, pulling production to the target markets.
- **Value-to-weight ratio**: Logistics costs are driven by the weight and volume of products. If value-to-weight ratio is low (e.g. beer or cement), there is great pressure to manufacture the product in multiple locations; if it is high (e.g. luxury goods), logistics costs do not pose a barrier to production in a single location from which the product is exported to other parts of the world.
- **Product-specific country-of-origin image**: Country-of-origin image advantages are only relevant for certain industries, like high-tech products from Japan or the USA, highly reliable products from Germany or Switzerland, or design-oriented products from Italy.
- **Minimum efficient scale of production:** In some industries, fixed costs (e.g. for setting up a manufacturing plant) are very high and the minimum efficient scale (the level at which most economies of scale are exploited) is also high. In these cases, a company is more likely to centralize its production in a small number of plants.
- **Separability of production stages**: The company must examine whether the production process can be separated into different stages. If it can, this allows a location choice for each stage separately, while one continuous and indivisible process often leads to concentrated production in the home country.

In addition, **country-related issues** have to be examined. The home country of the company plays a major role in location decisions and the home country market is in most cases the point of reference. Companies from industrialized countries, like Germany or Switzerland, have access to a skilled, but expensive labor force. The decision for relocation or home-country production will depend on their needs. Companies from developing countries might have to relocate to more expensive regions to enjoy country-of-origin advantages. The relative importance of each foreign country market to the company (e.g. measured by the percentage of foreign sales) is an important influence on the decision to relocate in the proximity of these countries. In addition, if the home country is included in regional trade agreements (like the NAFTA or the EU) or free-trade agreements, this will affect the relevance of trade barriers. Furthermore, the characteristics of host countries play a role in location decisions. These include competitiveness, country risk, host government influences, corruption, trade barriers, regional integration agreements, national culture and many more.

In addition, configuration decisions depend on the **company** itself, its characteristics and its strategy. For example, the competitive strategy (low price or differentiation), the production and inventory strategy (such as just-in-time), the international strategic orientation (global strategy or multinational strategy), and the configuration of the other value-added activities (R&D, etc.) will all help to determine the optimal configuration of production facilities.

Finally, **customer- and marketing-oriented factors** also influence the optimal configuration decision. For example, if the company intends to be seen as a local player in its host markets, this favors decentralized production. If there are few national differences in consumer taste and preference for products, the need for local responsiveness is reduced, facilitating centralized manufacturing of homogeneous products. In contrast, if products need to be locally adapted, this favors decentralization. The need for flexibility in production and the importance of delivery times (as in the high-fashion industry) will shift production closer to the target markets. If a company wants to exploit a country-of-origin image, then this element of the marketing strategy will also influence the configuration. For B2B, customers' production strategies may make it necessary to locate the company's production facility close to the customer.

16.4.2.2 Conditions influencing the operation mode

Conditions that influence the choice of the different operation modes have already been highlighted in Chapter 7 and Chapter 10. The most important conditions are company factors, product factors, venture-specific factors and host country factors.

16.4.3   Process for developing an operation strategy

Figure 16.3 shows the proposed process for developing an operation strategy. We next describe the various steps.

In **Step 1** the company decides which products and country markets the operation strategy is for. There are four possibilities.
- The operation strategy applies to all products and country markets.
- The operation strategy applies to a single industry market, focussing, for example, on chocolate products, or infant food products.
- The operation strategy applies to a particular region, such as East Asia.
- The operation strategy applies to a single industry market in a specific region, such as chocolate in East Asia.

The solution chosen will depend on the size and complexity of the business as well as the chosen level of integration and responsiveness.

In **Step 2** the current situation has to be analyzed. The current production flows, the current sourcing, production and logistics costs and the current operation modes must all be known. Based on these facts, an evaluation of the current situation is possible, identifying strengths and weaknesses.

In **Step 3** the future sales volumes are forecast for the different products in each of the markets served. The reason for this is that the operation strategy has to serve the demand in the different country markets optimally.

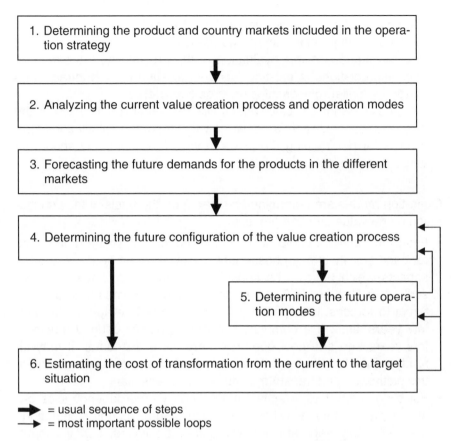

1. Determining the product and country markets included in the operation strategy

2. Analyzing the current value creation process and operation modes

3. Forecasting the future demands for the products in the different markets

4. Determining the future configuration of the value creation process

5. Determining the future operation modes

6. Estimating the cost of transformation from the current to the target situation

➡ = usual sequence of steps
→ = most important possible loops

Figure 16.3: Process for developing an operations strategy

Step 4 requires the value creation process to be determined:

- First, for each product group the company must determine whether the production process can be split into different stages.
- Next, the linkages between the different production stages of each product group have to be examined, along with the linkages between the production processes of the different product groups.
- After this, for each product group one basic type of production configuration should be chosen. If this is cross-border production, then the company must also determine which steps will be carried out in which country or countries. This is the ideal configuration that the company would establish if it could start from scratch.
- In the next step, a calculation should be made based on the ideal configuration for the company. In this calculation, the financial con-

sequences of the transformation from the existing configuration to the ideal configuration have to be identified and the profitability has to be evaluated. In this evaluation of the profitability, the extraordinary depreciations in existing facilities, existing labor contracts and existing supplier relationships must be considered.

- It is possible that the calculations will show that a full switch to the new ideal configuration is not worthwhile. If so, the calculations form a basis for determining the areas in which the company should diverge from the ideal configuration.

Operation modes are determined in **Step 5** on the basis of the configuration of the value creation process:

- First, the optimal bundle of operation modes should be determined for each activity in each host country. How this can be done and the aspects which have to be considered in this step, have been described in Section 16.3 above. In addition, a company should attempt to forecast the operation mode which will be appropriate in a few years' time. If a company entered a specific country market a few years ago and now operates there via a distributor, it may already be evident that in a few years it will be necessary to acquire this distributor and transform it into a sales subsidiary.
- For a company that is active internationally, interdependencies between the country activities may occur. Some country operations may be totally separate but others may be linked, e.g. via input-output relationships. For others, the same partner may be available in different countries. In the case of Renault, Nissan, its long-term partner, is available as a partner in certain foreign countries. These interdependencies have to be identified and their influence on the operation modes in the different countries evaluated.

In **Step 6** financial feasibility must be checked. Usually the corporate strategy sets a framework for investment in operations. If the planned measures go beyond what this framework makes possible, then there will be a loop in the process. As a result, exceptions to the ideal configuration and ideal operation modes will need to be envisaged. However, in this case, the reason for making exceptions is not to be found in the profitability, but simply in lack of resources to finance all the possible improvements.

17 The process of strategic planning in an international company

17.1 Preliminary remarks

For an international company, strategic planning is a highly complex task. If a company serves a number of different geographical markets and/or produces in more than one country, this makes strategic planning considerably more difficult than in a domestic company. In order to develop strategies for its future, the international company has to resolve issues that the domestic company simply does not have:

- To what extent should the different countries be autonomous? (see Chapter 12)
- To what extent should products and services be adapted to the needs of the different markets? (see Chapter 15)
- Will the products be procured or manufactured inside the different countries or will there be cross-border production? (see Chapter 16)

Beyond this, tasks such as defining the strategic businesses (see Chapter 13) and determining the strategic objectives (see Chapter 14) are more difficult to carry out for an international company. This is because of the added dimension of internationality.

Although strategic planning in an international company is more complex than in a domestic company, the recommended process is the same. The process introduced in Chapter 3 can be used to develop strategies for an international company too. Of course there will be additional issues to confront within each step of the process, and this will make the planning a more difficult task.

17.2 Overview of the process

Figure 17.1 presents the recommended process for strategic planning. Each step in the process is described below.

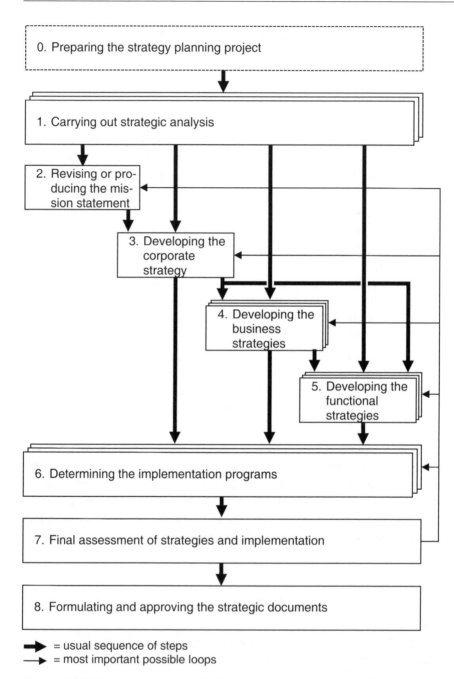

Figure 17.1: Process of strategic planning in an international company
(adapted from Grünig/Kühn, 2011, p. 47)

17.3   Step 0: Preparing the strategy planning project

Step 0 is to get the strategy planning project underway. A number of decisions are required to prepare the way for an efficient and targeted project.

The first and most important task consists in **naming the questions initiating the strategic planning**. Strategic planning, unlike budgeting, should not be a regular annual function. A company only needs new strategies if opportunities and/or threats become apparent which the company needs to react to. In the absence of any such opportunities or threats, existing strategies can continue. Sometimes they may require slight adjustment, but this does not require a process of the type presented in **Figure 17.1**.

Inset 17.1 gives examples of the kinds of questions which might initiate a strategy planning project for an international company.

Inset 17.1: Examples of questions initiating a strategy planning project in an international company

If, alongside its profitable markets, an international company also has some markets which do not make sufficient contribution margins, then three central strategic questions arise:

- Is the company offering products in some of its other markets which could also be introduced in the unsatisfactory markets?
- Could the costs of serving a market be reduced by changing the operation mode, using a sales representative, for example, rather than maintaining a sales subsidiary?
- Could the costs of the products be reduced, perhaps by buying them in rather than manufacturing them directly?

After a phase of growth propelled by acquisitions, a company is often faced with a situation in which different, locally produced or locally procured products are offered in each market. This situation raises the following questions:

- Can the products be standardized?
- Could economies of scale or of scope be achieved by combining operation units?

An international company may be faced with growing fixed costs for development and/or for marketing. The questions to answer are:

- How can the sales and contribution margins in each market be increased?
- Are there attractive new markets to enter?
- Could costs be significantly reduced by introducing production and/or sourcing in countries where the company does not yet operate?

In addition to formulating the key questions, Step 0, "Preparing the strategy planning project", deals with five other issues:

- Specifying the **conditions**
- Setting up the **project organisation**
- Deciding whether to mandate **consultants**
- Determining the **project procedure** and timetable
- Fixing the **budget** for the strategy planning project

How to deal with these issues is explained in detail in Section 8.2 and need not be repeated here.

17.4   Step 1: Carrying out strategic analysis

The first step in the strategy planning project is strategic analysis. The purpose of this analysis is to create a comprehensive view of the current situation together with developments that can be expected.

For an international company, the overview will have many facets. **Figure 17.2** displays the numerous areas for analysis in tabular form, for FFA presented in **Inset 14.1**. With regard to this table, we offer a number of comments:

- The strategic analysis is divided into three main areas: the environment, industry markets and the company itself. The analysis also distinguishes between the different countries in which the company produces or sells its products. The analysis is required to take an individual focus on these countries, but a worldwide view is also needed. Sometimes significant shifts in demand and in market offers in an industry lie outside the company's current fields of activity. They should nevertheless be included in the strategic analysis.

- As the figure shows, even for a company active in only four different geographical markets, three industries, and with three production countries there are many separate areas for analysis. Along with existing markets and resources, potential future markets and resources must also be analysed. In this case, the company plans to enter the Indonesian market with the products A and C. This move requires analyses of customers, distribution channels and competitors in that country. The planned market entry also requires an investigation of the sales organization that will be needed in Indonesia, one that will have to be built up from zero.

Coun-tries	Global environ-ment	Industry markets			Company		
		A	B	C	Sales	Produc-tion	Comp. in general
Austria	e	e	e	e	e	e	e
Germany	e		e		e	e	
Czech Rep.	e						
China	e	e			e	e	
Indonesia	p	p		p	p		
World	e	e	e	e			

☐ = main analysis field   ◸ = additional analysis field

e = existing market or resources   p = potential market or resources

Figure 17.2: Fields of analysis for FFA

- The strategy management literature offers a number of practical tools for the analysis of each field. There is not space in the present book to describe these. For an overview of tools for strategic analysis see Grünig and Kühn (2011, pp. 65 ff.)

At this stage, the main objective is to gather facts and figures relevant to the current situation and to future developments. However, some initial conclusions may also be justified:

- The analysis reveals opportunities and risks in each industry market and country market, as well as for the company as a whole. But the results are to be regarded as provisional at this stage. In later stages these preliminary findings can be strengthened or revised.
- The analysis should indicate whether the key questions formulated in Step 0 were pointing in the right direction. If there is a contradiction between the opportunities and threats revealed by the strategic analysis and the issues formulated at the outset, then the key issues must be revised and brought in line with the new understanding of the situation.

17.5   Step 2: Revising or producing the mission statement

Step 2 delivers a normative basis for the strategic planning. The company's overriding objectives and values must be specified, together with its relationship with the stakeholders.

Most companies have a mission statement, sometimes referred to as a vision or charter. It is necessary to check whether the existing mission statement is a complete and accurate statement of the company's true intentions. If the company has only recently begun internationalizing, the mission statement may well be incomplete as regards the following issues:

- What will our attitude be to the host countries? How much of our profits do we intend to repatriate?
- What will be our wages policy in the foreign countries? To what extent will the company voluntarily make social contributions?

- What will be our attitude to the environment in the foreign country? Will we apply the same standards as at home? If not, what modifications of these standards are we willing to accept, and where?
- How far will we offer the same product quality in developing countries? Will we provide the same level of information about our products abroad as we do at home?

If there is no available mission statement, or if the existing one is not considered usable, then a mission statement must be produced within Step 2. **Figure 17.3** gives a suggested structure.

1. Corporate identity / raison d'être of the company
2. Overriding objectives and values
3. Areas of activity
4. Relation to specific stakeholder groups
5. If any: Principles governing specific tasks

Figure 17.3: Table of contents of a mission statement
(adapted from Grünig/Kühn, 2011, p. 114)

17.6   Step 3: Developing the corporate strategy

17.6.1 Overview

The corporate strategy sets out long-term goals and investment priorities for the international company. The corporate strategy also sets important conditions for the business strategies and functional strategies which have subsequently to be worked out. This makes the corporate strategy the most important strategic document.

Figure 17.4 outlines the content of the corporate strategy of an international company. Each of these features is now described.

1.	Level of integration and responsiveness
2.	Strategic businesses
3.	Strategic objectives
4.	If needed: Level of standardization and differentiation of market offers
5.	If needed: Configuration of the value creation process and operation modes
6.	Required business strategies and functional strategies

Figure 17.4: Table of contents of a corporate strategy

17.6.2 Level of integration and responsiveness

The differences between low and high levels of integration and respon-siveness were described in detail in Chapter 12, which also explained the criteria a company can use when choosing between a multinational strategy, a global strategy and a transnational strategy.

One solution is to choose differing levels of integration and responsive-ness for the different industry markets. As **Inset 17.2** shows, this is a path that has been chosen by Nestlé. But for small and medium-sized companies we recommend choosing one of the three types, multina-tional, global or transnational. A number of advantages ensue:

- A single overall strategic approach is simpler and easier to manage.
- A company-wide global or transnational strategy allows the concen-tration of production at cost-efficient sites which leads to economies of scale and scope.
- If a multinational strategy is followed for all product groups, with pro-duction and sales in the different host countries, the locations for these can be the same. Furthermore, a strong presence in the host country gives the company more weight in its dealings with the gov-ernment. Sometimes tax concessions and other advantages can re-sult.

Inset 17.2: Different levels of integration and responsiveness at Nestlé

Nestlé is divided into seven operating segments:

- Europe
- America
- Asia, Oceania and Africa
- Waters
- Nutrition
- Other food and beverages
- Pharmaceutical products

The majority of the products can be found within the three geographically determined operating segments. The remaining four operating segments are responsible for the minority of products which Nestlé markets in a worldwide coordinated way (Nestlé, 2010, pp. 16 ff.).

From our perspective, the four product-based operating segments follow a global orientation. Nespresso is a well-known example. The Nespresso concept has been applied all over the world in almost the same form. Development, production and marketing are all highly centralized, leading to economies of scale.

The three geographically determined operating segments make it possible for the company to adapt the products to different regional needs and conditions. These segments might be following either a multinational or a transnational strategy. But the high degree of coordination and the great efficiency in production suggest that these are in fact transnational strategies.

17.6.3 Strategic businesses

A second requirement within a corporate strategy is the definition of the strategic businesses.

Chapter 13 has shown how this begins with the identification of **strategic business units,** market offers which contribute critically to the success of the company. Business units can be product groups, customer groups or combinations of the two. Where the different countries form separate competitive arenas, then the business units are linked to the country markets. If the competitive arena is the world market, then the business units are global.

The next move is to group the strategic business units in **strategic business fields**. A business field is a group of market offers or business units which is largely autonomous in terms of markets served and resources required. They can be considered as companies within the company. How business fields are defined will depend on whether their competitive arenas are the country markets or the world market. As **Figure 17.5** shows, the level of integration and responsiveness influences the business fields too:

- For companies following a multinational strategy, production is decentralized. Resources are divided among regions.
- In contrast, companies following a global or transnational strategy aim at economies of scale through the concentration of production and sometimes also at economies of scope. In this approach production resources are not allocated by country.

An example may help to make this clear. We return to FFA of **Inset 14.1**:

- The company follows a transnational strategy. The products and their marketing are adjusted to a certain degree to the national markets.
- Products B and C are each produced in separate world-market factories. In contrast, Product A is manufactured in two different facilities: the more expensive version, A1, is produced in Austria, while a cheaper variant, A2, is made in China. The company is planning, however, to move into cross-border production. In future each factory will be devoted to different steps in the production process, rather than to a different product.

Competitive arena / Level of integration and responsiveness	Country markets as competitive arenas	World market as competitive arena
Multinational strategy	▪ Business fields according to regions and industries ▪ Business fields according to regions	
Transnational strategy	▪ Business fields according to industries ▪ No business fields	
Global strategy	▪ Business fields according to industries ▪ No business fields	▪ Business fields according to industries ▪ No business fields

Figure 17.5: Business field patterns in international companies and their drivers

- **Figure 17.6** gives the business structure: the business units are all product-country combinations. As the company organizes production separately for each industry market, most of the resources are allocated by industry market. Thus the company has three business fields corresponding to the three industry markets.

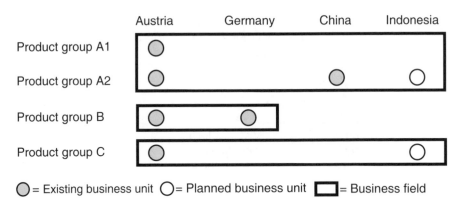

Figure 17.6: Businesses of FFA

17.6.4 Strategic objectives

The third element in a corporate strategy is strategic objectives. Chapter 14 showed how to define the strategic objectives for an international company.

If data is available giving the market shares for the company's businesses, and for those of its main competitors, then it is possible to display the target market positions in the form of a target portfolio using the Boston Consulting Group method. But this should only be done if the data are available for the relevant industry segments. Data for the market as a whole is not sufficient: a portfolio based only on data for the industry as a whole usually gives a false picture of the competitive situation.

Figure 17.7 gives the portfolio for FFA from **Inset 14.1**:

- The portfolio shows that the company has a strong position in its home market for all four products. These market shares must be preserved. But there will be little growth in turnover, as the Austrian economy is stagnant.
- The company is aiming to increase its sales in Germany by gaining market share at the expense of competitors.

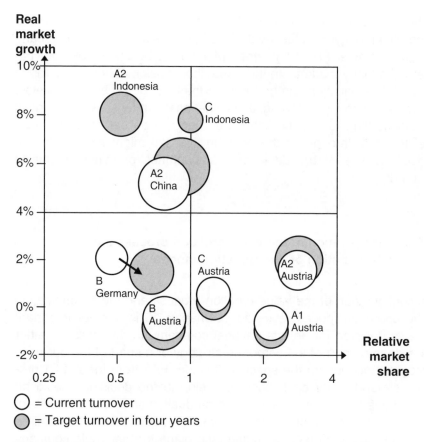

Figure 17.7: Target Boston Consulting Group portfolio for FFA

- Above average rates of growth in China and Indonesia can bring a powerful increase in turnover. For this reason the company is strengthening its market position in China and entering Indonesia with two products.

17.6.5 Level of standardization and differentiation of market offers

As Chapter 15 revealed, choosing the levels of standardization and differentiation of market offers represents an important strategic decision for an international company. Depending on the business structure of the company, this decision will be made either at the level of the corporate strategy or at the level of the business strategies. A company like our example, FFA from **Inset 14.1**, forms business fields for the different industry markets. In this case, the decision about standardization and differentiation can be made at the level of the business fields. But for a company following a multinational strategy, with business fields according to regions, standards need to be set at a corporate level to apply throughout the company. These might include, for instance, the use of brands in several countries or minimum quality standards.

17.6.6 Configuration of the value creation process and determination of the operation modes

The configuration of the value creation process and the determination of the operation modes reviewed in Chapter 16 is another important strategic decision for an international company. In this case, whether this is done as part of the corporate strategy or as part of the business strategies depends on the specific situation. FFA from **Inset 14.1** produces separately for each business field, so the decision should be taken at this level. But if some of the production steps are centralized, then the configuration of the value creation process and the determination of the operation modes should take place for the whole company and be set out in the corporate strategy.

17.6.7 Required business strategies and functional strategies

The final part of the corporate strategy is a specification of the required business strategies and functional strategies.

One obvious approach to this is to produce a business strategy for each of the businesses. But even with a medium-sized company, this may mean rather a large number of different strategies. To avoid this we recommend creating a business strategy for each business field. Individual business units can be addressed separately within the strategy for the business field as a whole. In this way the number of strategic documents is reduced and it becomes easier to create a consistent set of strategies.

With functional strategies too, less may be more. Only those functions which urgently require long term aims and measures require a strategy. This may be true, for example, of management development. If a company is following a policy of growth through acquisitions, then developing executives will be required not just to fill existing positions in the company, but also to create a pool of executives who can be sent into newly acquired companies.

As Chapter 5 explains, an international company typically requires operations strategies. They determine for the longer term how the value creation process will be structured and where value activities will be located. Looking at FFA from **Inset 14.1** once more, it might be necessary to develop an operations strategy for business field A. This operations strategy would define how the production would be divided in the long term between the facilities in Austria and China as well as the logistics issues raised by this decentralized production. In contrast, there seems little point in having an operations strategy for the business fields B and C. Each has only a single factory. Operations issues can be specified more appropriately within the business strategies.

17.7   Step 4: Developing the business strategies

In Step 4 the business strategies are developed. In the preceding section we recommended that a business strategy should be produced for each of the business fields and that the strategic prescriptions for the separate business units be included within the relevant business field strategy. We continue based on this recommendation.

Figure 17.8 lists the content for a business field strategy. Each item is briefly reviewed below.

The **strategic objectives** for the business field and the business units within it are set by the corporate strategy. The development of the

---

- ▪ Strategic objectives

- ▪ Generic business strategy

- ▪ If needed: Standardization and differentiation of the market offers

- ▪ Competitive advantages of the market offers

- ▪ Strategy of business unit A

- ▪ Strategy of business unit B

- ▪ Competitive advantages of resources and processes

- ▪ If needed: Operations strategy

Figure 17.8: Table of contents of a business field strategy

business field strategy can sometimes lead to a revision of these objectives, whose target market positions may prove to be either too ambitious or not ambitious enough.

Next, one of Porter's **generic business strategy** options must be selected (1980, p. 39). **Figure 17.9** gives the four possible choices.

For the sake of simplicity and to allow synergies to be exploited fully, each business field should, if possible, concentrate on a single generic strategy. But if there are a number of different country markets in the business field, as is the case with the Austrian producer of consumer goods, different generic strategies may be pursued in different country markets.

As we saw in Section 17.6, the corporate strategy may set out the ground rules for the standardization or differentiation of the market offers. This will occur when the business fields represent countries or groups of countries. But if the business fields are formed according to different industry markets, as is the case for FFA of **Inset 14.4**, then decisions about the **standardization and differentiation of the market offers** should be made at the level of the business field. For the different country markets, which will typically form different business units, the business field strategy will formulate policies relating to the products. These policies must indicate clearly which issues are determined for all business units at the level of the business field and where

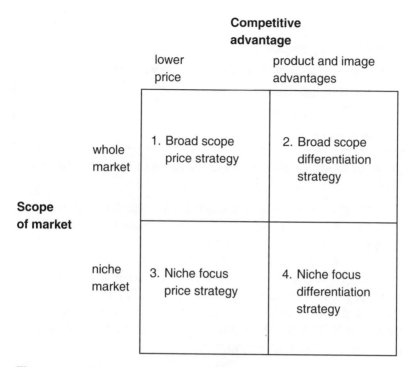

Figure 17.9: Generic business strategies
(adapted from Porter 1980, p. 39, by Grünig/Kühn, 2011, p. 223)

there may be freedom for individual country markets. Chapter 15 looked in detail at standardization and differentiation of the market offers and we do not repeat this information here.

The **competitive advantages of the market offers** must be defined according to the selected generic business strategy and to the indications concerning standardization and differentiation. They explain concretely why a potential customer should buy the company's product rather than a competing product. To answer this critical question, generalities will not suffice. Competitive advantages must be comprehensively and specifically defined. **Figure 17.10** gives the most important competitive advantages for Victorinox pocket knives. As Victorinox follows a global strategy (see **Inset 12.1**), these competitive advantages apply worldwide.

- Top quality products
- Multifunctional products
- Broad range of traditional and innovative pocket knives
- Uniform product design
- Swiss cross emphasizing Swissness
- Well-known brand

Figure 17.10: Competitive advantages of the pocket knives of Victorinox

For the business units within the business field – typically combinations of product groups and country markets or of customer groups and country markets – **business unit strategies** must be formulated. These should make more specific what has already been stated for the business field as a whole. If the business field strategy plans for differentiation of the products sold in the different countries, then the specifications for the products must be included in the business unit strategies. In addition, it is usual to include country-specific prescriptions for communication and distribution channels.

Irrespective of whether or not production policy is managed at the level of the business field, the business field strategy must define the target **competitive advantages of resources and processes**. As Section 3.2 explains, strong market positions and competitive advantages in the offer are based on competitive advantages in resources and processes.

The **operations strategy** may be a separate document or a section within the business field strategy. If, for the business field, there is one factory producing all the products, then a section within the business strategy will be sufficient. But if production is dispersed across a number of factories in different countries, or if production is entwined with the production for other business fields, then a separated operations strategy seems reasonable.

The content required for an operations strategy was presented in Chapter 16.

17.8   Step 5: Developing the functional strategies

In Step 5 the functional strategies are developed. The decisions as to which functions require a strategy were taken as part of the development of corporate strategy in Step 3.

The purpose of functional strategies is to allow an international company to carry out cross-border activities in a targeted and efficient manner. Management development, communication and the creation of a corporate identity are all functions carried out at the corporate level. With these functions, if each business field or country goes its own way, negative synergies will result.

As we have seen, for an international company the operations strategies are a crucial subtype of functional strategies. Operations strategies allow the coordination of production in complex situations. Such complex production structures can occur in two types of context:

- For a number of different business fields production is completely or partly combined.
- For one or more business fields, value creation takes place in a cross-border process.

Details on how to develop an operations strategy are given in Chapter 16.

17.9   Step 6: Determining the implementation programs

In order to implement the strategies developed in Steps 3, 4 and 5, clearly defined implementation measures are needed. This is the task of Step 6.

Strategic programs must be drawn up to enable the content of the strategic planning to be implemented rapidly and in a bundled manner. **Figure 17.11** illustrates possible strategic programs for FFA from **Inset 14.1:**

- Five of the twelve programs concern Indonesia. Entry into a new

Corporate level	Business field A	Business field B	Business field C
Building up a sales subsidiary in Indonesia *	Introduction of product group A2 in Indonesia	Replacing the sales representative in Germany by a sales subsidiary	Introduction of product group C in Indonesia
Introduction of a holding structure	Entering central and western China with product group A2	Marketing campaign in Germany	Building up * logistics for Indonesia
	Building up * logistics for Indonesia	Implementing rationalizations in the Czech factory	
	Building up logistics for Central and Western China		
	Shifting production steps for product group A1 from Austria to China		

* Must be coordinated with each other

Figure 17.11: Strategic programs of FFA

market demands a concentration of human and financial resources over a period of two or three years. And it is much more effective to invest heavily for a shorter period, than to proceed in a hesitant manner.

- As the Figure shows, cost reduction measures are also planned. In business field B there will be investment in rationalization, while for business field A it is planned to transfer some production steps for Product A1 from Austria to China. These will be production steps which are labor-intensive and not too complex.

Each of the implementation programs requires clear objectives, milestones and a budget. Each also requires a program leader, someone with the necessary knowledge and experience and who can devote the required time to the program.

Program leaders should report directly to the CEO or to a business field manager. In this way decisions can be made quickly and, if necessary, additional resources can be mobilized rapidly to overcome any snags or hold-ups.

17.10   Step 7: Final assessment of strategies and implementation

Steps 3 to 6 of this process generated and assessed different options for the individual tasks, but what has been missing so far is an overall assessment. At the conclusion of Step 6 all the elements of the future strategy are in place and it becomes possible to proceed to a final assessment.

For the final assessment of strategies and implementation it is necessary to look at the results of the strategic planning with some distance. There are four questions to answer:

- Do the strategies and the implementation programs answer the questions posed in Step 0?
- Will the strategies and implementation programs make it possible for the company to be successful and to continue to develop?
- Can the implementation programs be financed?

- Have the risks or critical aspects of the strategies been identified? Is it clear how these critical points will be monitored during the implementation phase?

If it is possible to answer positively to all four questions, then the work can move to Step 8. If one or more questions produce a "no", then the strategies and implementation must be revised. This is then a loop in the process.

The fourth question implicitly assumes that strategies contain risks or critical factors. Sometimes important moves can only be made if a company is prepared to accept risks. But these risks should never be so great that the company itself is endangered. And it is crucial that critical factors are monitored so that it quickly becomes known if a target is being missed. For this reason the monitoring must be focussed on the critical factors.

17.11   Step 8: Formulating and approving the strategic documents

In the process of strategic planning loops tend to occur again and again. For this reason, it is wise to leave the production of documents to the very end of the process. Up to Step 7, it is enough to use presentation slides and spread sheets. Once the final assessment has confirmed that the result is a viable strategy, then documents are needed which are concise and clear. In addition, the results of the analysis must be displayed in a clear form.

For a medium-sized international company, the results of strategic planning can usually be presented in relatively few documents. It is clear, however, that a large international corporation will require rather more extensive documentation of the results of its strategic planning.

Once the documents have been produced, they need to be formally approved at the highest levels of the company. Mission statement and corporate strategy will usually be approved by the board of directors. The rest of the documentation will be presented either to the CEO or to the board of management.

Once the documents have been approved, they should be discussed with all the leading executives. Here the objective is to make sure that all the managers know the content of the documents and have full awareness of their individual roles in the implementation. One-way communication is not enough. Workshops are needed, as these allow wide-ranging interactive discussion.

Figure 17.12 lists the documents for FFA from **Inset 14.1**:

- The mission statement creates the normative basis.
- The corporate strategy defines future businesses and their objectives. It also includes guidelines for the standardization of products and the value creation process. Thus it creates a framework for the business field strategies.

  The Austrian company has three business fields, corresponding to three industry markets. The three business field strategies define the competitive strategy for the business fields as a whole and for the individual business units grouped within each of the three business

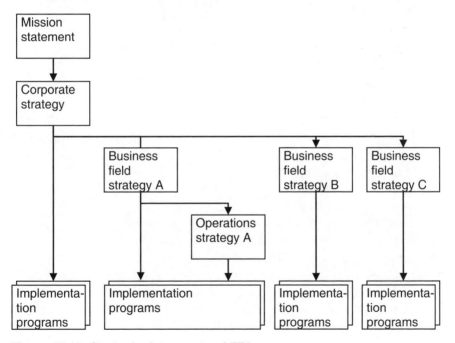

Figure 17.12: Strategic documents of FFA

fields. **Figure 17.6** gives an overview of the business units. The business field strategies for B and C also specify operations. As business field A has two factories and therefore a more complex production structure, operations for business field A are specified in a separate document.

- The implementation programs were given earlier in **Figure 17.11**.
- Missing from **Figure 17.12** are the results of the analysis. These results should be provided in an appropriate form, so that all the vital information they contain about customers, distributors, competitors, legal requirements and so on, is kept in the spotlight.

Finally this figure also shows that the selection of which strategic documents to produce will depend on each company's specific individual situation.

18   Closing remarks

As we made clear in our introduction, this book is aimed at executives and at master and EMBA students as future executives. In line with the needs of this audience, the focus of this book has been on practical recommendations. We began by devoting Parts I and II of the book to a comprehensive introduction to internationalization itself and to strategic planning. The last three parts of the book show how strategies for going and being international can be developed. Part III looked at going international for new markets, Part VI at developing an internationalization strategy for production and sourcing and Part V examined strategic planning in international companies.

In each of Parts III, IV and V, essential building blocks were developed. Finally these building blocks were assembled into an overall process. We, the authors, sincerely hope that we have provided information here which will allow the reader to develop clear and feasible strategies. Our effort has been guided by two main preoccupations:

- We wanted to insist on and facilitate a systematic approach. The required overview can be quickly lost if the process does not proceed step by step in a systematic way. The result will then be strategies which are incomplete and unclear.
- Secondly, we wanted to make sure that strategy development is based on facts. Strategies can only be implemented if they are based on reality. To improve the market position and performance of a company, strategies are needed which are feasible.

Our hope is that this book is a contribution to the development of clear and feasible strategies. In this way a contribution can be made to the successful future of the company. But we realise that while clear and feasible strategies are a necessary condition for success, they do not guarantee it. Good strategies are of little use unless the managers of the company are committed to them. What this means is that developing strategies is not only a complex set of tasks at the level of its content, but that this process also requires leadership. The board of directors and/or the CEO must succeed in persuading the managers of the company, right down to the level of team leaders, that these are the right strategies and that they will bring success. This can only happen if the managers themselves take part in the strategy planning process.

They need to own the strategies. This book concentrates on the content and leaves the difficult task of motivating the managers to the users.

To conclude, we wish the reader every success in developing and implementing international strategies.

Index

Bibliography

Anheuser-Busch InBev (2011): About AB InBev, www.ab-inbev.com/go/about_abinbev.cfmwww, accessed on 01.06.2011

Andersen, O. (1997): Internationalization and market entry mode: a review of theories and conceptual framework in: Management International Review No. 2/1997, pp. 27-42

Ansoff, H. I. (1965): Corporate strategy: An Analytic Approach to Business Policy for Growth and Expansion, New York etc.

Appel, H.; Hein, C. (2010): Am seidenen Faden, in: FAZ.net 10.07.2010, accessed 12.7.2010

Armaka (2011): Armaka AG – Wer wir sind, www.armaka.ch, accessed 01.03.2011

Armstrong, G., Kotler, P. (2007): Marketing – An Introduction, 8th edition, Upper Saddle River

Backhaus, K., Büschken, J., Voeth, M. (2003): Internationales Marketing, 4th edition, Stuttgart

Baizhu, C. (2011): Paradise reconsidered, in: China Economic Review 03.05.2011, http://newcer.chinaeconomicreview.com, accessed on 09.05.2011

Barney, J., Hesterly, W. (2010): Strategic Management and Competitive Advantage, 3rd edition, Upper Saddle River

Bartlett, C., Beamish, P. (2011): Transnational Management, 6th edition, New York

Bartlett, C., Ghoshal, S., Beamish, P. (2008): Transnational Management, 5th edition, New York

BERI (ed.) (2007): Business risk service user guide, info@beri.com

BERI (ed.) (2009): China's ratings, Business risk service 2009-I, info@beri.com

BERI (ed.) (2011): Business environment risk intelligence, http://www.beri.com/brs.asp, accessed 10.01.2011

Berman, B., Evans, J. (2010): Retail Management, 11th edition, Upper Saddle River

BMW (ed.) (2007): BMW Group eröffnet internationales Einkaufsbüro für Zentral- und Osteuropa, Press Release 20.09.2007

BMW (ed.) (2011): Manufacturing Facilities – Assembly Plants, www.bmwgroup.com, accessed 05.03.2011

Bradley, F. (2005): International Marketing Strategy, 5th edition, Harlow

Brouthers, K., Brouthers, L., Werner, S. (2008): Real options, international entry mode choice and performance, in: Journal of Management Studies No. 4/2008, pp. 936-960

Burr, W., Herstatt, C., Marquardt, G., Walch, S. (2011): Lizenzierung als Eintrittsstrategie in internationale Märkte, in: Zentes, J. Swoboda, B., Morschett, D. (eds.): Fallstudien zum Internationalen Management, 4th edition, Wiesbaden, pp. 357-370

Carlsberg (2011): Company, www.carlsberggroup.com/Company, accessed on 01.06.11

Carpenter, M., Sanders, G. (2009): Strategic Management, 2nd edition, Upper Saddle River

Cateora, P., Gilly, M., Graham, J. (2009): International Marketing, 14th edition, New York

Child, J. (1972): Organizational structure and strategies of control: The role of strategic choice, in: Sociology 1972, pp. 1-22

Cooper, R., Kaplan, R. (1988): Measure Cost Right: Make the Right Decisions, in: HBR September-October 1988, pp. 96-103

Coulter, M. (2010): Strategic Management in Action, 5th edition, Boston etc.

Czinkota, M., Ronkainen, I. (2008): International Marketing, Mason

Deloitte (ed.) (2007): Sourcing in the Global Factory, London

Deloitte (ed.) (2011): Leaving home. Global Powers of Retailing, London

Devinney, T., Midgley, D., Venaik, S. (2000): The optimal performance of the global firm: Formalizing and extending the integration-responsiveness framework, in: Organization Science No. 6/2000, pp. 674-695

De Wit, B., Meyer, R. (2004): Strategy, 3rd edition, London

Dicken, P. (2009): Global shift, Mapping the changing contours of the world economy, 5th edition, London etc.

Doz, Y. (1980): Strategic management in multinational companies, in: Sloan Management Review No. 1/1980, pp. 27-46

Dreher, A. (2006): Does globalization affect growth? Evidence from a new index of globalization, in: Applied Economics 2006, pp. 1091-1110

Driscoll, A., Paliwoda, S. (1997): Dimensionalizing international market entry mode choice, in: Journal of Marketing Management No. 1/1997, pp. 57-87

Ecco (ed.) (2010): Ecco's Annual Report 2009, http://www.ecco.com, accessed 18.07.2010

Electrolux (ed.) (2005): Electrolux Annual Report 2004, Stockholm

ETC group (ed.) (2005): Oligopoly, Communiqué 91, http://www.etcgroup.org, accessed 11.01.2011

European Foundation for the Improvement of Living and Working Conditions (ed.) (2008): ERM case studies: The employment impact of relocation within the EU, Dublin

Ewing, J. (2011): VW Focuses on U.S. Market in Bid to Be World's No. 1 Automaker, in: New York Times 08.01.2011, p. B2.

FAZ (ed.) (2009): Daimler verlagert Produktion nach Amerika, in: FAZ.net, www.faz.de, 09.12.2009, accessed 30.04.2011

FAZ (ed.) (2010): Ricola hadert mit Euro und Dollar, in: FAZ.net, www.faz.de, 13.12.2010, accessed 30.04.2011

Federation of the Swiss Watch Industry (ed.) (2010a): Information specially prepared for the authors, Bienne

Federation of the Swiss Watch Industry (ed.) (2010b): Swiss Made, http://www.fhs.ch/fr/swissmade.php, accessed 28.06.2010

Fraunhofer Institut (ed.) (2009): Produktionsverlagerung und Rückverlagerung in der Krise, Mitteilungen aus der ISI-Erhebung, Issue 52

Gälweiler, A. (2005): Strategische Unternehmensführung, 3rd edition, Frankfurt and New York

Gerber, J. (2005): International Economics, 3rd edition, Boston

Geyskens, I., Steenkamp, J., Kumar, N. (2006): Make, buy, or ally: A transaction cost theory meta-analysis, in: Academy of Management Journal No. 3/2006, pp. 519-543

Ghauri, P., Cateora, P. (2006): International Marketing, 2nd edition, New York

Ghoshal, S., Nohria, N. (1993): Horses for courses: Organizational forms for multinational corporations, in: Sloan Management Review No. 2/1993, pp. 23-35

Graham, E. (1997): Working Together: Foreign Direct Investment and Trade, in: Economic Reform Today No. 3/1997, pp. 29-32

Grant, R. (2010): Contemporary strategy analysis, 7th edition, Chichester

Grünig, R. (2011): Case study Southwest Airlines, Teaching document, Fribourg

Grünig, R., Kühn, R., (2009): Successful Decision-making, 2nd edition, Berlin and Heidelberg

Grünig, R., Kühn, R. (2011): Process-based Strategic Planning, 6th edition, Berlin and Heidelberg

Gupta, A., Govindarajan, P. (2000): Knowledge Flows within Multinational Corporations, in: Strategic Management Journal No. 4/2000, pp. 473-496

Haberberg, A., Rieple, A. (2008): Strategic Management, Oxford

Harzing, A. (2000): An empirical analysis and extension of the Bartlett and Goshal typology of multinational companies in: Journal of International Business Studies No. 1/2000, pp. 101-120

Hedley, B. (1977): Strategy and the Business Portfolio, in: Long Range Planning No. 1/1977, pp. 9-15

Heritage Foundation (ed.) (2011): Economic Freedom, www.heritage.org, accessed 12.03.2011

Hill, C. (2008): Global Business Today, 5th edition, Boston

Hill, C. (2009): International Business - Competing in the Global Marketplace, 7th edition, Boston etc.

Hill, C., Jones, G. (2008): Strategic Management, 8th edition, Boston

Hill, C., Hwang, P., Kim, W. C. (1990): An eclectic theory of the choice of international entry mode, in: Strategic Management Journal No. 2/1990, pp. 117-128

Hofer, C., Schendel, D. (1978): Strategy Formulation: Analytical Concepts, St. Paul

Hofstede, G. Hofstede, G. (2005): Cultures and Organizations, 2nd edition, New York

Hollensen, S. (2011): Global Marketing – A Decision-oriented Approach, Harlow

Holtbrügge, D., Welge, M. (2010): Internationales Management, 5th edition, Stuttgart

Horngren, C., Datar, S., Foster, G., Rajan, M., Ittner, C. (2009): Cost Accounting, 13th edition, Upper Saddle River

Inma, C. (2005): Purposeful franchising: Re-thinking the Franchising Rational, in: Singapore Management Review No. 1/2005, pp. 27-48

Institut der Deutschen Wirtschaft (ed.) (2010): Arbeitskosten – Von wegen Dumping, in: iwd No. 38/2010

Janetzke, C. (2008): Maquiladora belebt sich wieder in Mexico, Information von Germany Trade and Invest, 10.07.2008

Johanson, J., Vahlne, J. (1977): The internationalization process of the firm – A model of knowledge development and increasing foreign market commitment, in: Journal of International Business Studies No. 1/1977, pp. 23-32

Johnson, G., Scholes, K., Whittington, R. (2008): Exploring Corporate Strategy, 8th edition, New York etc.

Keegan, W., Green, M. (2008): Global Marketing, 5th edition, Upper Saddle River

Knüppel, A. (1997): Beschaffung, Produktion und Absatz in multinationalen Industrieunternehmungen, PhD Thesis University of Göttingen, Cologne

KOF (ed.) (2010a): KOF Index of Globalization: Press Release 2010, http://globalization.kof.ethz.ch/static/pdf/press_release_2010_en.pdf, accessed 15.06.2010

KOF (ed.) (2010b): KOF Index of Globalization: Calculation 2010, http://globalization.kof.ethz.ch/static/pdf/method_2010.pdf, accessed 15.06.2010

KOF (ed.) (2010c): KOF Index of Globalization: Index Development World, http://globalization.kof.ethz.ch/aggregation, accessed 21.05.2010

KOF (ed.) (2010d): KOF Index of Globalization: Index Development Switzerland and Vietnam, http://globalization.kof.ethz.ch/query, accessed 21.05.2010

KOF (ed.) (2010e): KOF Index of Globalization: Country Rankings 2007, http://globalization.kof.ethz.ch/static/pdf/rankings_2010.pdf, accessed 15.06.2010

Kogut, B., Zander, U. (1993): Knowledge of the firm and the evolutionary theory of the multinational corporation, in: Journal of International Business Studies No. 4/1993, pp. 625-646

Kotabe, M., Helsen, K. (2008): Global Marketing Management, 4th edition, Hoboken

Krugman, P., Obstfeld, M. (2009): International economics: theory and policy, 8th edition, Boston

Kutschker, M. (1999): Das internationale Unternehmen in: M. Kutschker M. (ed.), Perspektiven der internationalen Wirtschaft, Wiesbaden, pp. 101-126

Kutschker, M., Schmid, S. (2011): Internationales Management, 7th edition, München

Lantal (2011): http://www.lantal.ch, accessed 28.03.11 and interviews with Kreuzer M.

Lebensmittel Zeitung (ed.) (2011): Ricola stärkt Marktposition, in: Lebensmittel Zeitung No. 18/2011, p. 84

Levitt, T. (1983): The globalization of markets in: Harvard Business Review No. 3/1983, pp. 92-102

Lynch, R. (2000): Corporate Strategy, 2nd edition, London

Malhotra, N., Agarwal, J., Ulgado, F. (2004): Internationalization and entry modes: A multitheoretical framework and research propositions, in: Journal of International Marketing No. 4/2004, pp. 1-31

MAN Diesel & Turbo (ed.) (2011): Company Profile, http://mandieselturbo.com, accessed 03.03.2011

McCarthy, E. (1960): Basic Marketing, A Managerial Approach, Homewood

Migros (ed.) (2009): Noch schöner wohnen, Press Release of the Migros Group, 22.01.2009.

Miller, A., Dess, G. (1996): Strategic Management, 2nd edition, New York etc.

Mintzberg, H. (1994): The rise and fall of strategic planning, New York

Monteiro, J. (2010): Essays on investments and environment: A spatial econometrics perspective, PhD Thesis University of Neuchatel, Neuchatel

Morschett, D., Donath, A. (2007): Institutionalisierung und Steuerung von Auslandseinheiten – Analyse von Industrie- und Dienstleistungsunternehmen, Wiesbaden

Morschett, D. (2011): Die Globale Strategie von Flextronics, in: Zentes, J., Swoboda, B., Morschett, D. (eds.): Fallstudien zum Internationalen Management, 4th edition, Wiesbaden, pp. 221-228

Morschett, D., Donath, A., Fisch, J.-H., Schramm-Klein, H. (2009): Influence factors, barriers and effects of international divestment - A review, Presentation at the Annual Meeting of the Academy of International Business 2009

Morschett, D., Schramm-Klein, H., Swoboda, B. (2010): Decades of research on market entry modes: What do we really know about external antecedents of entry mode choice? in: Journal of International Management 1/2010, pp. 60-77

Morschett, D., Schramm-Klein, H., Zentes, J. (2010): Strategic International Management, 2nd edition, Wiesbaden

Mühlbacher, H., Dahringer, L., Leihs, H. (2006): International Marketing - A Global Perspective, 3rd edition, London

Müller, S., Gelbrich, K. (2004): Interkulturelles Marketing, München

Narimpex (ed.) (2010): Unpublished company documents, Bienne

Nestlé (ed.) (2010): Annual Report 2009, Vevey

OECD (ed.) (2010): Comparative advantages 2005, http://stats.oecd.org, accessed 15.08.2010

Palich, L., Cardinal, B., Miller, C. (2000): Curvilinearity in the diversification-performance linking, in: Strategic Management Journal No. 2/2000, pp. 155-174

Perlmutter, H. (1969): The tortuous evolution of the multinational corporation in: Columbia Journal of World Business No. 1/1969, pp. 9-18

Pfeffer, J., Salancik, G. (1978): The external control of organizations: A resource dependency perspective, New York

Pham, T. K. N. (2008): Strategies for Internationalization: A Comparative Study of Thai and Vietnamese Companies in Two Industries, Fribourg

Porter, M. (1980): Competitive strategy, New York

Porter, M. (1985): Competitive advantage, New York

Porter, M. (1990): The competitive Advantage of Nations, New York

Prahalad, C., Doz, Y. (1987): The Multinational Mission: Balancing Local Demands and Global Vision, New York

Raffée, H., Effenberger, J., Fritz, W. (1994): Strategieprofile als Faktoren des Unternehmenserfolgs, in: DBW No. 3/1994, pp. 383-396

Ramasamy, B. (2010): Wer löst China als Billiglohnland ab?, in: Wirtschaftswoche Online 06.10.2010, www.wiwo.de, accessed on 09.05.2011

Rohde, R. (2011): China – Neues Sozialversicherungsgesetz: höhere Lohnnebenkosten, in: Asienkurier No. 5/2011, www.asienkurier.com, accessed on 09.05.2011

Root, F. (1994): Entry Strategies for International Markets, 2nd edition, San Francisco

Rugman, A., Verbeke, A. (2001): Subsidiary-specific advantages in multinational enterprises, in: Strategic Management Journal No. 3/2001, p. 237-250

Sanyal, R. (2001): International Management, A Strategic Perspective, Upper Saddle River

Schindler (ed.) (2011): Fact Sheet Schindler Group, http://www.schindler.com, accessed 08.02.2011

Schmid, S., Grosche, P. (2008): Management internationaler Wertschöpfung in der Automobilindustrie, Gütersloh

Shah, A., Sterret, C. (2001): Southwest Airlines 2000, in: David F. (ed.): Strategic Management Cases, Upper Saddle River, pp. 200-208

Shenkar, O., Luo, Y. (2008): International Business, 2nd edition, Los Angeles

Shirong, C. (2009): China rural-urban gap widens, in: BBC News, http://newsvote.bbc.co.uk, accessed on 01.05.2011

Simflexgroup (ed.) (2011): www.simflexgroup.com, accessed 21.04.2011

Sollberger, R. (2010a): Europa ist nicht die ganze Welt, in: Handelszeitung 08.07.2010, p. 9

Sollberger, R. (2010b): Expandieren ist auf Dauer besser als jammern, in: Handelszeitung 08.07.2010, p. 9

Swiss Automotive Group (ed.) (2011): Unpublished company documents, Cham

Swoboda, B., Foscht, T., Maloles III, C., Morschett, D. (2006): Increasing and decreasing foreign involvement: A look at managerial reasons for change, Presentation at the Annual Meeting at the Academy of International Business 2006

Textilwirtschaft (ed.) (2010): China wird zu teuer, in: Textilwirtschaft No. 27/2010, p. 49

Thahabi, E. (2010): Die Bildung von strategischen Geschäften in mittleren, international tätigen Unternehmen, Wiesbaden

Thompson, A., Strickland, A. (2003): Strategic Management, 13th edition, New York

Transparency International (ed.) (2010): Annual Report 2009, Berlin

Tulikivi (ed.) (2011): Distributors, www.tulikivi.com, accessed 01.03.2011

Welch, L., Benito, G., Petersen, B. (2007): Foreign Operation Methods – Theory, Analysis, Strategy, Cheltenham

Wheelen, T., Hunger, J. (2010): Strategic Management and Business Policy, 12th edition, New Jersey

World Bank (ed.) (2010): World Development Indicators & Global Development Finance, http://databank.worldbank.org/ddp/home.do, accessed 19.06.2010

World Economic Forum (ed.) (2010): World Competitiveness Report 2010-2011, Geneva

WTO (ed.) (2010): The World Trade Organization, http://www.wto.org, accessed 17.12.2010

Yip, G. (1991): Do American Businesses Use Global Strategy?, in: Report No. 91-101 of the Marketing Science Institute, Cambridge

Zentes, J. (1993): Eintritts- und Bearbeitungsstrategien für osteuropäische Konsumgütermärkte, in: Tietz, B., Zentes, J. (eds.), Ost-Marketing, Düsseldorf etc., pp. 63-101

Zentes, J., Swoboda, B., Morschett, D. (2004): Internationales Wertschöpfungsmanagement, München

Zentes, J., Swoboda, B.; Morschett, D. (2011): The Complexity and Dynamics of Electrolux' Internationalisation, in: Zentes, J.; Swoboda, B.; Morschett, D. (eds.): Fallstudien zum Internationalen Management, 4th edition, Wiesbaden, pp. 3-24

Zentes, J., Swoboda, B., Schramm-Klein, H. (2010): Internationales Marketing, 2nd edition, Munich

Printing: Ten Brink, Meppel, The Netherlands
Binding: Stürtz, Würzburg, Germany